THE FIREBRAND

WILLIAM KILBOURN

THE FIREBRAND

WILLIAM LYON MACKENZIE
AND THE REBELLION IN
UPPER CANADA

IRWIN PUBLISHING

Toronto, Canada

COPYRIGHT, CANADA, 1956

IRWIN PUBLISHING INC.
FORMERLY A
CLARKE, IRWIN & COMPANY LIMITED BOOK

Eighth printing in paperback format 1977

ISBN 0-7720-1179-6

Canadian Cataloguing in Publication Data

Kilbourn, William, 1926-
   The Firebrand

ISBN 0-7720-1179-6

1. Mackenzie, William Lyon, 1795–1861.
2. Canada—History—Rebellion, 1837–1838.
I. Title.

FC451.M3K5 1977   971.03'8   C77-001750-9
F1032.M148 1977

   3 4 5 / 86 85 84

Printed in Canada

FOR MY FATHER

PREFACE

TO TELL a story and to interpret a character have been the two principal objects in writing this book. The reason for binding both purposes together into a single history will become more apparent, it is hoped, in the reading. Mackenzie's character, in any case, and the story of how the rebellion came about, now seem to the author to be bound up with each other more closely than he would previously have guessed. As Henry James once remarked in speaking of the novel, those vivid glimpses one sometimes has of a person as "subject" seem to require one to select and piece out and imagine the situations and subsidiary characters most capable of bringing out all the "subject's" possibilities. Since the writing of history is a more intuitively and even arbitrarily selective affair than one usually likes to admit, perhaps I may be forgiven the temerity of using Henry James' observation as some sort of excuse for the kind of history writing here attempted; specifically, for the attempt to bring a subject to life by involving him rather more completely in the context of a selective account of the events and the characters of his times than would be tolerable if this book were offered as a full-scale definitive biography.

My interest in Mackenzie began as part of a general study of the role of the editor-politician in Canadian history. Surprisingly enough, in the case of Mackenzie, one of the most important of them all, there was no modern study or biography available, and indeed the only biography published to date is that written by Mackenzie's son-in-law in 1862. By the time I had finished reading the relevant

Preface

source material, I felt impelled to attempt a short study
of Mackenzie's life. It is as a sketch of my "subject",
evoked and worked out in the context of an historical narrative, that *The Firebrand* has been written.

I should like to thank Colonel Charles Lindsey for his
helpful suggestions and for permission to use the *Lindsey
Papers*, which contain the principal collection of unprinted
material relating to Mackenzie. I am most grateful to Mrs.
H. M. Lay, Mackenzie's granddaughter, for telling me a
number of lively and illuminating stories from Mackenzie
family history. For their kind assistance in finding material,
I should like to thank Dr. G. W. Spragge and Dr. Margaret
Banks of the Ontario Archives, Mr. P. C. Band, the staff
of Mackenzie House, Miss Violet Taylor and the staff of
the University of Toronto Library, and Miss Olive New-
combe of the Dundas Historical Society Museum. Dr. W.
Stewart Wallace provided me with some excellent advice
and guidance at the beginning of my labours; Professor G.
S. French of McMaster University has advised me on a
great many matters and was good enough to furnish me
with some unpublished material which bears on the conflict
between Mackenzie and Ryerson; Professor Sydney Jackman of Bates College, who has been preparing a study of
Sir Francis Head, has put at my disposal his solution to the
problem of Head's appointment to Upper Canada; the
Reverend P. A. Sawyer, Rector of Thorold, and Professors
Gerald Craig and James Eayrs of the University of Toronto,
have read the manuscript in its earlier stages and offered
much useful criticism; Professor D. G. Creighton kindly
undertook to read the manuscript in its next to final form,
at short notice, but at a stage when certain of his suggestions for improvement could still be acted upon; my colleague Dr. C. M. Johnston was good enough to read the
manuscript in a proof and offer a number of suggestions. For
these several kind services, as well as for the less specifiable
but not less welcome help of friends, and for the inspiration
of my former masters in Canadian history, I wish to offer
my sincere, if inadequate thanks.

I should like further to record a debt of gratitude to McMaster University for a research grant which enabled me to complete the book, and in particular to the Head of the Department of History, Professor E. T. Salmon, for undertaking a portion of my own teaching duties during the final stages of the book's production. One of my former students, Miss Nancy Nablo, has assisted me with the proofreading, and undertook the preparation of the index, for which I am most grateful.

I wish to acknowledge the use of the John Ross Robertson Collection in the Toronto Public Library, which afforded an invaluable preparation for the setting of certain scenes in the narrative. I have also used a number of selections from *Landmarks of Toronto,* for which permission I am indebted to the executors of the John Ross Robertson Estate.

I am obliged to J. M. Dent & Sons (Canada) Limited for permission to quote an extract from *Building the Canadian Nation* by George W. Brown.

My wife has provided me with the advantage of her knowledge and research in the history of Upper Canada and, more particularly, with the use of several small unpublished studies she did in 1953 of certain episodes in Mackenzie's career. She has both inspired and criticized my work at every stage of the writing. And, not least of her labours of love, she has decoded my hieroglyphic pencillings and typed them into fair copy.

WILLIAM KILBOURN

Dundas, Ontario
Feast of St. Michael and All Angels, 1956

INTRODUCTION

THERE was a time when Canadians found politics the most exciting thing in the world, and, next to religion and clearing land, the most important. The reader's father or grandfather, if he was born in Canada, will remember neighbouring Grits and Tories who crossed the street to avoid speaking to each other. He will perhaps recall a day in the schoolyard when his family's support of a particular party cost him a face-wash in the snow. Indeed, it is not wholly impossible that *his* grandfather was one of the gentlemen called from their beds by the church-bells one winter morning to defend Toronto from rebellion, or one of the farm lads who shouldered musket or pitchfork to march against the city from the villages and farms of York and Simcoe and the counties to the west. For there was a rebellion once, and even something of a battle, on a country slope near what is now the Eglinton terminal of the Toronto subway: Politics came to that, even in Canada.

The affair ended, of course, in comic ignominy. The battle itself was something that even the most ardent Canadian nationalist does his best to forget. As for the permanent effect of the rebels' downfall, it appears to have left the country without a strong radical tradition. It seems possible, in retrospect, that the lack of a successful revolution may have had some connection with the unimaginative and sober nature of Canadian politics during the first half of the twentieth century. The political issues of 1837—real ones despite their dénouement—have been exchanged for a permanent gloat over the gross national product. The old passions have given way to a compulsive self-congratulation on the achievement of a nationhood of whose existence there is still some cause for doubt.

The failure of the rebellion may well have stunted the growth of political folklore in Canada; the Laurentian shield, with respect to the mining prospectors and the Group of Seven, is no substitute for a race of gods and heroes.

Considerations of the sequel to 1837, however, need not much disturb our purposes here. The path of this story does not lead to the four-lane highway of Canadian national development. Its protagonist represents a way we did not take. He is the sort of character we most emphatically did not become. Canadians are a people of the law rather than the prophets, and those few of them who are genuinely seized with the spirit could do worse than prepare to pay the penalty of ostracism or exile or madness. William Lyon Mackenzie, for a lifetime of passionate unselfishness and outspoken denunciation of public wrong, was rewarded in some measure with all three.

As for Mackenzie's opponents, the other principals of our story, it is doubtful whether they, any more than he, made a truly creative and positive political contribution to the building of the Canadian nation. Their lives have little connection with those later achievements by which a great trinity of Sam Smiles-ian Liberal prime ministers have given us a title deed to the twentieth century. The members of the old Family Compact did little but dig their heels in against the day when Canada should achieve that solid wealth and solid worth of which the distillers, like the rest of us, are so justly proud.

What, after all, of Bishop Strachan and the young Tories he schooled, what else of Strachan the politician can one say than that it is the most difficult thing in the world to imagine there ever *was* such a man. Politically he believed (as Walter Bagehot said of Lord Eldon) in everything it is impossible to believe in.

The political ideals and practice of a Mackenzie or a Strachan have not shaped the last hundred years in Canadian history. These men are not really among the makers of Canada, nor are they entirely fitting subjects for Parliamentary pedestals and tourist piety and the rigid bronze company of the civic park. If we are to plot Mackenzie and his enemies on the main graph of Canadian history, it is largely as useful challenges who have long since met their responses. Or perhaps we may choose to remember them as ancient bogey-men, whose ambitions to turn us into a North American Chile or Peru were once and for all strangled by the strong clean hands of Lord Durham and Robert Baldwin.

It will even be possible, in most of this story, to ignore the graph which plots the growth of nationhood and responsible government. There are other things in history besides the main chance (or what the present has decided the main chance to be). The historian has other jobs besides tracking down and making posthumous awards to the men who turn out to have done most for their descendants. People, after all, are ultimately more interesting for what they are, than for what they cause. A person is to be valued, finally, for the quantity and quality of *being* in him, rather than for what he does or does not lead to. And the same can be said of the shapes and sense of the places which he has inhabited.

It can be said without apology, then, that this story does not lead anywhere. It is cut off from the present by a break in the chain of consequence, as well as by the gulf of time. It must suffice that its actors along with their buildings and their homely treasures and their very landscapes are as earth-sunk and dust-stopped as the liveliest subject that ever caught Krieghoff's eye or brush. They are quite vanished with all the early American crinolines and winters and Indians of Currier and Ives. They are gone the way of the cooper's and dressmakers' and children's hoops, the buggies and broughams and sheds in the churchyard. Like the hunters of passenger pigeon, they are extinct. The splendid isolation of the single colonial colonnade once shone luminous and white from each prominence along the Niagara frontier; but, like the four quarters of the moon in the old calendars, the tall mansions and their light have long since set forever.

It must suffice that a world and its people are utterly gone from the face of things—and that we shall try for a time to recall a part of it. We shall try to see its people alive and spontaneous in their acting and responding, free as they once really were to make other choices than the single one in which the passing of time has frozen them.

Particularly it is in their politics that we are to watch them. If we are to make abstractions at all, it will not be for the graph, but in search of man the political species. We pretend, in fact, to nothing less than a scrutiny of politics. The pretence of anyone to do anything of the kind is, of course, a vast one. Politics is one of the oldest and subtlest of all the arts, and both the noblest and most soiled of the professions. It runs the whole scale of human seriousness from Thucydidean tragedy to fifth-rate light opera. It bears the marks both of the back room poker game and the quest for the good life. And it is the only fit calling for the philosopher kings of Utopia.

Thoughts of this sort might more often give the professional political scientist cause to hesitate as he confidently plies his calipers and his computing machinery; might well stagger the amateur historian a little from the smooth path of his style and his slim volumes. But there is a still more humbling consideration. It is one which must move any student of public affairs to awe, and also perhaps the one which most lures him on. The pursuit and direction of power to desirable ends is an occupation to which Lenin, St. Louis, and Lorenzo the Magnificent each devoted a lifetime. It is that concern which binds into a single company Gladstone, Sam Gompers and the Patriarch of Constantinople; Solomon, Gandhi, and the pupil of Aristotle; Genghis Khan, Queen Victoria, Boss Tweed, and Mackenzie King; and, possessed of more of the Old Nick than most and more than their share of unsuccess, Wat Tyler, Tiberius Gracchus, Sam Adams, and William Cobbett. Somewhere among the crankier and shabbier ranks of this last contingent, we shall discover the rebel of 1837.

Real people, and political types, we shall be looking for.

But, of course, we shall eventually have to come to terms with the graph too. We shall have to follow what there is of the line that leads from William Lyon Mackenzie and his rivals down to us, and back again beyond them to the distances of their own past. Mackenzie's rebellion and its twin in Lower Canada, by spelling out the doom of the Second Empire, prepared the ground for the coming of Confederation and the Commonwealth. Deciding a man's place on the graph may be secondary to a study of the man himself, but it is not unimportant.

Meanwhile, however, there are our several characters from early Canadian history at hand, and in search of an author. There is a world now scattered in the archives and the dust, waiting for whoever wants to try putting it together again. With a reminder that Everyman is ultimately his own historian, the reader is invited, by means of such help as his own imagination and this bookful of incidents can give him, to make a whole past come to life again, and to tell himself in as lively a manner as he knows how, the story of William Lyon Mackenzie, and the Patriots and Loyalists of 1837.

THE FIREBRAND

CHAPTER ONE

IT HAPPENED in York, most of it, in the early eighteen-hundreds. York was the capital of the British colony of Upper Canada and one of its chief military posts. It was the biggest market centre for the farmers and merchants of the colony. It had as many schools and churches as Kingston, its only serious rival. Such was progress, indeed, that by 1825 the population of York had attained the grand total of two thousand souls.

York was best reached by boat. In rainy seasons, when stretches of the road disappeared into impassable bog, this was the only way. Coming in from Lake Ontario, the pilots made for the tall lighthouse on the Peninsula (it only became Toronto Island thirty years later, when a storm cut off the eastern end from the shore) and steered through the western gap into Toronto Bay.

The Bay was always busy: barges, bateaux, York boats; Durham boats with their big hulls and fat single sail; and the timber rafts, each an acre or two of floating camp with crew's shacks and sails stuck on at random like posters in a parade. Smokestack-topped, the immense new black hull of the sidewheeler *Frontenac,* one of the earliest steamers ever built, often lay anchored there. But the schooner was still queen of the Lakes, and the two tall masts and graceful expanse of white sail was the more familiar sight.

Across the Bay stood the town, a few lines of severely elegant frame buildings perched hopefully above the swampy shore on the little cliff which ran between Garrison Creek at the foot of Bathurst Street and the Don River mouth.

William Lyon Mackenzie

The flag of Fort York marked the one, the four huge arms of Gooderham's windmill and the desolate shell of the Parliament Buildings, burned in the American invasion, marked the other. Behind the town rose the solemn green-black of the endless forest, still the most inescapable fact that imposed itself upon existence in Upper Canada. A thin gap in the trees at the centre of the long ridge (familiar now as the sharp slope below St. Clair Avenue) showed where Yonge Street climbed Gallows Hill and picked its way northwards to the scattered farms and villages in the wilderness.

In front of the town, a jauntier forest met the eye: masts, rigging, sails, warehouses, and the bell-towers on the docks. The waterfront was noisy. The fishwives in the fish-market at the foot of Church Street cried their wares. The hammers and saws of the shipwrights were busy on the hulls of new ships. Captains of small ships, the truckers and taxi-men of their day, loudly offered to carry freight or cattle or passengers to any of the hundred tiny ports and creeks on the lake. A steamer signalled her arrival by cannon; there was no steam to spare for a whistle. The docking ship was boarded by a swarm of porters, each seeking to snatch a traveller's belongings and carry them ashore. Hotel runners competed to carry off the travellers themselves to their own employer's hostelry. It was quieter a few hundred yards west along the shore, where Fisty Masterson, lake captain and smuggler, maintained his cottage and rented punts to admiring schoolboys. Farther west again, just below the well designed Georgian length of new building which was to provide a permanent home for Parliament, the sentry post was kept, a reminder that only a dozen years earlier the Americans had landed here and captured the town.

In the eighteen-twenties York scarcely covered the small rectangle from Queen to Front and Simcoe to Parliament Streets which is now the base of downtown Toronto. The area where the big department stores now stand was on the far northwestern edge of town, and a traveller once lost his way in

4

a swamp for hours while hunting for an isolated dwelling in that neighbourhood. Beyond this spot, scattered among the woods, were the country homes and estates of the well-to-do members of the community. Before one reached the corner of Yonge and Bloor, where the village of Yorkville clustered around a toll-gate, one was well into the country of the first pioneer farms.

The countryside abounded in game and wild life which spilled over into the town. Waterfowl by the thousands inhabited York's bogs and marshes. Deer on the street were a common sight, and in the nearby fields they were sometimes so numerous that they pastured among the cattle. Mink and beaver, trout and salmon could be taken in the creeks that flowed through and about the town. At least one farmer, driving "a load of pork" before him to market, was chased, pigs and all, down Bay Street to the docks by a bear whose path had been crossed. Early settlers remembered swamps which were the haunt of wildcat and rattlesnake.

In appearance, the shops and houses and public buildings of colonial York were humble enough, and, seen in a cluster, faintly suggestive of barracks. Even so, they were constructed with a certain knack for that civilized clarity of proportion, that superb symmetry in windows and doors, which are the marks of eighteenth century design. Most of the important buildings were on King Street. Near the west end was the famous corner known as "Education, Legislation, Salvation, Damnation". It was occupied by Upper Canada College, Government House, a church, and a tavern. On the present site of a thirty-four-story skyscraper stood York's first Methodist meeting house, two stories high and constructed of logs. Just north of King and Yonge stood the home and tannery of Jesse Ketchum whose leather made many of the shoes in Upper Canada and whose profits built the first Protestant churches and schools in York for the benefit of those who were not fortunate enough to be of the town's leading families.

King Street East was adorned with several fine mansions,

5

perhaps the best of them that of the Canada Company, dealers in land and owners of a vast stretch of territory between Lake Erie and Lake Huron. Also on King East, the square in front of the Court House afforded space for the assembling of the Orangemen's parades, for the country throngs come in to watch a public hanging, for the promenade of people of fashion on a spring day, or for the small informal gatherings for gossip and talk and argument which are necessary if a collection of individuals is to become a true community.

Across the square stood St. James' Church of England. Although it was small, the classic simplicity of its proportions gave it an air of importance and proclaimed a God of Reason, Aristocracy and Good Taste. We shall want to look inside St. James'.

Let us assume for a moment, then, that it is 1826, because in that year, hardly a minute's trot from St. James', the incident occurred which made William Lyon Mackenzie the talk of the town and pushed him firmly and finally into public life. Let us assume, too, that it is a Sunday— Sunday morning at eleven o'clock, for at that time in one place we shall find conveniently assembled the villains of our piece. They are known as the Family Compact.

The Family Compact is in church. Excellent men these, educated, well-bred, the leaders of society and rulers of Upper Canada, not the sort of villains you can hiss at, unless you can be persuaded to think of them as a group bound by ties of wealth and family into a conspiracy against the common people. That was how William Lyon Mackenzie thought of them. But there will be more to say about them after they have been introduced.

The church is full of sunlight which is captured and enlivened by the brilliant white of the pews and the wall panelling. The elaborate, colourful dresses of the ladies and the men's frilled shirt-bosoms and white cravats—"not apologies for cravats but real envelopes for the neck"—are worn as if in defiance of the surrounding forest and the difficulties of life in a pioneer community.

6

Round the edges of the church are benches for the poor and for the red-coated soldiers who parade across town from the Fort York garrison with band blazing and colours flying on certain festive Sunday mornings through the year. In the centre, box-like pews are ranged in rank for persons of quality: one for members of Parliament, another for the judges, and a third for other officers and gentlemen and their families.

At the far end is the pew of state surmounted by a canopy on four square white pillars and emblazoned with the lion and the unicorn, the crown and the shield, of the royal coat of arms. Here sits the Lieutenant-Governor of Upper Canada, chosen representative of His Majesty King George IV. The pew of state appears somewhat large for its occupant whose melancholy, pear-shaped face and tightly curled, powdered white hair maintain the royal dignity as best they can. Major-General Sir Peregrine Maitland is a noble, humourless man with a soldier's capacity for command and obedience but with little ability to imagine himself in other people's shoes. Disrespectful persons sometimes refer to him as Peregrine Pickle behind his back.

Sir Peregrine had the good fortune to elope with the Lady Sarah Lennox, daughter of the Duke of Richmond. When the Duke was appointed Governor-in-Chief of the British colonies in North America, he packed up his son-in-law and brought him along to govern one of them. So now in St. James' Church, York, sharing the vice-regal splendour of her husband, sits the Lady Sarah, conveniently remote in manner, and a touch too exquisite for the society of a frontier capital.

The real, the awful presence in that assemblage is not to be found in the pew of state. Look instead to the pulpit, where the formidable robed figure of John Strachan, Archdeacon of York, and destined to be first Bishop of Toronto, looms above the polite society of York like some visible antiphon to the lectern's great eagle of St. John. If the Family Compact has a leader, it is this man. The whole bent of his powerful will and considerable intellect is turned to the

7

achievement of his vision. He sees another England in the wilderness of Upper Canada, with the Church as its heart and soul. The Church is to be provided by law with valuable lands, with political privileges, and with the sole right of solemnizing marriage and as many of the sacraments and ceremonies of society as she deems fit; her schools and universities are to provide an intelligent clergy for the churches and an aristocracy fit to rule the colony. That he believed it all possible is some indication of how bold and tough a man he was.

John Strachan was once a schoolmaster to the sons of the better families back in the 1800's. Now he and many of his former pupils sat in the councils or the courts of the colony to advise and assist the Lieutenant-Governor. Now, too, many of the same men sit listening to their old master's sermon. Perhaps it will be enough to mention only the most distinguished of them. This proves to be the tall young man whom any observer must have already singled out as much the handsomest person in the congregration. John Beverley Robinson is the present head of the town's leading family. A lawyer before he was twenty-one, at thirty-five he has already had the refusal of the Chief Justiceship. He remains the intimate adviser of the Lieutenant-Governor and leader of the government's supporters, the Tory party, in Parliament.

Archdeacon Strachan's aristocratic pupils are not the only Tories in church. There are possibly more merchants and bank directors and land agents than anything else, bound to the government by the financial privileges and social distinction they receive. In the case of the Family Compact money is even thicker than blood.

But look at that splendid old Irish gentleman in the corner. He is Dr. Baldwin, the squire of "Spadina", who has recently finished constructing Spadina Avenue to reach his estate on the rise above town. He was once a schoolmaster himself, as well as a medical man, but of late he has been practising law and, it is generally believed, holds some dangerously radical ideas about politics. If it were not for

Dr. Baldwin and his family, and perhaps a few opposition members from the legislature, one might apply the old saying, to this congregation at least, that the Church of England is the Tory party at prayer.

The inconspicuous young man in the sober dark suit beside Dr. Baldwin is his son Robert, devout, steadfast, well-read, but lacking, it is generally feared, the gifts and brilliance of the Doctor. You would scarely guess, as you watch the congregation of St. James' on this Sunday morning in 1826, that to young Robert Baldwin the finger of history will point with most particular attention.

If William Lyon Mackenzie was in church that morning, you would not have found him in the comfortable pews of St. James'. Instead he would have been listening to the longest and deepest and fearsomest sermon being preached in York. For Mackenzie was a Presbyterian. It must be admitted that his application of a good Presbyterian training was at times rather less than Christian; his newspaper's description of a political opponent might occasionally sound like a Presbyterian sermon on sin, and there were times when his bookstore window was decorated with unflattering portraits of the Lieutenant-Governor and several prominent members of St. James' Church being roasted by a red gentleman with a pitchfork.

But better not try to picture Mackenzie listening to a sermon. For one thing, it is hard to imagine him sitting still. You had best see him at work, at which, in one way or another, he spent almost every hour of the day and night. In a small plain structure built a generation earlier for Dr. Baldwin's family, and situated on the Bay just a few blocks from St. James', Mackenzie kept house, newspaper office, editorial room, printing press, and bookstore all together. We have noticed the unusual window display already. Over the door a small sign announced "The Colonial Advocate, Wm. Lyon Mackenzie Editor & Prop." Inside it was dim and smelt of printer's ink. Long after his apprentices had finished their work and departed, Mackenzie could still be found there, proof-reading perhaps, writing out an editorial or, if he was rushed, cramming the words right into the type case as they came to mind.

He was only five foot six and looked smaller because of a slight, wiry build and a large head and high brow. The prominence of chin, and the lips pressed together like a vice suggested a will that would not be broken. One observer particularly remembered the "keen, restless, piercing blue eyes which, when they met your gaze at all, seemed to read your innermost thoughts." His features announced plainly that he was honest through and through, and uncomfortably suggested that if you did not agree with their owner, you must be *dis*honest or something worse. He had lost his hair from a fever and covered his baldness with a loose, flame-red wig which in moments of jubilation he used to toss at a friend or hurl to the floor. It would be understating the matter to say that Mackenzie was excitable.

CHAPTER TWO

WILLIAM LYON MACKENZIE came from a long line of fierce Scottish highlanders, who, with a precision in historical calculation then commonly practiced, traced their story to the Flood and derived their pedigree from our common parent Noah. It will suffice for our present purposes, however, that both William Lyon's grandfathers were of the clan Mackenzie. Both fought with their chieftain and Bonnie Prince Charlie in "The '45" when the Highlands for the last time rose in arms against an English king. His father, Daniel, was a dark young man of twenty-seven when he married, eighteen years younger than his wife, reckless, improvident with the little money he made as a weaver, wild, and fond of dancing. Lyon's exuberance and love of a good time were inherited from his father, who delighted in the whine of the pipes and the swirl of the kilts and the shouts of the dancers. If Lyon was never solemn, he was fiercely serious about most things, and in this he was like his mother, Elizabeth, a tiny creature with intense black eyes and tight thin lips. For her, life was not a round of pleasure but matter of hard work and Christian devotion.

Her only child was born near Dundee, Scotland, in the late winter of 1795, and the baby was only three weeks old when his father, the dark young Daniel, died. Elizabeth Mackenzie, like so many highlanders, was content to remain poor but proudly independent. One of young Lyon's earliest memories was of his mother, during the terrible famine of 1810, taking a handsome Mackenzie tartan which she had spun and woven herself and selling it for a little barley meal for her small son's breakfast.

Mackenzie was proud of the humble independance in which he had been raised. It taught him contempt for those who made their way up in the world by being pleasant. He felt an almost physical loathing for people whose wealth or power or social position was derived from what he chose to call "fawning and cringing" in the right circles. Those born in high estate he was disposed to admire, at least until proved guilty, which by Mackenzie's exacting code of honour could happen easily enough. His greatest respect was reserved for those among the common people who even in adversity had not allowed a good name to turn prostitute.

When he saw grounds for doing so he would ascribe a noble action in a man to his possession of a good pedigree, and he valued the influence of noble blood upon character, the more so since he claimed a trace of it himself. His mother was closer kin than most of her countrymen to "some of the first families of Scotland". She infused in him a deep prejudice for the Mackenzie name and its history. The very demons, she believed, owed it a certain obeisance, and family folklore in their branch of the clan had established that a Mackenzie never died without being warned of the event by the unearthly wail of their tutelary banshee.

It was not easy for young William Lyon to reconcile his Mackenzie pride with the facts of immediate family circumstances. Daniel Mackenzie had married a woman a whole generation his senior, and as strict in her morals as he was relaxed. Nor did he apparently let marriage curb his freedom of action. If the former circumstance excited the gossips, the latter aroused the more terrible notice of the elders of the Kirk. As a crowning affront to common decency, Daniel had the bad grace suddenly to take ill, go blind, and die, just when it seemed that a year spent in getting his wife a child but no money, had put him into such clear debt to responsibility that he would at last be forced to pay up.

As she struggled with hard circumstance, old Elizabeth's standoffishness to all the world exacted a widespread respect. It also won the tribute of more tongue-wagging. She and her small son were a strange pair, with their like intensity of eye and the similar nervous activity of the facial muscles which was a lifelong trait in both of them. Widow and orphan together armed themselves for their struggle for existence with pride enough for a whole Scottish clan.

All of Mackenzie's later life can be seen as a search to satisfy the unfulfilled wants of his early years. Much of his wild talk and violent posturing was that of a person who cannot accept himself for what he is. If there is such a thing as the small man's inclination to be aggressive, Lyon possessed it: this Mackenzie, whose ancestors wielded the claymore in battle with tall and braw abandon, was accustomed to find himself the tiniest person in any group he entered.

It would be wrong to belabour the point. A rebel's idealism cannot simply be explained away as compensation for his lack of stature or father or the full social acceptance accorded to the normal. It is not necessarily revenge upon society for personal humiliation. To Mackenzie's difficult childhood and hard family circumstance we may ascribe the intensity of his idealism. We may explain thereby certain of its perversities. For its content, however, we shall have to seek elsewhere.

It will be enough for the present to credit him with a simple compassion for the poor and the underprivileged and the outcast. He was well equipped to understand their lot with a sensitive but unsentimental accuracy. And if the school of experience exerted a simple, powerful influence on the lifelong character of his idealism, so did his formal education. The principles in which Mackenzie was brought up were directly at work in everything he did.

Elizabeth Mackenzie was an ardent Calvinist. If her pride meant that her young son occasionally went to bed without his supper, he never went without his lessons and his prayers. He spent evenings learning to recite the psalms and the Presbyterian catechism. He knew the Bible thoroughly. His writing was to be filled with its language and with the power of its rhythms, though it was a power sometimes harnessed to incongruously small purposes. It was, however, an admirably workaday and practical, often polemic, use that Mackenzie made of Scripture. His Bible is much underlined and circled, even clipped out, especially where the text speaks of judgment upon the Lord's unprofitable servants, or of liberty, and of rewards for longsuffering righteousness.

His Calvinist training and his knowledge of the Bible were to be important sources of his later liberalism. He remained a faithful Presbyterian in his later days in spite of a brief period of moral rebellion in his youth, and with equal fervour he embraced the dogma of the current rationalist liberalism. He did not examine them sufficiently to find any real conflict between his two religions. It was enough for him that their urgent moral demands had much in common and that their practice was terribly absent from the world as he found it.

As for all Scottish children, Mackenzie's schooling was thorough and severe. He was very small when he went to the parish school, "a bright boy, with yellow hair, wearing a blue coat with yellow buttons" as an old schoolmate described him. He was soon able to head the class, and was quick to help the other children, particularly the girls, with their arithmetic lessons.

He was also quick at sketching a chalk face on the back of a coat, or pinning paper slogans on a classmate while helping him do a sum. One day he dressed up as the teacher with gown, birch rod, tawed leather whip, and fool's cap for good measure. The room was in an uproar when the teacher, a burly giant of six foot eight, walked in behind his diminutive capering mimic. Small Mackenzie was whipped with the taws until his face became spotted over and the bigger boys began hissing and shouting at the master. He was seated for further punishment in the "holy cup", a stone basin on the wall once used for holy water when the school room had been a Catholic chapel. From this gargoyle's perch on the wall it was his custom to excite further confusion in the classroom with the gestures of a monkey and grimaces grotesquely various enough to decorate a whole Gothic roof. Summonses to the master's sanctum were ineffective, for he always managed to return with an earsplitting grin.

At the age of ten he decided to run away from home. He persuaded some friends to go along and they set off towards an old castle in the hills above Dundee. Here the boys planned to live as lonely hermits, far from the world of grown-ups and lessons. They soon found that hermits were subject to hunger and the fear of spirits and fairies. They managed to stick it out for several days before deciding that home and fireside and a good dinner were the most essential things in life.

At Dundee the sea was close, an invitation to adventure for all boys, and for young Mackenzie a passion. The ships and the raw mist and the North Sea wind blew up the wide Firth of Tay to the town, and left a rubbing of salt under the skin of its inhabitants and a hardiness in the bone not so often bred among the land-locked.

The boy spent his hours after school down on the harbour admiring sea captains and planning to stow away. He would race to double the capstan, or outclimb his companions to a vessel's crosstrees and turn the vane. One wager in marbles nearly cost him his life. He dived into the Tay although he was scarcely able to swim, and went under twice before he was fished out with a boat hook.

Mackenzie never lost his quickness or his talent for acrobatics. Once, in his forties, when two constables climbed his stairs to arrest him, he let them reach the top, then, in one nimble motion, dived straight between them, tucked his head between his knees, and somersaulted down the staircase and out of the door to freedom.

When he was eleven, Mackenzie began to haunt the local library and to read everything he could find. He became by far the youngest member of the reading room of the

Dundee *Advertiser*. A belief in the importance of numbers, and a sense of order which resembled the filing clerk's rather than the systematic philosopher's, prompted him to make a list of the books he read from that time until, as a young man, he came out to Canada. There were "54 in Divinity, 38 on geography, 168 in history and biography, 52 on travels and voyages, 85 on peotry and drama, 41 on education, 51 on science and agriculture, 116 on other topics, and 352 novels"—a total of 957 books in all, most of which he had read thoroughly and summarized in his notes. It is not surprising that his mother was afraid "less the laddie read himsel' out o' his judgment".

Mackenzie may have read not wisely but too well. Certainly those voluminous notes, from which selections were often thrown helter-skelter together to press home some editorial point, filled many long columns of the *Colonial Advocate* in years to come. Someone has said, after reading through the *Advocate,* that it is difficult to know where Mackenzie the man leaves off and Mackenzie the filing system begins.

Except under the most extreme pressure of work he never again abandoned the regular course of reading which he had set himself, and he later acquired the ability to read in staggering quantities. On his travels he could scarcely enter a city or the home of a new acquaintance without making first for the library. On visiting Washington he was quite as excited by the Library of Congress as by an interview with President Jackson, the great Democrat whom he profoundly admired.

Although there was more of the glutton than the gourmet in his passion for reading, he could not help but derive a certain mental agility as well as a wide general knowledge. The love of books was to play an important part in his life. He wrote several himself, he printed others, and he was able to earn his living from the book-selling business he operated from time to time in Scotland and North America. It is not these facts in themselves which are remarkable but rather the tremendous reliance he placed upon the power of the printed word. He believed it to be the great educator in all virtue, and the sure means of stirring men to a fight for social justice. He seemed almost to transform himself into a Society for the Propagation of Useful Moral Knowledge. Books, pamphlets, collections of quotations, he was to disperse broadside by the thousand upon his Upper Canadian public because they were "efficient weapons in the hands of free men".

He used his books for personal as well as public combat. More than once he surrounded himself with a chest-high barricade built from the piled and place-marked volumes from which he planned to make his defence in court or legislature against a charge of libel.

After Mackenzie left school, he became a clerk in a large merchandising firm where he learned much about accounting and banking that was of great use to him later in public life. At the age of nineteen, just after the British victory over Napoleon at Waterloo and the end of war that had begun before he was born, Mackenzie was ready to go into business for himself. He managed to borrow the capital to run a general store and circulating library. It lasted for three years, until the post-war depression was too much for him, and the business failed.

He went south to wander through England, taking jobs where he could find them, the best of them as the accountant for an important canal company. Increasingly, he spent his time and his money, like the prodigal son, in riotous living. During a long stay in Paris particularly, he disported himself in a fashion which might best be described as untypically Scottish.

When a Scottish friend proposed that they emigrate to Canada and set up business there, Mackenzie quickly reformed his ways. The prospect of a new life and of adventure absorbed him completely. His most besetting vice, gambling, had led him to the brink of personal financial ruin. This indulgence he gave up completely, never to return to it. He resolved to rescue his mother from her poverty, and he gave solemn promises to his creditors which he later kept to the last jot. In the spring of 1820 he boarded the schooner *Psyche* and set off upon the long perilous journey to an unknown land.

Close by the towering citadel of Quebec they landed at last, as immigrants still do, beneath the famous Plains where Wolfe's victory had determined the fate of the continent sixty years before. Mackenzie, impatient as always, hurried on up the river by the first boat. He took a job as accountant for the Lachine Canal Company in Montreal where he worked for several weeks during the summer of his arrival. He aroused the ire of the construction workers by telling them they were not doing a fair day's work. Nor did he fail to let the management know that in his opinion they were not running the firm as it should be run.

He moved next to York where he and a partner opened a drug- and book-selling business, in which Mackenzie was to take the profit from the drugs. The partners soon announced the establishment of another store, to be managed by Mackenzie, in a more westerly part of the province: "Mackenzie and Lesslie, Druggists, and Dealers in Hardware, Jewellery, Toys, Carpenter's Tools, Nails, Groceries, Confections, Dye-Stuffs, Paints & Etc., at the Circulating Library, Dundas". Dundas was a pleasant town at the head of Lake Ontario, its Scottish stone houses settled comfortably in the valley at the meeting of the two escarpments. The competition from its enterprising young rival, the nearby village of Hamilton, had not yet disturbed its placid ways.

Here Mackenzie brought his bride in 1822. He had been to school with Isabel Baxter in Scotland, but they had each forgotten what the other looked like. Mackenzie must have remembered something about her but how and whether he persuaded her to come we do not know. Very possibly old Mrs. Mackenzie chose the wife for her son. The determining factor in such marriages was often as simple as the scarcity of women in Canada and of marriageable men in Scotland. She crossed the Atlantic in May, he met her in Quebec, and three weeks later they were married.

It was the beginning of a long and difficult married life for Isabel Mackenzie. She had thirteen children, six of whom died in childhood. As she grew older, the reward of her labour was poverty, persecution, and exile. Yet she always remained gracious and gentle, loving and faithful to the strange, impetuous little man to whom, after such a brief courtship, she had committed her life.

Old Elizabeth Mackenzie came out from Scotland at the same time as her prospective daughter-in-law. She brought with her to the household in Dundas the little boy whose upbringing she had undertaken. William Lyon's son, James, was born, to whom it is not known, a few years before Mackenzie came out to America. James was always the centre of his father's ambitions, and the relation between them always fond and close.

In spite of the obvious difficulties, Isabel and William Lyon Mackenzie's marriage was a happy one. In 1823 Isabel presented her husband with a daughter whom he fondly named after her. The business supported them well and was soon clearing a handsome profit of £100 a month. Mackenzie dissolved his partnersip with Lesslie after deciding it cramped his independence, and he continued alone in the business after that.

Mackenzie's talents were not well suited to manual labour. His hands were small and quick but they were not those of a craftsman. He made half a dozen motions where one would have been more effective. "I cannot boast a talent for mechanics," he wrote, stating that even the task of carving a turkey was too much for him. He more than compensated for this awkwardness with his hands by his ability to master quickly and accurately the operating principles of any technical subject he set his mind to, whether it was printing, or pharmacy, or drafting laws. In such matters, as his surviving copy-books well show, he had the accountant's passion for crisp efficiency. "System is everything," he later wrote, when he encountered the Upper Canadian legislature's antiquated formalities and chaotic rules of procedure, all of which passed, to his horror, for an accepted method of doing its business. It was only in the larger matters—his blueprints for a better society, or the framework of his own philosophy—that he lacked a sense of order, or else wanted the time and patience to allow his sense of order to take effect.

Mackenzie, in short, would have been perfectly capable of amassing a small fortune from his business had he ever seen fit to devote himself to the project. As it was, however, he found financial prosperity and a comfortable existence in Dundas unendurable.

In the spring of 1824 he moved his family to the handsome stone house which stood high on the slopes of Queenston overlooking the Niagara River, and sank his merchandising profits in a printing press. Mackenzie had decided he must publish a newspaper. It was to be a precarious business but, except for the briefest of intervals, one that he never deserted during the rest of his life.

We may well ask why he did it. It may have been that he could not be content to grow rich while he saw so much poverty around him. He believed, certainly, that the men with power and privilege, by holding back the development of the country in their own selfish interests, were responsible for that poverty. On top of this, the very existence of the Family Compact represented an affront to his own family pride. He may have received, too, a social rebuff from one of its members during his first residence in York. The little man's peculiar appearance and manner were such that his aloofness would pass in society, not as evidence of restraint from vulgar familiarity, but as a sign of boorishness.

One has heard it said that if Mackenzie had been admitted even to the outer circle of the colony's ruling class he would have never founded a newspaper: if the Robinsons could have seen fit to pay him a call, there would have been no rebellion in Upper Canada. Such propositions are tempting but untenable. In later years Mackenzie looked on several well-intentioned offers of favour or public office as little short of insulting. He rejected them all as subtle attempts to buy him off or to deprive him of the total liberty of expression which he considered proper to every free man, and most of all to a Mackenzie.

Yet he had a compelling need to be noticed. Writing editorials afforded what was for him an easier means to that end than the practice of the social graces. It also allowed him to use his encyclopaedic book learning by prescribing it out in apothecary's doses for the ills of society. Whatever his ultimate motives, however, Mackenzie could hardly have kept out of the newspaper business if he had tried. He had it in his blood to stir things up, and to do so as publicly as possible. He was the most unselfish of idealists; he was also a born muckraker and scandal-monger.

Mackenzie published the first issue of the *Colonial Advocate* on May 18, 1824, at Queenstown. He stated proudly that this was the westernmost newspaper in His Majesty's dominions. Every extreme had a natural attraction for him, and in the faintly stuffy atmosphere of Canadian society this natural attraction was to bloom to the proportions of a mania. He would confront the complacent narrow-mindedness of his environment with an extreme of indiscriminate denunciation which was peculiarly his own.

Mackenzie's newspaper was soon noticed by the rulers of Upper Canada. That his ideas and criticisms were not kindly received may be gathered from an incident which occurred in the summer of 1824. At the time of the *Colonial Advocate*'s first appearance, the monument to General Brock was being built on Queenston Heights, where he was killed in battle against the Americans. During a small ceremony for the laying of the cornerstone, certain pious worthies saw fit to send the General on his last dark journey in the company of a small bottle which contained, among other comforts, the first number of the *Colonial Advocate*. Sir Peregrine Maitland, when he heard of this, ordered that the work on the monument be stopped immediately and a quantity of newly erected masonry pulled down for the purpose of removing the bottle and its offensive contents. New stone, minus bottle and *Advocate*, was laid, the hero's remains were decently preserved, and Mackenzie's attacks on persons in authority increased, as did the number of his subscribers.

With moderate success Mackenzie was as usual dissatisfied. He decided to move again, this time to York. Here he would be at the centre of political life in Upper Canada and he could fire on his opponents at closer range. He brought his precious printing press across the lake in November of 1824. It was characteristic of Mackenzie that Christmastime should be spent in moving and settling his little family. Henceforth we shall find him in the small house and shop which we have already visited on Palace Street, overlooking Toronto Bay. One may well imagine that Sir Peregrine wrinkled his refined nose in disgust when he heard of the latest arrival in his capital.

CHAPTER THREE

UPPER CANADA in the eighteen-twenties and thirties was hardly the prosperous, bustling, forward-looking community which we sometimes imagine our pioneer forefathers to have enjoyed. One traveller called it a "stagnant backwater". Others confined themselves to more specific complaints: the roads were atrocious, the winters were hard and the summers fly-ridden, the hotels were "badly conducted, from the stage coach to the preservation of butter which instead of being, as in the States, hardened by means of ice, was an unclean fluid." For the merchants, business was generally slow and there was little money being invested in new enterprises. Those settlers who laboured to carve a farm from the wilderness seemed sometimes to be faced with a hopeless struggle. Often unused to farming, they would spend years clearing land that could only yield a few harvests before it turned into desert. Others had given up, and were content to sit about the wharves or the taverns or the general store and watch what there was of the world move past them.

The situation seemed all the worse by contrast with the young United States whose border was far closer to most Upper Canadians than their own capital of York. The optimism and the progress and the very numbers of the people in the frontier states provided a dramatic contrast to the stagnation of Upper Canada, and in the eyes of the dissatisfied served as a constant reproach.

What could account for the contrast? More than anything, perhaps, it was the indifference of British statesmen and the scarcity of British investment money, for on those things the fate of the colony ultimately depended. One reason that the American west was developing so rapidly was that the government and private businessmen were willing to foster that development by spending their money there. But to William Lyon Mackenzie there was a simpler and deeper answer than that: popular control of government in the United States and the lack of it in Upper Canada.

Why not bring American democracy across the border then? For the good reason that the original population of Upper Canada had come there to avoid it.

When the American colonies won their independence, Americans who had remained loyal to their King and Empire were compelled to change either their convictions or their country. Of those who made the second choice, a number came to Upper Canada, a vast wasteland dotted sparsely with Indian villages and a few military palisades. The decision meant for most of them the sacrifice of a crude frontier farm in Pennsylvania or Western New York and the doubtful advantage of a plot of forest far to the north, the exchange of a hard life for a harder one. A few, however, like the Robinsons, were giving up the elegance of a Boston house or a Virginia plantation and the civilized society of the drawing room. But, simple and cultivated alike, they made the terrible journey north to struggle with the Canadian wilderness for the sake of the flag that flew over it. These were the United Empire Loyalists, the people who cleared the farms and planted the orchards, and on the banks of Lake Ontario built York and Newark and Kingston, crude and simple replicas of the great towns they had left behind. They had scarcely settled when they were threatened again.

The war of 1812 was fought because American frontier politicians wanted to "liberate" Upper Canada from British rule and annex it to the United States. As one might expect, Upper Canadians felt no desire for this form of liberation. Led by British soldiers and good commanders like Isaac Brock, they beat back their liberators at a dozen points along the border and in hard-fought naval battles on the

Great Lakes. At its farthest point of advance an American army landed at York in 1813 and set fire to the Parliament Buildings. The American general planned originally to burn the rest of the town as well. It is very probable that the Reverend John Strachan helped to change his mind. Coupling a shrewd appraisal of his captor with his natural confidence in the God of battles and big battalions, Strachan bluntly threatened him, not with the future judgment of heaven, but with more immediate vengeance at the hands of the British army. The town was spared.

During the war the Loyalists had many of their worst suspicions confirmed. Certain democratic sympathizers in Upper Canada turned traitor and joined the Americans. After the war, as Tories and members of the Family Compact, the Loyalists naturally associated democracy with treason. They regarded the arrival of American democratic ideals in the new Parliament Buildings with as much enthusiasm as they had watched American soldiers set fire to the old ones. They were soon reinforced as a governing aristocracy by another important group of settlers. Many of the British officers who had served in the War of 1812 retired on half-pay and took up land in Upper Canada, notably around Peterborough and Lakefield where many of their handsome homes still stand. They lived, most of them, in dignified but poverty-ridden gentility. Often they failed to keep pace in farming with the husky farmer-immigrants from Britain and the United States who settled around them. They served as local justices, they took the title of Squire, and they kept the country British.

It was natural for these colonists, living in a military outpost in a period of war and truce, that their idea of Britain should be a military one. To them, as to later generations of Britons overseas, Britain meant, more than anything, the red-coated grenadier, the Union Jack, the crimson patches on the map of the globe, the sum of which stood for law and order and decency in a world that would go rapidly to the dogs without them.

It was a colonial attitude, often the view of the man

who called Britain "home" though he had never been there. It neglected, unfortunately, some of the best things about British civilization, from the habit of buying books to the parliamentary tradition of brilliant debate and high political integrity. It might be summed up in the old saying that "an ounce of loyalty is worth more than a pound of brains."

As one might expect, then, the government of Upper Canada was a loyal replica, at least in outward appearance, of the government in the old country.

At the top the Lieutenant-Governor, usually a British soldier like Sir Peregrine Maitland, represented the King. He received his orders from the British Secretary of State in London who directed the affairs of the whole Empire. Within the limits of these general orders, however, his power was supreme. To assist him at his good pleasure, he had an Executive Council chosen from among the leading persons in the colony. He was not bound to seek their advice, let alone take it, but his social affinity with them, and his unfamiliarity with the colony's affairs, often led him to accept their wishes and their point of view. "He arrived here," wrote Strachan in the course of praising Sir Peregrine Maitland, "with some ideas on the Executive Government not founded on sufficient evidence; but he now sees things more clearly."

The Executive Council differed from the modern cabinet in that its members were individually responsible to the governor rather than collectively responsible to the representatives of the people. They were not dependant upon the support of a majority in the lower house of the legislature nor were they usually members of that body. They were each chosen and appointed at the governor's pleasure and they were almost never asked to resign.

As far as administration was concerned, all Executive Councillors more or less participated in everything the government did, when and if the governor chose to ask for their advice. The departments of the civil service, not necessarily headed by members of the Council, were very small since the government did not attempt to do much towards the developing of the community. This in itself, of course, was a prominent cause for complaint from members of the legislature.

There are three parts to a legislature of British parentage: the royal person, and the two houses in which the whole community of the realm is virtually assembled. In Parliaments, then as now, a bill had to be passed by a majority of the members in both houses and signed by the king or his governor before it became law. In Upper Canada the upper house was called the Legislative Council and was modelled on the British House of Lords. Its members, however, were simply appointed for life by the Lieutenant-Governor, and so did not have the independence possessed by the Lords, most of whom inherited the right to sit from their fathers. It was inevitable that the Legislative Council, like the Executive Council, should be dominated by the Family Compact. Indeed, Archdeacon Strachan, who never did things by halves, thought it necessary and proper that he himself should be a member of both councils at the same time.

The lower house, the House of Assembly, was the place where the common people had a chance to express themselves through their own elected representatives. Even here, however, the Family Compact often held control, though the Compact's supporters were capable of a show of independence long since stifled by the party whip. They had two great advantages which often won elections for them. The first was the government's power to spend money on politically useful people and places. Were the Tories in danger of losing Glengarry? Let the tavern keepers be subsidized for their unstinting hospitality during election week. Was Sir Allan MacNab being given a close race in Hamilton? Let it be noised abroad that the government would present the city with a splendid post office if the electors would oblige Sir Allan. But the pork barrel is one of our more basic and permanent constitutional customs and needs no further description.

The second and more important Compact advantage was

the issue of loyalty. The Tories claimed, sometimes quite justly, that they were fully loyal to King and Empire, that their opponents were not, and that such loyalty was the ultimate test of political right and wrong. It was to be William Lyon Mackenzie's misfortune that in the crises most people were fully prepared to agree.

The Reform party had all the other advantages. They generally had the sympathies of the common people. They profited from bad times, unemployment, a crying lack of schools and roads, and from their demand that these things be remedied. Such a demand had little permanent effect, however. The Reformers might hold all the seats in the House of Assembly (for a time in 1829 they almost did so!) but the Tories stayed in power as long as the government and the British Colonial Office pleased. This led to irresponsible behaviour on both sides. The Tories did not have to justify their behaviour to anyone in the colony because they held office in spite of popular disapproval. The Reformers did not have to weigh their criticism or their promises because they would not be in a position to act upon them.

The solution to this problem, which would eventually become the basic principle of government in all the colonies, was as yet firmly and clearly fixed only in the minds of Doctor Baldwin and his son Robert. By the principle of responsible government a ministry must command the confidence of a majority in the House or make way for a ministry that can do so. And the governor must always act on the advice of his ministers. Out of sheer necessity something remotely like this already existed in England: a ministry could not long survive without the money voted to it by the House. But often in the colonies the salaries of the governor and other important officials were already provided for, and only the clerks' salaries and specific new expenditures depended on the vote of the popular house.

The feature of British society which the Family Compact chiefly wished to reproduce was even more fundamental than a system of government. It was the fact of aristocracy itself. There must be a governing class. Its members must supply the councillors, the judges, the professional men and the militia officers for the whole colony, the squire and the parson in every parish. Their duty would be the welfare of the people, whom they must care for as lovingly and sternly as fathers cared for their children. They must set an example in manners, in morals and in religious observance. They must foster art and music, poetry and drama. They must grace the countryside with beautiful houses and estates. If their duties were great, so were their privileges. They must have sufficient land and wealth and prestige to feel no need to grasp for more. They must have leisure to lead the cultivated life. They must be educated for their task in schools fit for gentlemen.

It was a noble ideal. It was also one that could not be realized in Upper Canada. The frontier imposed a democracy of its own and allowed a certain freedom to those who did not choose to be governed by an aristocracy. There was little leisure for those who aspired to be the aristocracy: Robert Gourlay, a Scottish critic of Upper Canadian society, suggested that a stranger might be informed to his surprise and dismay that a pair of yokels working in a hayfield, with pitchforks in hand, were the Duke of Ontario and the Marquis of Erie. The idea of an aristocracy lent itself too readily to ridicule. It also lent itself too readily to abuse. A born aristocrat might be an excellent thing but an aristocrat on the make was intolerable. Members of the Family Compact were, for the most part, of the latter variety. There was inevitably a struggle to acquire the privileges of aristocracy—the best lands, the best positions and favours of every description from the government. The duties of fatherly care for the people and intelligent patronage of piety and the arts had usually to be neglected. This criticism was not entirely applicable to Archdeacon Strachan and his fellow priests, whose labours for their scattered congregations and for the cause of higher education were of heroic proportions, but whose insistence on exclusive privileges for their own Church scarcely inspired non-

Anglicans with confidence in their motives or their sanctity.

Those who complained of neglect or who attacked the very idea of aristocracy and privilege were apt to run into trouble. Robert Gourlay had done both. For two years, soon after the War of 1812, he had written scathingly but intelligently of the backward state of Upper Canada. He circulated a list of questions among the common people asking precisely what changes were needed in each district. The authorities had him arrested and imprisoned, and, after a trial which was a mockery of British justice, he was banished from the colony forever. The next man to complain rudely and publicly of the condition and rules of Upper Canada was William Lyon Mackenzie.

"Another reptile of the Gourlay breed has sprung up among us," wrote John Beverley Robinson, on first seeing the *Colonial Advocate*. "What vermin!"

CHAPTER FOUR

"I HAD long seen the country in the hands of a few shrewd, crafty, covetous men under whose management one of the most lovely and desirable sections of America remained a comparative desert." So wrote Mackenzie of his early years in Upper Canada and his decision to publish a newspaper. When he got down to details, Mackenzie the editor sometimes changed his mind as to which were "the few shrewd, crafty, covetous men". In one *Colonial Advocate* it would be the members of the Assembly. In another it was reduced to a particular individual, no matter if he had been praised to the skies a few numbers before. More often Mackenzie was content to speak generally—of "the funguses" which grew in the shade of Government House, of flatterers, time-servers, defrauders of the people. Consistency and moderation were not among his virtues. His editorials spoke out whatever inspiration came into his head, whenever it came. He thought it hypocrisy to do anything else. To read the *Advocate* then, was to be sure of finding remarks that had been better left unsaid. The *Advocate* was widely read.

Another of the editor's faults also helped to sell the paper. He often failed to distinguish between the public and the private life of an opponent. A prominent Tory would be informed by the *Advocate* that a member of his family had been living in sin. One of the Governor's favourite councillors would be reminded that he was originally a cobbler's apprentice. The Robinsons, descendants of a long line of Virginian planter aristocrats before their U.E.L. days, were gratuitously advised that their "mothers came to America to try their luck and were purchased by their sires with tobacco according to the quality of the article."

Yet there was much to be said for Mackenzie's fault, in its less inspired and imaginative moments. The Family Compact itself, by definition, was such a close intermingling of the public and the private that it invited the kind of attack which did not distinguish between the two. With a kind of holy glee Mackenzie published lists of the Compact's members and their occupations: "No. 7. Peter, brother to No. 6" (No. 6 being John Beverley Robinson, at the time Chief Justice of Upper Canada) after which followed titles of Peter's several government positions and a note of his income.

Mackenzie at first exempted the King's representative from personal abuse, and indeed he remained through most of the 1820's a thorough royalist. But he proclaimed loudly that his loyalty to the King was no reason for him "to cringe" before "His Majesty's butcher or baker", as he called Robinson and Strachan. He was not long in adding the Lieutenant-Governor himself to the list of royal hired help. He was fonder still of characterizing Sir Peregrine as one of the lilies of the field, who toiled not neither did he spin. Notices were published in the *Advocate* every social season of Sir Peregrine's stately progresses from the sumptuous vice-regal mansion on the Niagara to Government House in York. Mackenzie announced the event as "the migration from the blue bed to the brown".

In his rude fashion, Mackenzie helped attract the attention and support of the common people to the one cause about which he never changed his mind. He was obsessed with the need for honest and efficient government and for government which would respond immediately to the criticism and the wishes and the welfare of the people. He did not find such a government in Upper Canada. In the end he never found it, for he persisted in expecting that human affairs should attain the condition of the kindom of heaven. But possibly it is part of the editor's calling, as it was the prophet's, to expect nothing less. At the very least he must be prepared to attack wickedness in high places and to condemn a generation which falls short of righteousness. In such preparation and such attack Mackenzie undeniably abounded.

In spite of denunciations and the occasional titbit of scandal, the early colonial newspaper was not a particularly exciting or sensational affair. By the standards of the yellow press, indeed, it had all the pace of a three-volume Victorian novel. It took an evening, not a glance, to do justice to the front page. The style was something of a cross between Old Farmer's Almanac and a threadbare Ciceronian rhetoric. In short, the paper was a matter for sustained attention as it was read aloud of a long winter's evening.

> Generally on the evening after the paper comes to hand, a few of the neighbours assemble in my house, and after our homely compliments are exchanged a *reader* is appointed, who, after drawing a chair up to the table, trimming the candle, coughing and clearing his throat, unceremoniously bawls out, "Silence"— and immediately all are attention. After the reading is over, then come the remarks.

"The remarks no doubt often went on into the night." The early newspaper and its politics made democracy possible at the level where it matters most—the exchange of ideas in the neighbourhood, the serious but not necessarily solemn conversation among friends.

Of course the *Colonial Advocate* was not all politics. Turn past the solid fine print—debates, reports and speeches —on the first page you will find odd bits of local news:

> A 3¼ lb. tooth has been found on the banks of the Don River together with many other bones of enormous size. There is every probability that they have lain there since the Flood, for it is hardly probable that 6 ft. of clay could have been thrown over them at any other period.

There are no big advertisements, just as there are no banner headlines, but in the personal column on a good day can be found almost any necessity from a fully-stocked farm to the wares offered by Mackenzie himself when he began to dispense medicines in conjunction with his small book business. He announced that he would be happy to supply the public with "Balm of Quito, Pectoral Balsam of Honey, Godfrey's Cordial, Harlem Oil, Essence of Lemon, Jesuits Drops, Mochrikufsky's Russia Oil, Cordial Cephalic Snuff, and Young's Vegetable Specific for Wounds and Ulcers" among other things, remedies which must have been wonderfully comforting to the imagination, whether they effected direct physical cures or not.

The newspaper's personal column asked regularly for such information as the whereabouts of a daughter (emigrated from the old country two years since), or gave notice of a one farthing reward for the return of a runaway apprentice, or announced a husband's refusal to honour bills contracted by a missing wife. The commonest item of all is announced by a small printed symbol of a cow:

Came within the enclosure of the subscriber at the head of Spadina Avenue, about three months ago, a large brindle cow with white face, and has calved within a day or two. The owner is requested to prove property, pay charges, and take her away. Wm. Burns

Sometimes subscribers themselves supplied the best copy in their letters to the editor:

Esquising Jany 8 1827

very Dear Sir,—I have taken upon me to write you a few Lines to let you know that the Scotts Bodys that Lives heare is all doing Tolerably well for the things of this world but I am afraid that few of them thinks a bout what will Come of their Soul when Death there days doth End for they have found a thing they Call Whiskey and a great many of them dabbales and drinks at it till they make themselves worce than an ox or an ass.

Now Sir I could tell you Bits of Stories but I am afraid that you put me in your Colonial Advicate I do

not Like to be put in prent I once wrot a bit of a letter
to my Son Robert to Scotland and my friend Jas. Hogg
the poet put it in Blackwoods Magzine and had me
through all North America before I New that my letter
was gone Home. Hogg poor man has spent must of
his life in coining Lies and if I read the Bible right I
think it says that all Liares is to have there pairt in the
Lake that Burns with fire and Brinston But they find
it a Loqarative trade for I belive that Hogg and Walter
Scott has got more money for Lieing than old Boston and
the Erskins got for all the Sermons ever they Wrote.

Now my the Blessing of God rest on you and all
Loers of his name is the sincer prayer of your Loving
Contry man old James Laidlaw

Esquising

Within a week of writing his letter, James Laidlaw was
in print once again. He wrote to Mackenzie, "This will
let you know that you have Done me a very Bad trick in
prenting my bit simpel Letter that I sent you ye are shurly
very Scarce of Mercy. I thought you had more honour than
expose an old Body like me shall say little more but if I
ever come to you, I shall give you your XXXX. I ould give
you my advice to read your Bible."

Mackenzie must have known how miserable his exposure
would make the poor old man, but once he laid hands on
good copy he was incapable of restraint, least of all when
its potential for damage was greater than in this instance,
or when the person most hurt by publication would likely
be himself. It has been said of Mackenzie that you could
trust him with your life but not with your secret.

One will search most of the newspapers of early Upper
Canada in vain for any semblance of an intelligent art,
music or drama review. Whatever other reasons there may
be for this, the lack of good art, music and drama in the
community will suffice. This journalistic gap was partially
filled however, by the sermon review, just as the sermon
itself in no small measure fulfilled the function of the public
theatre. It is true that the early Canadian sermon was all
too frequently little more than a stew of old-fashioned tur-

gidities, or, at the other extreme, became "a clamorous presentation of the obvious". Indeed in the hands of some few ancient journeymen of the mystery the sermon achieved an amazing organic fusion of both styles. Nevertheless, the continual oral recreation and elaboration of a single body of myth vitally enriched the culture, however impoverished it may have been in the higher art forms, and was an un-ending source of earthiness and subtlety and harsh vigorous music to the common speech. A language which lacks a Bible must invent one, and invented Bibles are apt to be very thin gruel. The sermon, too, besides providing the chief substance of that living oral tradition of which political rhetoric formed a part, served to feed those common instincts and assumptions which are embedded so deeply in the mind of the community that they are taken for truth by all its members. The words from the pulpit nourished the land and its culture in the manner of that rain which seeps down to underground tributaries for the supply of wells.

Mackenzie, in the best Scottish tradition, attended church twice on the first Sunday of the New Year, 1826. He came away with copy for the *Colonial Advocate*. He went first to the Presbyterian Church, but it was with an account of "the fascinating delivery", in the evening, of a young Methodist named Egerton Ryerson, who will soon loom large in our story, that he chose to fill his columns.

> When we entered the church that Sabbath night, they were singing a hymn, and we found ourselves in the midst of the largest congregation we had ever witnessed in Upper Canada. Beside Mr. Ryerson, in the pulpit, sat an aged and venerable man whose name we have not learnt. . . .
>
> During prayer all was still, save for the deep and sonorous voice of the minister, as he put up a petition to the Holy One of Israel in behalf of the humble supplicants under that roof, in behalf of the whole human race: fervently did he implore a God of Mercy, for the sake of Him who died on the accursed tree, to blot out

the transgressions, and forgive the backslidings of his people. Earnestly in the sermon did he call upon those who heard him to remember the shortness and uncertainty of time, to think of everlasting eternity, and to make up their peace with Jehovah—for to many, another New Year's day might never revolve on this side the grave. He impressed upon their minds the immortality of the soul,—every voice was hushed, except where some one deeply sensible of his own unworthiness in a soft whisper responded to the truths which fell from the lips of the servant of Christ.

> The SUN is but a spark of fire,
> A transient meteor in the sky;
> The SOUL, immortal as its Sire,
> SHALL NEVER DIE.

It is of great advantage to a preacher when he has read much, not only in the sacred scriptures, but also in that vast record of human perseverance, miscellaneous literature. That Mr. Ryerson has not been negligent in this respect is apparent from the tenor of his discourses—he touches every chord of the human heart, but he never forgets his index.

And so Mackenzie continued with his review, on into a discussion of the manner in which Mr. Ryerson dealt with his text, which was drawn from the eighth chapter of St. Luke's gospel, the parable of the sower.

For many people the newspaper was the chief tie with the capital they hoped one day to visit, and with the old homeland they knew they would never see again. A good deal of news three months cold was reprinted from the British newspapers. The doings of York were retailed somewhat more freshly. As for comics, crime, gossip, pictures and sports, one must be satisfied with more political fine print and an editorial or two. But then politics in those days had something of the character and interest of all those things put together. At least they did when Mackenzie wrote about them.

Part of Mackenzie's hold over the loyalty of the farmers of Upper Canada had little to do with the cut of his politics, however, or with his ability to flay the Compact and voice their sense of injustice. He was a good story-teller. He knew instinctively how to entertain his readers, as well as how to educate or preach at them. The antiquarian's nose for curiosities was one of his better-cultivated senses and it led him on his travels to the source of much new provender for his store of rural folklore.

A short time since, in an adjoining town, a happy pair were joined in wedlock by a facetious township squire whose fees totally exhausted the funds of the bridegroom. Not many days had elapsed before the parties who had been joined till death should them part, became mutually dissatisfied with their lot, and returned to the squire with their many tales of woe, beseeching him with all their eloquence to *unmarry them*; which he agreed to do, provided he was previously paid the sum of three dollars, double the fee of their first ceremony. This sum the bridegroom paid by a week's labour on the squire's farm. Then came the ceremony of the parting. The squire placed a block on the floor, on which was put a live cat; one pulled the head and the other the tail, while the squire with an axe severed the cat in twain, at the same time exclaiming "Death doth you part." The couple departed with the firm belief that the performance was strictly legal, and have not lived together since.

Mackenzie collected a great number of such stories from the *Advocate* and published them, along with new material, in the book called *Sketches of Canada and the United States*. His writing was not troubled by classical compunctions about form or a sense of order. His method in the *Sketches* approximated that of the medieval chronicler who said he had made a heap of all that he had found. Mackenzie's own interest and style imposed what unity the book had.

He retold the story of "an old curmudgeon whose brains were made of sawdust, hog's lard and molasses, but who on account of the spaciousness of his farm had been for years head of the school committee in his district", and of his daughter who tricked the old man into hiring her lover as schoolmaster.

For those who had not heard the man in person, Mackenzie printed a description of the Rev. Lorenzo "Crazy" Dow, a Methodist preacher, whose parish was North America, "wherein he itinerates at will, preaching by appointment from the tops of rocks". The Rev. Mr. Dow told every congregation he preached to that they were hearing his best sermon, and at least one congregation that he needed a wife and would a lady please rise, upon which he married the first volunteer.

Mackenzie watched, and then interviewed, the famous Mr. Sam Patch who specialized in leaping off things. On this occasion he had hurled himself 160 feet down into the whirling waters of the Niagara gorge, with the Falls for a backdrop and several thousand people looking on. Mackenzie's readers were gratified to learn that he "inhales when he leaps and says it does not hurt him in the least."

Among the stories, Mackenzie scattered accounts of his travels in America and through the Upper Canadian countryside he now knew so well. He gave advice to prospective immigrants on which crafts and trades were needed in Upper Canada, and which not, and exactly what trade conditions they could expect to find. He composed a short bucolic on the joys of an Upper Canadian farm, and surrounded it with much moralizing, in the manner of Benjamin Franklin's Poor Richard, on how the joys were to be achieved.

> Be diligent—persevere—neither eat, drink, nor wear anything that is not produce of your own farm—if you can avoid doing so—until your lands are payed for, and a freehold title recorded in your pocket. Rather make a good bargain than grasp at too much with the risk of getting into debt. If your clothes be plain and clean, never care although they be coarse. You will be valued by your conduct and not by your clothes. As to food, your own mutton and beef, and pork and veal, and butter and cheese, and potatoes and corn, and poultry &c. raised at home, will render you as independent as

King William IV. Drink good water, or plain family beer, (there is no malt-tax or exciseman to interfere with you) and look forward to the time when the orchard you have planted and enclosed will bear fruit abundantly, and enable you to refresh yourself and comfort a friend with an occasional tankard of racy, home-made cyder. As to tea, coffee, smoking or chewing tobacco, snuffing, and the vile practice of drinking spirits, be not tempted by the extraordinary lowness of price in America; "touch not, taste not, handle not."

But the thought of the new settlers and the land brought to mind the unjust way in which its sale was regulated, and Mackenzie's mind veered back like a magnet to thoughts on misgovernment. He printed in the *Sketches* a long letter from an old Scots shepherd, from which we have already quoted, telling of the rogues in the land offices who made it hard for a poor immigrant. The shepherd's sorry tale is, in type, though perhaps not in the manner of its telling, the tale of thousands who came from Britain to the British possessions in the New World.

America is a good country for a poor man if he is able to work but it is Country that is full of Rougs that is what I like it worst for there is very few but will Cheat you if they can if I had known it to be what it is it Should never have seen me but times being bad in Scotland after the Wars and old Shepherds Like me being not Much thought of when we get old I thought of coming to America and there was an Advertisement in one of the Edinburgh News Papers in the year 1816 that ony Body that wished to go to Canada Government would take them out free of Expense and they were to Write to a Mr Campble in Edinburgh so I Wrote Mr. Campble telling him what family I had that I had five sons and told him there age and I wanted to know how much land each of us ould get, so he wrote me that I was a very fit hand to go to America having so many sons and that I could get Two Hundred Acers for myself and Like ways for Every one of my sons that was come of age but I could not get away as stock was so low and it could not be turned into money but times was better in Two years So I sold all that I had and came away 1818 and I had to come out on my own Expense for by this time there was no word of Bringing ony to Canada So I came to work and went through all there offices according to acte of parlement I sopose and aye the other Dolor to pay but they ould only give us one Hundred acers Each,—and that was to be drawn Ballat if it was good Land we were the better of it and if Bad we bid Haud with it if there Map said it was capable of cultivation I believe the Cribblers in York ould tak the last Shilling that a poor man has before they ould do anything for him in the way of getting land for in one of there offices they were crying it is five and Sixpence and only Marking two or three words, but I will pass them for they are an avericeous Set. I am Realy feared that the Deil get the must part of them if they do not bethink themselves in time, I sopose that they never read the tenth commandment or they could not covet their niboures money

It does not much matter that the "Cribblers in York" were clerks doing their day's work or that the Canada Company justified their possession of huge tracts of land by bringing out settlers and providing a certain amount of help in the way of bridges and roads. It was a fact that the sale of Crown lands was not efficiently handled nor adequately regulated by law. Furthermore, the Canada Company who resold so much of it at a handsome profit, and the Commissioner of Crown lands, the Honourable Peter Robinson, grew rich, while those that worked the land did not. The undeveloped Crown and Clergy reserves in every township placed a greater burden of the taxes for local improvements upon the actual settlers. These things added up to the most substantial fact of all: a sense of injustice, and a willingness to subscribe to Mackenzie's belief in a conspiracy of the crafty covetous few.

Running a newspaper in Upper Canada was a precarious venture at best. Most of the early newspapers never survived past the first few issues. It was especially difficult for those whose object it was to be critical. Mackenzie complained with some justice that "four-fifths of the journals published in this colony are continually in raptures with the Lieutenant-Governor, the Councils, and the House of Assembly." His own violent attacks on public institutions, particularly the Post Office, did not make it any easier to publish and distribute his newspaper. In 1826 it looked as if the *Advocate* was finished. It appeared irregularly, only as often as Mackenzie could scrape together enough money to cover the cost of printing.

Another of the editor's problems was to persuade the subscribers to pay for their papers. Sometimes an editor took his payment in goods. One cold December in the 1830's the Cornwall *Observer* announced, "Our wood-paying subscribers will please send us a few cords of wood at their earliest convenience." Mackenzie held out for cash, which meant that he had to spend time trying to collect small bills, or else pay a collector to travel for him, into the far corners of the province.

We must not assume that the *Advocate* was lacking in public support. Mackenzie had a fairly effective network of political allies, including the Reform leader Marshall Spring Bidwell, who acted as *Advocate* agents in their localities, and who forwarded paid-up subscriptions by the batch. There were country folk willing to part with the only bit of cash they had seen in weeks in order to keep the *Advocate* alive. But inevitably in a far-flung and relatively poor community, many papers were not paid for. The greatest financial difficulty arose from the Post Office's practice of demanding from the publishers quarterly payments in advance, based on the maximum number of papers sent out through the mails, and at a very high rate per paper. No guarantee of delivery was given and thanks to the uncertainty of the post and the unfavourable disposition of Tory postmasters, the *Advocate* suffered. The system was such for a time that the more subscribers a paper listed, the more money it lost.

Mackenzie's health was never good, and the "dumb ague", a recurrent malarial fever he had contracted upon his arrival in Upper Canada, never left him. The strain of overwork aggravated the disposition to terrible chronic headache which he seems to have inherited from his mother. And in spite of everything he could do, his debts mounted and his creditors began threatening him.

Just when his situation had become desperate, Mackenzie's worst enemies came to his rescue. He celebrated the *Advocate's* second anniversary on May 18, 1826, by digging out what he believed were several skeletons from the closets of the better families and providing them with a loud public funeral. The issue also contained vicious personal attacks on several leading members of the Family Compact. Most of the persons concerned found the attack so wild as to be beneath notice. Some of the younger ones, however, decided to teach Mackenzie a lesson. One more issue of the *Advocate* appeared on June 8. It was much like the last.

That evening, just before a warm June sundown, the good people on the east side of town, their doors open and dinner over, were treated to the unusual sight of fifteen well-dressed young gentlemen marching Indian file in the direction of the Bay. On reaching Front Street, they turned, set of purpose, towards the office of the *Colonial Advocate*. It was closed. They shouted to be let in. Old Mrs. Mackenzie, upstairs having a late high tea with her young grandson James, was terrified. If Mackenzie himself had not been out of town, there would have been a violent scuffle then and there.

When they received no reply, the young gentlemen stove the door in, entered, and set to work destroying everything they could find. The press was broken. The type cases were smashed. The type was carted across the street and thrown into the Bay. Two of Mackenzie's apprentices rushed over to see what was the matter, but on being threatened with a club thought better of picking a fight. The only persons who could have stopped the destruction were the officials

43

and magistrates whom Mackenzie had been attacking. And of these the two who were on the scene were content to watch the whole affair. Colonel Heward, Auditor-General and clerk of the peace, out for an evening's stroll, and Mr. Justice the Honourable William Allan, who stood smoking his pipe in his doorway, were obviously enjoying themselves as much as their young friends and relations at work on the press.

Mackenzie, across the lake in Queenston, was quickly possessed of several accounts of the incident, and a plentiful supply of rumours. A reliable report came from Jesse Ketchum, the Reform-minded businessman, who wrote to say that public reaction was in Mackenzie's favour. Contrary to a spreading rumor, he would be safe in York and probably would recoup all his losses in a court settlement. But Ketchum could not refrain from adding an avuncular rap on the knuckles: "On your part you should not call Mr. Allan Shoe Black any more nor Mr. Mcally Barber." Mr. Macaulay was in point of fact a judge, and churchwarden of St. James', but like others of the Compact hypersensitive to unpleasant insinuations about the respectability of his family's early history.

Mackenzie replied firmly and cheerfully to the solicitude and friendly reproof of another acquaintance: " I have no fear for the future, none—I will surely get justice of the government people, and if so I will be able to pay all I owe and begin the world anew with a cargo of experience for my stock in trade. I am glad it is only with my journal you find fault, for as it is dead and drowned and ended you will of course scold W.L.M. no more."

Mackenzie often thought he was through with journalism. Reprieve from the gruelling business of being his own editor, reporter, proof-reader and circulation manager was something he solemnly promised himself a dozen times or more in the course of his lifetime, but it was a promise he never kept. The destruction of its press and the watering of a fair portion of its stock was by no means the end of Mackenzie's newspaper business.

As he had expected, public opinion and the verdict in his

law suit both proved favourable to Mackenzie. At the trial, the jury decided that the young gentlemen—or in other words their fathers and friends—should pay him £625 in damages.

Justice had clearly been done. But the result did nothing to increase Mackenzie's respect for the existing system or to change his opinion about the liberty of the subject in Upper Canada. "It may be said that I am proof of the freedom that exists. Far from it; where I have survived hundreds have sunk to rise no more. Trial by jury is in the sheriff's power, the sheriff is in the governor's power, the governor is in the power of his advisers." In the exceptional case of the destruction of the press the trespass against Mackenzie was so public and so clearly illegal that there was no possibility of finding a jury who would decide in favour of the self-constituted posse of young gentlemen.

In fairness to many members of the Compact we should register their sincere concern to act upon what they conceived to be the principles of British justice and fair play. The Surveyor-General, for example, was found several hundred pounds short on his accounts, a defalcation infinitesimally small by modern democratic standards. Nevertheless he resigned immediately (a custom in such circumstances which is possibly no longer part of Canadian constitutional practice), and his brother made good the difference out of family capital.

Mackenzie, however, was substantially right about the bias in the Compact's manner of running the province. Their self-interest was too narrowly conceived to allow their sense of honour and their respect for the constitution to carry them very far along the road to judical impartiality.

Out of the damages awarded to him Mackenzie bought new type, paid off old debts, and soon had the *Advocate* press running again. He never let the public forget that the destroyers of his press had included the confidential secretary of the Lieutenant-Governor and members of some of the best families in York. And, of course, the publicity of the trial was good for business. As the rumour spread of the Compact's attempt to buy off Mackenzie, as the tales of witnesses and the dramatic monologues of counsel and the story of the jury's thirty-two hour vigil were retailed, suitably embellished, by newspaper and word of mouth throughout the province, Mackenzie became a famous man in Upper Canada. It was a propitious time for the next step in his quarrel with the Compact. He would become a politician himself.

CHAPTER FIVE

SOME months before the elections of 1828, the editor of the *Colonial Advocate,* unsolicited by so much as a single political convention or delegation of public worthies, surprised the voters of York County with the announcement that he would seek to represent them in the legislature. As in most things, Mackenzie went about his politics differently from everyone else. It was usual to have a supply of "needful"—tap money for innkeepers, treats for supporters, and the odd shilling to lure a voter who was poor but would not drink. Mackenzie flatly stated that this was a vicious custom. There would be no treats from him. It was usual to run as Tory or a Reformer, or, since party lines were not clear in those days, to hint to the appropriate people of both sympathies that you were well disposed towards them. Mackenzie said he would run as an independent and that there were things he disliked about both sides. Before previous elections, in fact, he made up lists of Assemblymen who had voted the wrong way on crucial issues, and, with appropriate black marks beside each name, the lists were circulated among the voters. It was usual that such a niggardly campaigner as Mackenzie would come at the bottom of the list. Mackenzie was elected with a large plurality. One of his defeated rivals was the lawyer who had won him his case in court after the destruction of the press.

There was excitement about the shops and public houses of York as the newly-elected members arrived in town to take their places in the House of Assembly. On the appointed afternoon in January of 1829, "a crowd of some hundred people in all manner of strange defences against the piercing frost, intermingled with military costumes, and a few Indians lounging by in their blanket-coats and war-plumes" gathered outside the Parliament Buildings, at the foot of York Street to welcome the new Governor and to watch what they could of the opening of Parliament. Behind them lay the frozen expanse of the Bay; immediately before was the moving coloured confusion of small sleighs, the horses curvetting and kicking up the snow, in which the legislators and the ladies of York society were arriving.

Within, in the gilded and scarlet upper chamber, where the Legislative Councillors are ranged facing each other in formal anticipation, the elevated throne, with the judges leonine thereunder, is empty, the galleries are crowded and given over to the chatter and perfumery and pretty toilettes of the feminine portion of the aristocracy. All is in readiness for the occasion's liturgy to be set moving by the guns and the coming of the Governor. Black Rod's clattering on the bolted doors of the lower chamber, the summoning of the commoners to their throne speech standing-ground below the bar of the upper house, these and other points in the solemn historical-comical little game have scarcely changed their form since the days of Charles Stuart, and their significance since the time when the Plantagenets gathered round them the communities of medieval England to get money and consent for their statecraft.

Among the figures of the Assemblymen who stand listening to the speech from the throne we can single out the portly amiable bearing of the philanthropic tanner, Jesse Ketchum, the acute and intelligent mien of old Dr. Baldwin, the sage of Spadina, and in front centre, rising over the bar, the burning blue eyes and the flaming wig, worn like an outsize artist's beret, of William Lyon Mackenzie. A number of rustic turkey necks bulge from ill-fitting and roughly handsome homespun suits, one of them belonging to that outspoken radical, thick of speech and thumb, Peter Perry of Ernestown. Mark the contrast of such figures as these with the superb acuity of John Beverley Robinson, another member of the House, who for the moment is not standing at the bar but, as a law officer of the Crown, is seated beside the judges immediately below the throne. Among his fellow members in the House of Assembly, he is a Sir Thomas Lawrence portrait surrounded by Hogarths and Daumiers. Possessed of such features and such a bearing, together with "the most pleasing and insinuating voice I ever heard", Robinson is magnificently out of place. Or is it perhaps that his presence lends a displaced air to all the other members?

To the fashionable ladies in the gallery, several of the more rustic Assemblymen at the bar are the very picture of that disturbing new phenomenon called democracy, an observation perhaps prompted by the fact that they looked sufficiently attached to their headpieces to have slept in them. At any event it was obvious that a sizable portion of the lower classes of British North America believed that the condition of independence from Europe's code of customs included the right to keep a hat on in any presence and on all occasions.

As for the national origins of the Assemblymen, of all the many species of Celts and Saxons obviously present, the numerous sandy complexions and growths of heather thrusting thick as the Gaelic from ears and nostrils suggest that Scottish is the predominant one. However, after observing more than one of those lank, black-locked figures with a redolence of the Puritan in their tailoring and the comportment of a drawl, we shall not be surprised to learn from the 1829 Assembly records that it contained no less than fifteen immigrant Yankees. This in itself gives promise of a large majority for Reform and of a stormy session in the new Assembly. Yet as they straggle herd-like back through the corridor into the Assemblyroom, the members have that air of stolid bovine masculinity that imparts a quality of the uttermost conservatism to any ordinary mass of men, however wildly each individual therein may be possessed of radical opinions or eccentric private sensibilities.

The rumour had been circulating for several days that there was a huge majority for the Reformers, the first they had ever received. But no one knew for certain until the first vote in the House. The test would come when the House chose its speaker. Within the House presiding over its business and its debates, without its spokesman to King and Governor, the Speaker was important to the small world of Upper Canadian politics as he had been to the English House of Commons in its early struggle for independence. Like the Speaker of the American House of Representatives, he was the real leader of the popular house. The Reformer's choice for Speaker was a bold one and an affront to the Governor and his advisers.

A certain Barnabas Bidwell, born and bred a Yankee, was elected in 1821 to the House of Assembly. His experience in American politics (he had been Attorney-General of Massachusetts) and his admiration for Thomas Jefferson, the first Democrat, made him critical of any government which was not efficiently exercised in the interests of all the people. But the Empire had just fought a war to keep American invaders out of Canada. In the opinion of the gentlemen who ruled Upper Canada, it was also a war to save their colony from democracy and the likes of Barnabas Bidwell. In the postwar years that salvation seemed more and more precarious as settlers poured across the border, bringing their American political instincts and expectations with them. The steadily increasing number of Reformers in the Assembly between 1815 and 1830 was a good measure of the climbing tide of American influence. Among William Lyon Mackenzie's most faithful supporters were to be farmers who had migrated from the United States.

The issue of Barnabas Bidwell's possession of public office appeared to the Family Compact as one with the issue of whether their Canada was to be British or American. Ways and means were sought to bar him from the Assembly. Their legality was brought into question by some of the more delicate-minded of the Tories, but Dr. Strachan shoved scruple aside. "Never mind the law," he told his old schoolboys, "toorn him oot!" And out he went.

The voters of Lennox and Addington replied by returning his son at the next election. Marshall Spring Bidwell, Yankee-born like his father, was soon the leading critic of the government. He was as quiet and steady as Mackenzie was erratic and excitable, but strong in the cause of Reform. As the Assembly began its business in 1829, Bidwell was nominated for the office of Speaker. The Reform members, joined by Mackenzie, voted for him and won. This victory decided the fence-sitters; for the rest of that session Attorney-General Robinson was the only consistent supporter of the government left in the House.

The next step was a direct challenge. The House moved its disapproval of the Lieutenant-Governor's advisers and policies, thirty-seven votes to one. The lop-sided majority was a fair reflection of public opinion. The government had undertaken few constructive public improvements at a time when they were desperately needed, and most of its positive actions were highly offensive. Archdeacon Strachan's attempt to establish the Anglican Church had aroused the Methodists into becoming the major political force which they were to remain for the rest of the century. Great numbers of American-born people, like the Bidwells, had been alarmed by a series of Tory attempts to deprive them of their land and their right to vote. Intelligent men everywhere, many United Empire Loyalists among them, were offended by the high-handed manner in which the government had behaved in several delicate situations. A judge who had not acted in a particularly judicious manner, for instance, had been dismissed a month before the election. People were very much aware that he was a friend of the Reformer Dr. Baldwin and that he had crossed words with Attorney-General Robinson. The editor of the *Canadian Freeman*, a paper whose abusive language and talent for creative fiction consistently surpassed that of the *Advocate*, was prosecuted by the Attorney-General for a libel, of which the alleged victim was the Attorney-General himself. The judge, whom the defendant impudently called "our old customer", practically compelled the jury to return a verdict of guilty, after which he passed a savage sentence of imprisonment without time limit. Fears for the rights of the subject, as well as for the freedom of the press, were also raised by the government's refusal to pay money voted to Mackenzie by the Assembly for printing its debates. And the destruction of the *Advocate* press was not quickly forgotten in Upper Canada.

Perhaps the rankest piece of injustice involved a retired artillery officer, Captain Matthews from County Middlesex, who was a leading Reform member of the last Assembly. His pension was cut off and he was ordered back to England for asking a company of American actors to sing "Yankee Doodle" and "Hail Columbia!" at a New Year's Eve theatre party. The British military authorities in Upper Canada, of whom Sir Peregrine Maitland was at this time a fairly typical example, were not altogether sensible of the limits to which the issue of loyalty could be pressed.

Before his final and unlamented departure on a bleak day in November soon after the 1828 elections, Maitland himself warned his successor and the world at large that "men who were notoriously disloyal, and whose characters are really detestable are now degrading the legislature of the country by their presence." Members of the government agreed with this description, or found it convenient, and continued to pay little regard to the Assembly's wishes.

Since the Assembly could not remedy abuses, it had to be content with exposing them. Mackenzie followed closely the issues that came up in the House and presided over no less than five of its investigating committees. Why, he wanted to know, did it cost seven shillings or more (several dollars to us today) to send a letter to England? Why were the roads between York and Montreal in such bad condition that the mail coach could hardly make the trip? Did the House know that election officials could be bribed and that elections were held in inconvenient places? What was the Bank of Upper Canada but a source of gain to a few rich merchants and of political influence for the government? Why were the government contractors making so much money building the Welland Canal? Why was Archdeacon

Strachan, variously described by Mackenzie as "demon", "hypocrite", and "the Governor's jackal", allowed to pick an Anglican chaplain for the House Assembly? Why were female lunatics chained together in the filthy cellar of the County jail?

Mackenzie worked himself ragged during the session. When it was over he wrote to a fellow editor in Quebec:

> I can truly say that I have come home from the House night after night at 8 or 10 or 12 p.m. after a 'twelve hours' attendance so tired and worn out that when I went to bed I could not sleep for perfect fatigue. I am a diminutive little creature and I really could not have conceived it possible that I could have undergone the fatigue I have endured during the last ten weeks. I had to write all the original matter necessary for my paper, reports of proceedings etc. as we publish from 30 to 35 quires of news each week. I got involved thereby with other business and when the lieutenant-governor got through with his closing speech I felt like a bird escaped from a cage.

The Reformers' attack was tireless and spirited, but unorganized. They failed to distinguish between big issues and little ones. It would have been better to channel public resentment and their own efforts upon one or two major pieces of reform legislation. No real leadership was provided in the House and even if it had been, Mackenzie, who dearly loved to follow his own nose, was probably incapable of accepting it.

It might appear that the Reform Assembly had been talking to no purpose. Allan MacNab's Gore *Mercury* used that line of attack:

> For months this ribald conclave
> Retailed their vulgar prate,
> And charged two dollars each per day
> For spouting billingsgate.

In the opinion of one observer, to see the legislature in action was the best cure for admiring it.

> I have paid our legislators another visit, [wrote John Langton] and have heard a long rigmarole from the opposition; one of them commenced as follows: "Several Honorable gentlemen has rose in this 'Ouse"—a very fair sample of the oration. I feel myself fast growing a Tory. There is a singular incongruity in the *tout ensemble* of the House; the court dress and sword of the Sergeant at Arms and the cocked hat of the Speaker all seem as if they intend to be imposing; but the appearance of the members themselves writing their letters or reading their newspapers at their several desks, whilst a little boy is running about bringing them plates of sandwiches etc. reminded me much of a coffee house. During the whole of the five or six speeches I listened to, not a single member appeared to think of anything but his own business; and when one speaker sat down and another rose, very few even condescended to look up from their papers to see who it might be.

Mackenzie himself once wrote: "Many of these Legislators are qualified to sign their names; but as to framing and carrying through a bill on any subject whatever, the half of them wisely never attempted such a herculean task." There was, in fact, little inducement for them to make the attempt or to learn how to do it properly, since almost all their bills for reform were lost or mangled in the upper house. Where positive action on an important matter was required, it was the will of the governor, or of the British Colonial Office, which alone mattered.

In 1829 a change for the better occurred at Government House. The new Lieutenant-Governor, Sir John Colborne, was not only one of Britain's best soldiers, but also quite literally a gentleman, a Christian, and an educated man. It is true that he was a High Tory of the Duke of Wellington's stamp. He was thoroughly out of sympathy with the demand for popular government and out of touch with the need for social reform. Like the Duke, however, he was ready and able to conduct a skilful retreating action before a tide of liberal public opinion. He was less a prisoner of the Family Compact and a narrow mind than his predecessor, and infinitely more tactful.

Colborne shared the Compact's alarm over the dangers of American immigration into Upper Canada. Soon after his arrival he appealed to London for more British settlers to act as a counterweight. One of his aims in founding Upper Canada College in 1829 was to preserve the aristocratic tradition in the colony against the influence of American democracy. Before Colborne's governorship was very old the Tory party was to enjoy a signal triumph in Upper Canada.

With the unlamented decease of George IV in 1830 the life of the sitting Assembly automatically ended. Writs were issued in King William's name for a general election for all his Parliaments. It was to be a year of destiny for the cause of liberalism throughout the world. A revolution in France toppled the autocratic Bourbons from their throne for the last time. Jacksonian democracy entered its first full year in the American presidency, girding itself for the crucial struggle with big business and the United States Bank. In the newly-elected English House of Commons there was a majority for parliamentary reform and the country was ready to rebel if the Lords should attempt to frustrate its desire for change. But the liberal infection was not catching in Upper Canada.

In the minds of the recent British settlers particularly, the Reform cause was identified with the unruly but ineffectual sessions of the last Assembly, and with the foreboding overtones of Yankee republicanism in certain Reform demands. The Tories on the other hand stood solidly for the principle that the King's government must be carried on. They were prepared to co-operate with the new Governor who was himself the very model of the things which were most obviously British. A small general increase in the Tory vote and some discouraged abstention from the Reformers was enough to win a majority in the new House for the Tories.

They celebrated their triumph by granting the Governor a permanent civil list, so that several of the official salaries, including his own, would be paid regularly and perpetually without the usual grant of funds from the Assembly. The Assembly's only practical means of changing the government's mind was thus seriously weakened. The Reformers called it the Everlasting Salary Bill, but it was passed in spite of their objections.

Two of their number were notably missing from the new Assembly. Young Robert Baldwin, who had lost the seat won the year before at a by-election for York town, and John Rolph, the discursive subtle English doctor-lawyer who had led the Reformers during the 1820's, were no longer members of the House. But Mackenzie was returned to his place, with Jesse Ketchum, by the voters of York County. So were Bidwell and Peter Perry from the County of Lennox and Addington.

The first session of the new House opened in January of 1831. Within a few weeks the government law officers, Boulton and Hagerman, found Mackenzie's presence in the House so intolerable that they determined to find a way to be rid of him. There was no doubt that he was by that time the most ardent and noisy of all the opposition members. Every day of the session, with a cockiness which so nettled the Attorney-General that he once nearly charged across the floor to throttle him, "the little mannikin from York" urged motions of censure, bills for public improvement, demands for an investigation; offered passionate declarations of principle, lists of statistics, questions about the operations of the government and the governing classes and all their works.

An apt minister of vengeance for all this busy impertinence quickly appeared in the new member for Wentworth. Allan Napier MacNab began his public career while still a struggling young Hamilton lawyer, by committing a calculated breach of privilege against the Assembly of 1829-30, for which the Reform members, on a motion of Mackenzie, condemned him and put him into custody of the sergeant-at-arms. Before he was through with his career,

MacNab had added to its lustre many another quarrel with the Reformers, including the battles of 1837, and, for valour in the cause, had been adorned with a high militia command, a baronetcy, a castle, the Tory lead in Parliament, and in the end the prime ministership of the united Canadas. He determined from the beginning to be one of the Family Compact's adopted sons, and it was not long before he could surpass any of them in the outspoken courage, or if you prefer, the loud bombast, of his Toryism.

MacNab now declared Mackenzie in his turn to be guilty of a breach of privilege. He put forward a motion which would lead to Mackenzie's expulsion from the House, if it passed. Unfortunately for MacNab the only breach he could find was Mackenzie's distribution to the public of verbatim reports of an Assembly debate. Tory editors had done the same sort of thing many times. Although MacNab and his government supporters were technically correct, it would clearly cause widespread embarrassment if this traditional parliamentary privilege were now resurrected from obsolescence. A few of the more independent Tories joined the Reformers in the lobby to defeat MacNab's motion by five votes.

In the course of the six months' adjournment which followed, MacNab and the government cast about for some better means of catching Mackenzie. And Mackenzie spent the interval in activity which gave them more cause than ever for wishing to end his political career.

His first adventure was innocent enough of politics. While he was making a trip to Quebec City, his ship was caught and smashed in the spring ice of the St. Lawrence River. Mackenzie was absolutely devoid of fear, and almost seemed to relish the general excitement and danger. He was the last person off the ship. After the captain had left, he clambered back into his cabin to fetch his valuables and several pieces of baggage. The passengers made their separate ways to shore over a mile of ice hillocks and water holes. In spite of his huge load, Mackenzie overtook a couple who were making their way with the great difficulty.

A long crevice of water opened between one poor woman and the shore. Mackenzie dropped his things and helped her across the gap. When all were safe ashore, the nearest habitant village lavished upon them a profusion of hospitality and good cheer.

In Quebec City, Mackenzie visited churches, a theatre, and a crowded immigrant ship. He rejoiced in the abundance of books in the town's libraries. The number of soldiers from the Citadel prompted him to remark that Canadians must be a very valuable people to require so many keepers. He was fascinated by the dog-carts in Quebec. The dogs negotiated the steep cobbled slopes and heavy snow so nimbly that he was tempted to try rigging up a pair at home.

He was shown round the college with every courtesy by its superior, and he found the monastic simplicity of the place, like the austere perpendicular beauty of the town itself, very much to his taste. Of all the things he liked about French Canada, perhaps it was the closeness of the Church to the people, and the unassuming manner of the clergy he had met, that impressed Mackenzie most. From this impression, in any case, invidious comparisons with Strachan and the Anglican Church in Upper Canada were drawn for the benefit of subscribers to the *Colonial Advocate*.

The purpose of his trip was to visit Reform leaders in Lower Canada. Their party was able to maintain a constant and overwhelming majority in the provincial Assembly, thanks to the support of the French Canadians. They were vociferously opposed to the government and the Chateau Clique, as the Family Compact was called in Lower Canada, and Mackenzie hoped to learn some lessons in opposition from them. He also wished to effect closer relations between Reformers in the two provinces. For several years he had been corresponding with John Neilson, who was the editor of the Quebec *Gazette* and a member of the Assembly. But when his friend Neilson, a year or so after his visit, broke with the French Canadian Reformers for fear of the extremes to which they might go, Mackenzie reproved Neilson and threw his full support to Papineau and the uncompromising opponents of the government. Mackenzie was in fact the first English-speaking Upper Canadian to hit upon the idea of an alliance between the Reformers of both races and both provinces. Unlike some of the French leaders, he was not a republican. He was still convinced that the British Empire and the monarchy were compatible with a better state of things in Canada. But he kept in touch with Papineau, and when the day of decision arrived in 1837, it was his immediate response to Papineau's appeal that set afoot Mackenzie's first definite plan to overthrow the government of Upper Canada by force.

Mackenzie's next trip was closer to home, largely in his own riding of York in fact, but it took him longer, and over more ground. He walked and rode that summer of 1831 all through the forest settlements and remote villages and farms of the country beyond the northern ridges. In Georgina township, on the Lake Simcoe shore, the settlers told him he was the first of their representatives to visit them since the province was settled, though they always made the fifty mile journey south to cast their votes.

The ostensible purpose of Mackenzie's journey was to gather grievance petitions for an appeal to England against the perpetrators of misrule in the colony. This he did, gathering signatures by the thousand. Township meetings were called upon the occasion of his visits: "Mr. Bogart's son called the town meeting," he wrote later of one such visit, "and the father (with whom I breakfasted) presided; Mr. Eck who has a farm and tannery in the next concession acting as secretary."

As with all his trips to the hinterlands, however, Mackenzie was driven by other motives beside the desire to force governmental reform or to mend his political fences. He did not walk with blinkers on, nor shut off his senses from the pleasures and surprises of the forest. He delighted in the abundance of deer and partridge, fox and bear; with much content he noted each variety of brilliant weed and

wild flower; tasted the midsummer bounty of the goose-
berry bush and the cherries of the stunted sloe; with the
apothecary's curious eye picked out the medicinal herbs and
roots as he passed them on the trail. At the end of the day's
journey there was always another meeting, and then the
welcome of a settler's cabin for the evening.

> The supper [he wrote] consisted of viands the growth
> and produce of the place. On the table were placed
> curds and cream, cheese, butter, new potatoes, new
> bread, of flour the growth and manufacture of 1831,
> Caledon-made wine, sugar of the Canada maple. . . .
> After supper, in accordance with the time-honoured
> usage of his country, Mr. M'Naughton took down the
> venerable folio Bible, his partner in life's pains and
> pleasures; his family of eleven gathered round him,
> and in this distant wilderness, were the solemn strains
> of Scottish melody heard ascending from his lowly roof,
> in honour and praise of the Almighty Creator, pre-
> server, and bountiful benefactor of the world. The
> eldest son then read a chapter from the sacred volume;
> and the family of the settler concluded the services of
> the day by bowing the knee in prayer to their God.
> Surely this is happiness on earth?

Mackenzie's trip through the country beyond the ridges was
a kind of personal research into the anatomy of paradise,
and a temporary indulgence of its bliss.

But if the settlers in the wilderness, by dint of much
hard work, could achieve a few moments of idylic joy,
Mackenzie was all the more keenly aware of man-made
boundaries that had been erected against the perfecting of
their happiness. He saw huge tracts of the best land kept
idle for clergy reserves, or for the speculative profit of
distant owners in London or York. Mackenzie was a pure
naturalist only in passing; nature improved by man's labour
was his greater passion. The wilderness was delightful, but
there was too much of it. It was the enemy of the roads
and schools which only large areas of contiguous settlement
could support. Mackenzie frequently cast a practical im-

proving glance about him: "This river could be made navigable with no great expense," he observed, "and five-acre lots all the way to town." Or in another township: "These marshes might be drained with ease, thought I, if we had a population adequate to the task, but it cannot be while a few irresponsible individuals have the management of the lands." Always the distant government, the wealthy monopolists, the local justices of the peace—in effect, the Family Compact—stood firmly in the path of Mackenzie's hopes.

He returned to York in the fall of 1831, ready to hurl new charges from his editor's desk and from his place in the Legislative Assembly.

It has become the accepted opinion of Mackenzie that he was not one of the leaders of the Reform party; that he never achieved the confidence of his fellow Reformers in the Assembly, and, in their judgement, had no great stature as a politician. In a sense this opinion is quite true. Dr. John Rolph, the Oxford graduate, was more capable of seeing all sides of an issue and of persuading solid men that the side he chose was the best. In the 1820's he was accepted as the Reform leader by both Tory and Reformer alike. Bidwell replaced him in the 1830's as the steadiest, most acute, and broad-minded of the Reformers. Jesse Ketchum and Peter Perry were always more widely respected in York than Mackenzie. Robert Baldwin was more fastidious and more intelligent. And old Dr. Baldwin, his father, was both the elder statesman and the intellectual leader of the party. But there was a power of leadership in which Mackenzie far outstripped the others. None of them knew the country as intimately as he did. None of them enjoyed so widespread a personal following. Those qualities which prevented him from gaining a position of influence among important men were often the very ones that excited the sympathy and support of the rest. He was both passionately outspoken and minutely specific in his complaints, often to the point of unbalance. He could not be content with the subtleties or the small tangible gains of a compromise. Above all, he could personify abstract abuse into

61

this or that particular member of the ruling class. "Gentle-folk talk about things, servants talk about people," says the old Victorian maxim. It was Mackenzie's unique source of political strength that for all his booklearning, he often spoke more like a servant than a gentleman.

Soon after the Assembly met again, late in 1831, the Tories decided to catch Mackenzie on a charge of libel. They selected for their purpose an issue of the *Colonial Advocate* in which he called the House "a sycophantic office for registering the decrees of as mean and mercenary an Executive as ever was given as punishment for the sins of any part of North America in the nineteenth century".

On December 11th, 1831, the Assembly met to hear Mackenzie defend himself. The Tories came with throats well tuned for groans and catcalls, satisfied that he would do nothing but rave back at them. Bidwell and Ketchum who had done what they could to defend Mackenzie, now simply waited in the hope that he would not provoke a scene or use language that might justify the Tories.

Mackenzie began calmly and nobly with an appeal to the principles which are the very foundation of a free society.

> The articles complained of contain opinions unfavourable to the political character of members who compose the majority of this House and the executive council of this colony. It is alleged that to propagate such opinions is criminal and deserves punishment. Undoubtedly, if there is a rule or law it is wrong to transgress it. But I know no law that is transgressed by propagating these opinions. Let it even be supposed for the sake of argument, that the opinions are false, though I firmly believe they are perfectly true; if all false quotations and false opinions are improper, then all discussion, either in this House or through the press must also be improper, for one set of opinions must be wrong. And if none but true opinions can be given or quoted by either party, then there can be no argument. How are the people to know when to approve or to disapprove of the conduct of their rulers, if the freedom

of expressing all opinions concerning public men be checked?

If the government is acting wrongly, it ought to be checked. Censure of government causes inquiry and produces discontent among the people, and this discontent is the only means known to me of removing the defects of a vicious government and inducing the rulers to remedy the abuses. Thus the press, by its power of censure, is the best safeguard of the interests of mankind. . . .

Be assured, Mr. Speaker, that were every representative on this floor to join in condemning the articles you have selected as libellous, I would republish them the following Thursday.

Mackenzie was warming to his task. Striding back and forth, wagging his ludicrously large head, twitching an angry finger at his accusers, he launched into a more personal aspect of his speech.

I must not call things by their right names in the paper caller the *Advocate*; but either praise the most undeserving of public men, be silent as death, or go back to the freeholders of the country with the brand of a "false, atrocious, and malicious libeller" on my forehead. If such shall be your measure of justice, I will not shrink from the appeal to the country.

Not one word do I retract; I offer no apology; for what you call libel I believe to be the solemn truth, fit to be published from one end of the province to the other. I certainly should not have availed myself of my privilege, or made use of the language complained of on the floor; but since I am called to avow or disavow that language, as an independent public journalist, I declare I think it mild and gentle; for be it remembered, Mr. Speaker, I see for myself how matters are carried on here.

He began calling out, like an incantation, a long list of the reforms which had been recommended in the popular petitions of 1831. He drove them home with swinging strokes of the fist, as if he were nailing a coffin, and with all the strength of his enraged small frame. Blow by blow he sang out for

> economy and retrenchment, for the regulation of wild lands sales by law, for the abolition of Crown and Clergy Reserves, and all reservations except for education, for an abolition of banking monopolies, for a reduction of law fees and a simplification of law practice, for assuring control of the whole public revenue, for a revision of the corrupt jury-packing system, for the repeal of the everlasting salary bill, for disqualifying priests and bishops from holding seats in the two councils, for taking the free-holders votes at convenient places, for allowing the people control over the local taxes, for inquiring into the trade law of last April, for the abolition of the tea monopoly, and for an equal representation of the people in this House. . . .

Towards the end of the speech Mackenzie brought down a hubbub on his ears with a personal attack on another member of the House, an editor from Kingston, and the Speaker had to call him to order several times. The next morning Mackenzie was refused permission to continue, and, after the law officers of the Crown had described him as a "reptile" and a "spaniel dog", he was duly expelled on a straight party vote for having libelled the character of the Assembly of Upper Canada. A writ was issued for a by-election in York County.

Mackenzie left in high and gleeful fury, hell-bent for his pulpit among the inkpots and his printer's devils, and having thrown defiance into the type-case, made off in his sleigh to the hinterland of his constituency. There, beyond the ridges above the town, up and down the length of Yonge Street, lived the farmers and village mechanics who were his most fervent admirers. It was there and for them that he fought his hardest political battles, and there, in the end, he led them in rebellion.

CHAPTER SIX

YONGE Street of a century ago cut its way through the heart of Upper Canada. Down Yonge Street came the farmers from York and Simcoe and the counties nearby, bringing their vegetables and grain and pigs to town. Past the broad flat marshes of Holland Landing they came, down Richmond Hill, through the swamp at Hogg's Hollow, past the Eglinton crossroads where Montgomery's tavern sat square and comfortable, a haven for tired travellers, down Gallows Hill toward Bloor Street. After a rest at the Red Lion Inn they paid their toll at the Bloor tollgate, and with the chimneys of York in sight, moved down the gentle slope to the town limits, over to higher ground on the eastern side to avoid the ankle- and knee-deep quagmires of lower Yonge Street, through the King Street traffic of oxen, carts, carriages and horsemen, down to the St. Lawrence market and the brink of Toronto Bay.

On the second day of the new year 1832, Yonge Street seemed busier than usual. Sleighing was excellent; everywhere the snow lay firm and smooth, and the jangle of sleighbells filled the air. There was noticeable excitement about the passengers whose sleighs were bringing them to the Red Lion Inn. Around the rambling old white stucco building with its low roofs and gables and mullioned windows, a crowd had been gathering since daybreak. The big red British lion that swung above the door was a familiar sight to many of the farmers. They often stayed there overnight on their trips so that they could go into York and back within the day and so avoid a double toll at Bloor

Street. There too, they had read by candlelight their copies of the *Colonial Advocate* and talked of its vigorous little editor who had so stirred the bowels of Tory wrath. Now that MacNab and his friends had thrown him out of the House of Assembly, a by-election to fill the vacant seat for York County had become necessary. This was the cause of the present excitement in and about the Red Lion Inn.

By ten o'clock of the bright January morning, a huge crowd had gathered round the hustings, a rough wooden platform in the snowy yard. Suddenly, the skirl of bagpipes pierced the air and William Lyon Mackenzie appeared riding the top deck of a large two-storey sleigh supplied by Mr. Montgomery, owner of the tavern at the Eglinton crossroads. Mackenzie and his Tory opponent, Mr. Street, were nominated and the balloting began. Through the short winter way it continued, person after person mounting the hustings and declaring his choice. By three o'clock one hundred and nineteen votes had been cast for Mackenzie, only one for Street. Mr. Street conceded the election and the polls were closed. It was said that if the voting had continued for a week, as it often did in those days, Mackenzie would have received five thousand votes.

The excitement of the day was far from over. The crowd that had helped to elect Mackenzie now pressed into the large ballroom of the inn which had so often rung with the voice of the square-dance caller and the stamp of feet and the high tune of the fiddle. Now a tremendous shout went up as Mackenzie came forward to receive an immense gold medal and chain presented to him by his loyal supporters of the County of York. It was said the medal was worth £250 easy, and all not counting the work that went into it. A committee member reminded people around him that the motto on the medal proclaimed Mackenzie's dearest ideals, King and Reform. As Mackenzie placed it around his neck, his fierce blue eyes blazed with pride.

The medal became one of the few material things to which he was ever greatly attached. As it turned out, Mackenzie was never to know a happier day than this. Perhaps in later years he treasured its memory for all the things that might have been. It must have seemed certain then to the common people that their hero would one day arrange things at Government House and that they would exchange their lives of hardship for a crown of joy. The evil men would be put down in that day, the unused lands of the rich divided among those that would work them, and a mill and a school and a church be built in every township. How precisely it was all to happen they were not certain. Nor, to tell the truth, was Mackenzie.

After the speeches were finished, the crowd, heated with drink and excitement, were glad to get out into the frosty air and the sleighs that waited for them. Mackenzie and the committee men climbed back into the two-storey sleigh, the driver's whip cracked over four teams of steaming horses, and to the drone and scream of the pipes, they moved off down Yonge Street. It was a gay procession which followed: horses drawing their sleighs with that air and step of self-importance which animals assume for occasions; boys snowballing, tumbling, fighting for a place on the end of a runner; some of the men jogging beside the sleighs, their step big-booted and a little staggery from the snow or twenty-cent-a-gallon whiskey; and over a hundred sleigh-fuls of cheering voters with huge crimson banners floating their slogans aloft and, in inspired needlework and imaginative spelling, proclaiming that the Heavens themselves had gone Reform.

A covered sleigh carried a small printing press which was heated from beneath by a small furnace to keep the printer's ink from freezing. Several boys were printing Mackenzie's New Year's Message, cranking the press by hand, and throwing copies at the little knots of people who braved the cold to stand by the road side.

When the parade reached the town, it turned west, and stopped in front of Government House and the new Parliament Buildings, the crowd cheering in good-natured defiance. By the light of blazing torches, Mackenzie was driven home, borne aloft to the door, and deposited among friends in his big front parlour. In his excitement, he threw his gold chain at one of the girls ("quick as lightning", she said), hurled his red wig to the floor, and flung his arms around his mother's neck and kissed her.

It had been a day of triumph. But was the loyal support of the farmers of the Home Counties enough to win the reforms he had hoped for? He may have wondered, as he watched their sleighs prepare to leave, if he could count on their loyalty in a sterner test than this.

The stars were bright overhead and the faint jingle of the sleighbells floated in the frosty air as the sleighs sped, one by one, along Yonge Street, by Bloor and the Red Lion Inn, up Gallows Hill, past Montgomery's tavern, up Richmond Hill, on and on, to the quiet farms waiting in the darkness.

Mackenzie's battle with the Assembly rumbled with indistinct but ominous threats for his political future. Of this fact he had the occasional intimation when he was withdrawn a little from the joyous hubbub of wellwishing and support. But Mackenzie lived sufficient for the day; the present moment, to the point of recklessness, was his only real concern.

Besides his New Year's triumph at the polls, he now enjoyed a rare measure of domestic felicity, free from the visitation of the dark angel that had carried off three of his infants during the early years in York.

His small bookselling and printing business might now almost be called prosperous. While he was never wealthy by the standards of merchant or gentleman, Mackenzie was able to live in the style of a townsman who was not of the labouring classes.

Some time after 1830, following a period of residence on Church Street, Mackenzie moved his family to a two-storey brick house at the west end of town near the splendidly classical home of the Law Society of Upper Canada, Osgoode Hall. Though Mackenzie's place contained five upstairs bedrooms and a fully used cellar, it was modest by the standards of nineteenth century York. At the back, however, there was a large and well-kept garden, "filled with choice fruit trees, currants, gooseberries, grapes, and a well of purest water, which is always in abundance". There was "a yard and a shed and stabling for two horses".

It was a well-populated household. One of the help usually stayed with them. Mackenzie's mother-in-law and his eighty-year-old mother lived there, and Lyon and Isabel were now the parents of three small daughters. Of the three others who died in infancy, their firstborn, a little girl of almost two, caught smallpox on the ship during the Mackenzie's move from Queenston to York in 1824. There is a pathetic letter among Mackenzie's papers informing him that there is no way of answering his earnest plea for hospital accommodation for the sick child. She died at their home, above the *Advocate* office on Palace Street, four days before Christmas of 1824.

Mackenzie was full of tricks enough for the liveliest of small daughters. If he was home from work before bedtime the whole house was instantly transformed into a gigantic playroom. It sometimes seemed Papa would never be caught at tag or touch last, even as he hopped and dodged just inches from the grasp of six small hands, until suddenly and mysteriously they would all catch hold at once, and the prize of a shoulder ride each or the secret of a new trick was securely won. As for birthdays and birthday presents, these were things Papa never, never forgot. And in the mornings if they found him lying abed they climbed the hillock of knees and heard the verse that was still recited in the family when the grandson who was to be Prime Minister, and his sisters, were small:

> A lady sat on a castle wall
> High, high high
> The winds did blow and the rains did fall
> And lowering looked the sky.
> At last the castle wall gave way
> And down *down* DOWN went she.

Mackenzie was the fondest and best of fathers to his family of females, when he spent time with them at all. But he had been hoping for ten years that Isabel would get him sons. It is scarcely remarkable that the darling of his ambitions was the little boy Mackenzie's mother reared for him in Scotland, his son James.

Besides his immediate family, Mackenzie had other charges. Some ten or eleven journeymen and apprentices worked in his printing office. If Mackenzie drove them hard, he was also a good master to them, and the young ones he cared for and disciplined as if they were his sons. One of them was a lad named Charles French who had tried to stop the press raiders in 1826, and was the chief witness for the prosecution at the trial. Two years later, French became involved in very serious trouble himself. Mackenzie was deeply disturbed and committed himself utterly to saving the unfortunate young man.

The trouble began when French fell in with companions who divided their idle evenings between the dram-shop, for heavy drinking, and the theatre. Of the former type of establishment York's population of two thousand supported no less than sixty, and of theatres usually only one, very intermittently operated and regarded by the respectable majority, if they made distinction at all among the springes of the Arch-Tempter, as the more deadly.

Mackenzie did not partake of any of the more stiff-necked orthodoxies on the questions of the theatre and alcohol, but to drunkeness and much wasting of time he had objections which were both Puritan and severely practical. Whether or not, as one suspects, the impulses to Puritanism and practicality were in their origin the same, and were only separated by the Victorians, nevertheless in Mackenzie's make-up the two characteristics were intimately related. He believed in frugal living for the purposes of good workmanship, a sentiment which he was not slow in conveying to young French. In disciplinary matters he did not practice a Scottish Calvinist sternness, but he was almost unnecessarily outspoken in his verbal reproofs. French, who by now had apparently finished his apprentiship and become a journeyman, continued to behave as before. One night when he returned home drunk, there was a noisy quarrel with his employer, and French was sacked.

It was soon after this that the young man became involved in the incident which spelled the finish of the theatre in York for the next six years, and consequences far worse for poor French. When French and his companions arrived in their seats at the theatre one evening in June, they found themselves behind a huge bear of a man by the name of Nolan, who had recently threatened French's life, and who indulged in the unsociable habit of carrying round with him a large pair of ugly iron tongs. French had been drinking heavily and the sight of Nolan with his tongs protruding from a big coat pocket provoked him into borrowing a pistol from a friend, picking a fight and shooting Nolan in the side. Nolan walked home to his boarding hotel and told the barman, "I am shot; squint-eyed French has shot me," and with that took his hand from his ribs and let the blood stream over the bar. He died the following day.

French awoke with a headache, and a case of total amnesia with respect to his activities the night before. To his surprise he found Mr. Wiman, the chairmaker and acting constable, in his room placing him under arrest. He was summarily convicted of murder and sentenced to be hanged.

Mackenzie pleaded unceasingly to the very day and hour of the execution for a commutation or a reprieve from the Governor. The scaffold was built in the square in front of the jail. The crowds assembled for their little festival of death, the gallows rising from the rough pine altar above them. And still Mackenzie kept up his vigil in Sheriff Jarvis' room, waiting for word from the Governor which never came. Finally Jarvis had to announce that there was no further reason for delay, and sent word to bring out the prisoner.

Mackenzie left the terrible scene just before the execution, his gaze fixed with grief, the large head turning slowly from side to side on his light frame, which as always seemed to be towed along a half step behind, but for once without a trace of the habitual scurry. A young Anglican priest who was there remembered seeing Mackenzie with a stream of tears running down either cheek and on to his big white collars as he walked away.

It was during the time immediately after this incident and in the early 1830's that Mackenzie enjoyed his period of relative success in politics and business, and the solstice in the long season of his personal sorrow. He was still subject of the fearful headaches, and the chronic fits of trembling and fever which continued to visit him periodically during the rest of his life, but he had long since come to expect physical pain and excruciatingly long working hours, as an ingrained part of existence.

The newspaper itself lost money as usual, and the political pamphlets and documents he circulated were paid for out of his own pocket. But this was not of prime concern to Mackenzie, so long as they continued to be useful in the cause of reform. He would have liked to put aside the continual burden of publishing the *Advocate*, so that he might devote more energy to his career in the Assembly and among his constituents. He may well have been looking to the day when his son James could take responsibility for the newspaper.

James was trained in the printer's craft, with the other apprentices, and worked for his father from an early age. By the mid-thirties James was reporting Assembly debates. He signed a contract, together with his father, for the printing of the Assembly's *Journal of Proceedings*. After 1837, when the rebellion reprisals smashed Mackenzie's business for good and sent the family into exile in the United States, James set up his own printing establishment and newspaper in a small town in upstate New York.

James was much attached to his father, and showed a lasting affection and deep filial respect. He was distinctly conscious of an intellect more powerful and original than his, nimbler in argument, voluminously stored with book learning of all kinds and possessed of an expert technical knowledge of a half dozen different trades. When it came to common sense, however, James preferred his own counsels.

As a boy he regarded with mingled feelings of embarrassment and pride the everlasting spectacle of his father engaged, often with the hottest personal animus, in continuous battle against rival editors, suitors for libel, political adversaries, and the best society in York. He gradually became aware of the growing reputation for instability and crankiness which his father enjoyed among acquaintances and enemies alike.

He learned by reaction to exercise a careful prudence of his own, and to take an almost paternal responsibility for the elder Mackenzie who himself had never known a father. James often attempted to protect his parent from the consequences of recklessness, although he suspected he was pleading a lost cause. Typical of his earnest counsels of caution and regard for self-interest is one of the many letters he wrote to his father in 1838 when they had just begun their American exile:

> My dear Father,
>
> Why embroil yourself in the question of the currency at a time when the voice of the people is fearfully in the balance against your principle? That your principle may be correct I am not politician or financier enough to dispute—that your motives are pure I know—but that it is policy or prudent I deny.
>
> Interested personal considerations have never weighed enough with you—nor will any influence change an opinion you form. Even in Canada you cannot but recollect how your friends looked aghast at the absurdity of your attacking the interested whether friend or foe.
>
> We must speak the truth but not the whole truth at all times. Perhaps I am Jesuitical and imitate Talleyrand when he said the murder of d'Enghien was worse than a crime—it was a political error. Judge for yourself. I have meant well.
>
> I am, dear Father,
>
> > Respectfully yours,
> >
> > > James Mackenzie.

On this, as on other occasions, James' pleading was received with admiration for the boy's powers of persuasion and a tender appreciation of his solicitude, and then with a mental resolve to achieve wisdom in old age, the counsel was blithely and totally ignored. To the very end, with Mackenzie, politics was never the art of the possible, nor the practice of worldly wisdom a thing of which he was capable.

Mackenzie celebrated his return to the House the day after his triumphant re-election by publishing a violent attack on the members who voted for his expulsion. A new libel charge was laid and Mackenzie was called upon to make his defence. Before beginning, he glared defiantly around him, and when all eyes were upon him he placed round his neck the great gold medal and chain just given him by the freeholders of County York.

Because he quoted at length from the speeches of English parliamentarians to prove his case, the Speaker ruled him out of order. To which Mackenzie said he would defend himself properly or not at all. With the Tories hooting after him like a flock of crows, he strode out of the House. The Tory majority expelled him again, and then with complete disregard for precedent and good political judgment, they also declared him incapable of sitting in the Assembly again during the present session.

Mackenzie thrived on this sort of treatment. He could stand on a stump or a wagon and harangue a crowd into a conviction like nobody else in the history of English-Canadian politics. He had the power of communicating righteous indignation; and the results were terrible indeed for opponents who were as patently in the wrong as the Assemblymen who found him unfit for their company. Mackenzie was promptly returned for a third time to the same Parliament by the voters of York County.

His martyrdom gave him the chance to agitate throughout the province. But he was nowhere more at home than among the farmers from beyond the ridges, who filled the streets of York on market day.

"Every market day," one witness recalled, "when business was all done before the farmers went home, there would be a crowd around him as he talked from the top of a wagon. He made great speeches, I can tell you. I happened to be there once through a person who was staying in his house. We turned down by the church and waited at the market below King Street where he was standing in a wagon talking and you should have seen how the people listened."

His popular success was such that a few of his enemies decided to use more direct means of silencing him. After a stormy political meeting in front of the Court House in the Tory town of Hamilton, several threats were made on his life and a plot was laid to maim or murder him. His friends urged him to leave town before dark for fear of what might happen. But Mackenzie said he had business to transact there that evening and would have to stay until the 11 o'clock stage. He went with a fellow newspaperman to the home of an acquaintance in Court House Square. As the two men sat writing in an upstairs study, a wealthy gentleman by the name of William Kerr, Justice of the Peace, Member of The Assembly, and government canal manager, walked in. Mr. Kerr refused to take a seat, but in a friendly way asked Mackenzie if he had yet settled all the grievances of Upper Canada. He then beckoned Mackenzie towards the door, as if he would have a few words with him outside. Mr. Kerr was one of the Tories who had threatened Mackenzie that very afternoon. But in matters affecting his personal safety, as opposed to questions of other men's political motives, Mackenzie was of an entirely unsuspicious nature. Even if he suspected what might happen to him, however, he would have doubtless thought it out of keeping with his own dignity to refuse the properly delivered invitation of a gentleman. He lit the way downstairs by candle and opened the front door. Three men stood waiting there. Kerr introduced Mackenzie with the words, "This is your man." Mackenzie shrieked, "Murder!" and grabbed the door post. He was felled by one mighty crack from someone's stick, luckily softened by grazing the door lintel on the way down. He was dragged into the street and was being kicked and beaten when a group of friends came to the rescue.

Mr. Kerr, one of the more prominent local members of the Family Compact, was let off with a small fine and a reprimand by the judge for his part in the unsuccessful attempt to remove Mackenzie from Upper Canadian politics. There can scarely be any doubt that if the situation had been reversed, if friends of Mackenzie had been caught in the attempted assassination of, say, Colonel Allan MacNab, the defendants would have been fortunate to escape with a heavy jail sentence. That sort of politics Mackenzie and his friends scrupulously avoided. But such a vicious attack and miscarriage of justice did not serve to strengthen what little inclination Mackenzie had for presenting his case against the Compact in a judicious and coherent manner. He informed his newspaper readers that the Assembly was now, among other things, "a nest of unclean birds".

Mackenzie was back into the rough-and-tumble four days later. According to the Tory *York Courier* which relished Mackenzie's discomfiture, he was haranguing a large crowd in York from the usual rostrum of a wagon, with Jesse Ketchum and other Reformers standing by him, when "some twenty or thirty Irish lads dashed into the middle of the mob, seized the wagon and galloped off with it, patriots and all. The wagon orators finding themselves thus unexpectedly in the hands of the Philistines, scattered themselves out of the wagon, some by jumping and some by tumbling, amid the abundant salutes of rotten eggs." Meanwhile the Tory mob from a rival meeting decided to uphold the English constitution by making for the office of the *Colonial Advocate* and, in an outburst of loyalty, smashing its windows.

By spring of 1832 Mackenzie had gathered nearly twenty-five thousand signatures on petitions from all parts of the province to the authorities in England. He had been appointed the agent of a score of local Reform organizations. He was determined to appeal against his colonial enemies to the men who ruled the Empire. King William was popularly supposed to be a reformer at heart, and the new Whig ministry was on the point of routing the Tories by passing the most revolutionary law of the nineteenth century. Surely a Whig Colonial Secretary would act for the cause of reform in Canada. "If those persons in office in England could but enter into the feelings of the farmers here," he had told the crowds, "and properly understood the effects of the exclusive system, it would be altered. *And it will be altered.*" Mackenzie set off from York on his mission hopefully, with the warmest of wishes from his supporters, and some rousing bad verse to cheer him on his way:

> Now Willie's awa' frae the field o' contention
> Frae the Land o' misrule, and the friends o' dissension
> He's gane owre the waves, as an agent befittin'
> Our claims to support in the councils o' Britain.
>
> There, there, the REFORMERS shall cordially meet him
> An' there his great namesake, KING WILLIE, shall greet him;
> Our PATRIOT MONARCH, whose name shall be written,
> Wi' letters o' gowd in the Records o' Britain.
>
> Gae Canada's Patriot, gae, strang in your mission,
> Gae bear to our Sov'rein, his subjects' Petition;
> Our Despots unmask—shaw the deeds they're committin'
> Pervertin' the blest Institutions o' Britain.

In April, Mackenzie and his family boarded the packet *Ontario* out of New York and set sail for England.

CHAPTER SEVEN

AN OCEAN voyage by sail in a small ship was once the common experience of every traveller. It is now just barely imaginable: the crashing silence of a still wide noon, until the wind shakes the canvas and tugs at the riggings and the sea glides close by the low hull; or the mountainous heave of the black waves and the howl of the dark wind all but drowning the sound of bell and gull and sailor's cry above them.

It was a fair trip for the packet *Ontario*, and a chance for Mackenzie to disburden his waspish buzzing brain of politics for a few weeks and look at the stars. He gorged himself on novels—a frivolous pastime in those days—for the first time since leaving Scotland. He found the company good and the port and Madeira excellent. His good spirits, not to mention the champagne every other day, led him to picture himself as a gentleman of stature and influence, "the equal of any person on board", and to confess to himself that he had something of the aristocrat in him.

The political winds of London were also blowing strong and fair. Mackenzie arrived at the peak of the excitement over the great Reform Bill. This bill would abolish the rotten boroughs whose Parlimentary seats were often sold like commodities on the free market and were the means of many brilliant as well as many comfortable political careers, and it would give the vote to some of the more substantial people in the new industrial towns. Although the provisions were moderate enough, the bill would begin to admit the dangerous Benthamite principle of "one man one vote" within the sacred folds of the unreformed constitution. It would be the first statuory pronouncement of doom upon the paternal aristocracy of Merrie England and the village families who asked their Ultimate Overlord to

> Bless the squire and his relations
> And keep us all in our proper stations.

The Great Reform Bill bore the seeds of the harvest of Labour votes which firmly and finally made England an industrial democracy in 1945.

In the late spring of 1832, the feelings of the country were aroused as scarcely ever before or since, and there was talk of revolution if the bill were defeated. At the beginning of June, Mackenzie wrote home in his letter to the *Advocate* that he had seen the Duke of Wellington, "the hero of Waterloo, pelted with mud and fish heads in the streets of London. Tory peers were hissed, hooted, and groaned at as they entered their carriages" coming from the House of Lords. Already the Radicals had claimed they had prevented the Tories from forming a government by threatening a run on the banks. "To stop the Duke, go for gold!"

Mackenzie was hustled off by Joseph Hume, M.P., the Scottish radical who spent his life airing colonial grievances, to meet the author of that slogan. Francis Place was a self-educated tailor whose library in the back of his shop in Charing Cross Road was the political headquarters of English radicalism. Place was a republican, a democrat, a believer in a severely rational legal system, and had taken upon himself the job of educating a generation of members of Parliament in these Benthamite ideas.

"My library," he said, "was a sort of gossiping shop to such persons as were any way engaged in public matters having the benefit of the people as their object and was frequented very much in the manner of a common coffee-house room." Contemporary Whigs and Tories, neither of whom Place cared for unless and until they were prepared to listen to him, had a healthy regard for his parliamentary influence. "Give me *place* for my fulcrum and I will move the world."

His most diligent though not his most brilliant disciple was Mackenzie's friend, Joseph Hume. Hume was known in the House for his gauche expressions and his long speeches, but he and his Radical friends were a force to be reckoned with by a shaky ministry when the country was roused. As self-appointed "watchdog of the Treasury" he made trouble for more than one minister who proposed to spend money, and his knowledge of colonial affairs was a source of some anxiety to a long succession of Colonial Secretaries.

A London magazine sketched for its readers a vivid cartoon of Place as the intense, impeccable little philosopher perched on his tailor's stool with his earnest pudgy pupil, Hume, at his feet, all attention: "There upon that three-footed stool, gowned in wholesome grey, with an absolute avalanche of schemes, scraps, and calculations ; ound him, sits the philosophic sage, delivering his golden rules with the slowness and the certainty of the choicest alembic; and yonder, squatted upon a pile of unread pamphlets, sits the substantial pupil, with his whole countenance perked into one gigantic ear of astonishment and delight. 'The wild ass quaffing the spring in the desert,' says the Arabian proverb, 'is not so lovely as the countenance of him who drinketh understanding.' "

Inevitably Mackenzie was taken to the master's busy sanctum and introduced. He could scarcely believe his ears when Place told Hume how he had that very day completed work on the detail of his plans for a rebellion if the Bill were finally turned down in the House of Lords. The tailor's shop was in fact the centre of the agitation for the Reform Bill, an encouraging thought to a bookseller-printer who, like Place, had schooled himself on the political ideas of the Philosophical Radicals, and preached them to his countrymen.

Mackenzie watched from the gallery the night the Lords surrendered, under King William's reluctant threat to create new Whig peers, and passed the Bill by a small majority. He wished a similar threat could be applied to the upper house in Canada. But of course in Canada a Reform ministry never came to power as it did in England —which in a sense was precisely why he was here. Joseph Hume put Mackenzie's petition before the House of Commons and arranged a meeting with Lord Goderich, a former Prime Minister and now the Whig Colonial Secretary.

Lieutenant-Governor Colborne had already supplied him with an introduction. "Mr. Mackenzie has now laboured for more than seven years," he wrote in a dispatch to the Colonial Office, "to create discontent in the province. He possesses that cunning and effrontery which will generally attract the attention of some part of the populace, and ensure the success of any demagogue. He has had recourse to every species of falsehood and deception which would promote his views and get his journal into circulation."

Lord Goderich was not one to believe everything an ultra-Tory general told him, and was quite prepared to hear, if not to accept, the other side of the story. Furthermore, with the tide of public opinion running so strongly to reform, the Whig government found it expedient to make concessions to Joseph Hume and his Radical friends. Mackenzie was accompanied to the Colonial Office by Hume, Denis Viger the agent of the Assembly of Lower Canada, and the Reverend George Ryerson, who was pleading for the religious and educational rights of the Methodists and other nonconformists in Canada.

It was a strange meeting. The passionate little Scots-Canadian—"five foot nothing and very like a baboon, but the O'Connell of Canada"—pouring out his grievances by the hour, while Goderich, urbane and unshockable, sat listening, now and again interjecting a pointed remark or a wry smile, but wearing always the mask of polite attention. He wrote later that "he was perfectly satisfied from the conduct of the individual that Mr. Mackenzie was as vain and shallow a person as he had ever encountered. If the conference alluded to by Mr. Mackenzie was only two hours' duration, he must say it was the longest two hours he had ever known."

Further meetings were arranged, for which Mackenzie was to put his charges in writing. Through the summer and fall of 1832 Goderich was inundated with letters and papers on the state of Upper Canada from Mackenzie. Once he stayed up writing day and night for a week, at intervals switching his pen, to avoid a cramp, from one hand to the other, since he had trained himself to write equally well with either. He had often advised his Upper Canadian readers, in the manner of Poor Richard's Almanac, about the need for early rising and hard work, and the folly of wasting time. "When mind and body are active it is surprising how little sleep we require. There are many persons who lose a day each week by sleeping in bed too long in the morning." In London, he more than lived by his own homiletic. So much so, indeed, that if he could have persuaded himself to reduce his activity by half, the remainder might have been more effective. But the feverish concern over wasted time coursed in his very veins and was one virus he possessed in common with all the rising busy men in America.

After months of apparently futile activity, he wrote back to the *Advocate*, "The longer I remain here the more clearly I see that Whigs and Tories are neither more nor less than two factions of wealthy and influential men who have conspired to plunder the great body of the people time about—the Whigs taking the helm when the Tories become too detestable to be endured, and going below whenever Toryism had got a refreshed character by a few years' pretended opposition to misrule." He retracted these remarks when he finally learned, in March of 1833, that the Colonial Secretary had done something after all.

Goderich was sufficiently conscientious to read all Mackenzie's papers and intelligent enough to act upon them. Indeed, in spite of Mackenzie's bias and bravura rhetoric, it was the best detailed information on Upper Canada which Goderich could get hold of, since Colborne's military eye imposed a sense of order on everything he saw and his dispatches were of a Caesarean brevity. In November, 1832, Goderich sent out a long dispatch, accompanied by Mackenzie's submissions, which Colborne was instructed to make public. Mackenzie's exaggerations and irrelevancies were noted, his charges about the malicious intentions of His Majesty's government in Upper Canada were denied, and his request that the Secretary of State interfere with the Assembly was firmly turned down.

To Mackenzie's strictures about freedom of the press, he wryly remarked, "It is needless to look beyond Mr. Mackenzie's journal to be convinced that there is no latitude which the most ardent lover of free discussion ever claimed which is not at present enjoyed with perfect impunity in Upper Canada."

But for other abuses, Goderich suggested remedies. If the Canadian upper house, for example, proved as obstructive as the English, Colborne should add new members; and Archdeacon Strachan and the Roman Catholic Bishop Macdonell were invited to resign their places in that body. (They did not, as it turned out, choose to accept the invitation.) In other matters, Goderich acted himself. Mackenzie's bitter complaint about the Post Office brought the first decisive step in eliminating graft and in reducing the letter rate from one dollar or more to the two cents that became standard in 1898. Mackenzie's attack on the Bank of Upper Canada as a friend of big business and a means of undue political influence persuaded the British government to veto the Bank Acts passed by the two Houses and signed by Colborne.

The Colonial Secretary's actions and his dispatch, though by no means an endorsement of Mackenzie, were greeted by the Tories with outbursts of indignation. "An elegant piece of fiddle-faddle", "stupidity" and "condescending impertinence". It was shocking that Lord Goderich had chosen so much as to speak to the man whom they had just expelled for the third time from the Assembly, let alone to hear him out and reply to his submissions.

The Legislative Council refused to put the despatch on

their journals, and instead sent it back to the Governor declaring it unworthy of their serious attention. The Assembly hesitated to commit such a deliberate insult and tabled the dispatch without Mackenzie's submissions. The Colonial Office replied swiftly to this foolish behaviour. For their discreditable part in the affair, as well as for leading the House in Mackenzie's expulsion, the two law officers of the Crown, Attorney-General Boulton and Solicitor-General Hagerman, were dismissed from office.

The official newspapers now pulled out all the stops in their blasts at the British government. The *Courier* announced that the affections of those who mattered in Upper Canada were "more than half-alienated" from the mother country; "they already begin to cast about for some new state of political existence." It was thus not only Mackenzie but also some of the Tories who in the course of the eighteen-thirties threatened to break away from the Empire. Their language on this occasion was some measure of their readiness to use imperial loyalty as a personal convenience.

Altogether, Mackenzie got more satisfaction out of the Colonial Office than any other Canadian who went there as a suppliant. An interview with the Secretary was in itself a rarity. And Mackenzie had seen two of his chief enemies in the government fired, his attack on big business crowned by the Bank Bills' veto, his complaint about the Post Office swiftly acted upon, and strong language used by the Secretary to the Lieutenant-Governor on more than a dozen other matters, including his own expulsion from the Assembly.

Events which followed, however, soon showed the futility of building a reform policy on what the *Courier* called "the lottery" of British politics. It could not be the permanent function of a successful opposition to attack His Majesty's government in Upper Canada at a distance of three thousand miles through the practice of the gentle art of lobbying in the corridors of Whitehall. The whole situation was an invitation to irresponsible behaviour on both sides and indicates what a blessed necessity the introduction of responsible government was to be.

What faith Mackenzie had in appeals to the British government as a solution to the problems of Upper Canada was quickly shaken. Goderich was replaced at the Colonial Office by a man who himself resigned when a Tory government came to power. There were in fact no fewer than ten Colonial Secretaries within a space of ten years. It was the period of the *laissez-faire* Second Empire, when the public no longer cared about the Empire and left it to a few soldiers and civil servants to manage as best they could; when the future imperialist Disraeli spoke of "those wretched colonies" as "millstones round our necks", and the apostle of the new industrial capitalism in England, Richard Cobden, said he would as soon send troops to defend the colonies as to defend the national debt.

Charles Buller, who later became Lord Durham's secretary and intimate adviser on his famous mission to Canada, was one of the few Englishmen of that time who did care about the Empire. He wrote of the frustration of the poor Colonial at the mercy of "Mr. Mother Country", an industrious and obscure official residing in one of the suburbs of London and travelling daily to Whitehall to govern the Empire. "There are rooms in the Colonial Office with old and meagre furniture, bookcases crammed with *Colonial Gazettes* and newspapers, tables covered with baize, and some old and faded chairs scattered about, in which those who have personal applications to make are doomed to wait until the interview can be obtained. These are men with colonial grievances. The very messengers know them, their business, and its hopelessness, and eye them with pity as they bid them wait their long and habitual period of attendance."

For Mackenzie, the first shock came one May morning as he was preparing at last to finish his mission in England. He met the unspeakable Hagerman entering the Colonial Office just as he himself was leaving. A month before his departure Mackenzie learned that the new Secretary had given Hagerman his job back and awarded Boulton a consolation prize of the Chief Justiceship of Newfoundland. Worse was to follow. All Goderich's strongly-phrased

advice about reform in Upper Canada could now be safely
circumvented by the Compact men, even though Colborne
himself made a few gestures in the direction of his former
chief's wishes. In England, the Whigs grew weary of their
reforming role. Many of them had supported the great Reform Bill only because they hoped it would finish once and
for all the popular demand for reform. A future Colonial
Secretary, Lord John Russell, was nicknamed Finality Jack
because of his view on the matter. The lethargic Lord Mel-
bourne succeeded Grey as Prime Minister, and the radicals like Joseph Hume found themselves more and more
out of sorts with the government.

Mackenzie more than once considered parliamentary
union with England as a solution to the Upper Canadian
problem. In 1827 he had even sent an open letter to the
Governor-in-Chief of British North America proposing it.
He dearly loved the play of wit and intelligence in the Lord's
and Commons' debates and he had a sense of their moment-
ous significance. The stale torpor and stupidity and crankiness of a Canadian parliament made English politics seem
like some afterglow of the Arthurian legend.

One wonders whether, as he sat looking down from the
gallery on the House of Lords in session, he did not see himself on the front bench as a member of a future Reform
ministry, or holding forth in Pitt-like philippic against the
imperial policy of a bungling government. But the journalist's quick eye kept his mind from taking off entirely for
outer space. The readers of his letters to the *Advocate*,
after being duly improved by a rapturous description of
the Prime Minister, the Earl Grey, were treated to the
gratifying but scarcely verifiable titbit of information that
the House of Lords contained three to one more bald pates
than any legislature in America. Mackenzie was always
more of a gossip than a dreamer.

Now with the frustration of this year's vigil outside the
Colonial Office, Mackenzie was readier to agree with the
opinions of his friends, Hume and Place, that Canada might
be better off running her own affairs and independent of

Great Britain. There was also little reason to stay longer in England.

The year had been a difficult one for the Mackenzie family. Their London quarters in Brunswick Square were not large and the joyfully welcomed arrival of a baby boy, Joseph Hume Mackenzie, did not make life any more commodious. A half-bucket of coal a week and a miniscule grate whose heat sped skyward as surely as a river seeks the sea were not proof against the soul-and-bone dampening English winter weather, at least to North Americans spoiled with having all the wood they could burn. "I would rather spend a winter in Upper Canada than in London," wrote Mackenzie with conviction. "I have tried both." The organizations which sent Mackenzie to England only paid one quarter of his "total" expenses, with the result that he was often in financial difficulties. He naturally was not able to run the *Advocate* and the bookstore himself, and this of course meant a smaller income. He entered more deeply into the practice of heavy borrowing from acquaintances, a habit of which he was never entirely free, and which became something of a chronic vice with him in later years when it was the only means of satisfying his urge to incessant publication.

On the strength of recent loans, and particularly one from the Rev. George Ryerson, Mackenzie managed to travel north, and to satisfy his sense of honour by paying off all his old debts in Scotland. He visited his native Dundee for the last time, and in the summer of 1833 left the British Isles forever.

The greater part of the Mackenzies' fellow travellers on the return journey were not now returning British officials or businessmen, but poor emigrant families, crammed into pitching, choleraic steerage quarters often occupied by timber or wheat on the eastward voyage, men and women and children who had given up forever the familiar hardships and comfortable custom-bound certainties of a thousand-year-old village for the hope and terror of the unknown. Mackenzie no longer entertained himself with confident hopes and thoughts about the omniscient benevolence of the persons who ruled the Empire, nor was he as certain as he had been at twenty-five on his first adventure on the Atlantic that only a Mackenzie knew how to be loyal. This trip meant committing himself as irrevocably to the New World as the humble folk that travelled with him.

Seven weeks out of port, at length, from the infinity of sky and sea came the land. For the emigrant for whom the village over the next hill meant "far" and the market town, for practical purposes, the end of the world, the first sight of their adopted country, where it did not freeze the senses into incomprehension, must surely have been awesome. Day after day the great shores of the gulf lay aloof from the frail busy society of the small ship, now all but disappearing from sight, now pressing in until the sheer black perpendicular mile of Capes Trinity and Eternity skidded vertiginously above them. How could anyone who knew the Thames or the Dee, who judged rivers by their human, civilized banks, accept the St. Lawrence? Only a few miles from where these others join the sea, kings have ridden on their waters—Saxon Edgar rowed by his thanes; Elizabeth in her royal barge greeted by Leicester; gouty periwigged George saluted by the "Water Music" of his court composer, Mr. Handel. But the coming together of the St. Lawrence and the Atlantic is hooded in the perpetual mists of the sub-Arctic.

Into the high sun of the gulf, the inhuman tallness of the blue and cirrocumulus sky, it is the same. Islands a day's journey in the passing lie like the sleeping form of some species of monster unknown to Greek mythology or some giant never met by the gods of Valhalla. Beyond, on the shore, a forest bleaker by far than the haunted Teutonic woods that scared the Romans so. And the shore itself, the edge of a continental shield that would sternly test the man who believed he was the measure of all things. Gulf, sky, shore, each the infinitely receding and advancing perspective in the brain, the rim of madness, in a land still unthinkably abstract and virgin.

CHAPTER EIGHT

THE society to which Mackenzie returned was at its roots an American one, as nearly alien to Europe as the land itself. It was most American where the immigrants came to live with the daily struggles and the freedom of the wilderness. For they were free, free from the rule of class and culture, squire and parson, if not always of mortgage and debt, in a way that Europeans were not. The original deposit of immigrants was predominantly Tory and loyalist in sentiment, and rightly dubbed "His Majesty's Yankees". But they were eventually outnumbered by the settlers who were simply looking for land. These later arrivals cared little for loyalties to London or even to Washington and were scarcely conscious of having crossed a border. Whether they cared or not, they brought with them American ideas and habits which a still later tide of immigrants from Britain in the 1830's found there and accepted, when they were not well warned, as easily as they breathed the new air.

The constant flow of trade also kept Upper Canada in touch with the United States. The fact that the province was a peninsula planted deep in the heart of the American midwest, in winter and spring cut off from England, except through New York, by the barrier of the frozen St. Lawrence, ensured that the Strachans and Robinsons would never succeed in recreating the social hierarchy or the gentle good life of England's green and pleasant land amid the rock and coarse grass and cedar swamp of southern Ontario. "Rational freedom must now prevail on the whole continent of America," wrote Mackenzie, quoting a Canadian newspaper. "It is indigenous to its soil."

After his return to Canada, Mackenzie no longer referred to the Old Country as "home". He was more certain now that the salvation of the land and its people could be worked out with the help of the institutions and practices of American democracy. He remembered his visit to Washington and the White House in 1829, and the genial greeting and rough graceful informality of its occupant, Andrew Jackson of frontier Tennessee. Mackenzie had been surprised that a chief of state should be attended not by a troup of liveried lackeys, but only "by an agile little Irish lad who appeared to me the very antipodes of ceremony and parade". He was amazed to find the President completely free of access to the meanest citizen who chose to pay him a call.

Mackenzie recalled, too, an incident which befell a traveller in Vermont:

> I saw a sturdy-looking farmer pass the inn, driving a one-horse cart on which he was seated. He drove to a store, shouldered his bales of wool, one after another, and placed them in the merchant's shop. Who do you think he was? Palmer, the present governor of the state of Vermont!

"Who would not willingly exchange General Colborne for a governor of this sort?" Mackenzie asked his readers.

Mackenzie's admiration for American democracy grew as rapidly during the 1830's as his affection for British rule declined. Two years after his return, Mackenzie aptly summed up his position when he wrote to a fellow editor, John Neilson of Quebec City, "I am less loyal then I was."

The question of loyalty and of the future form of Canadian society was not far from the centre of the next battle Mackenzie fought. He landed at Quebec in August of 1833 where he refused the tribute of a public banquet proffered to him by the Reformers of Lower Canada, although he was pleased by the gesture. In late August he slipped quietly back into York and his editor's desk at the *Advocate* without so much as a notice in the paper announcing his return. As his severest modern critic has fairly said, Mackenzie was never a self-advertiser for the sake of self-advertising. But with him the self had wide and flexible boundaries. Let persons fall below the standard of public righteousness which Mackenzie expected of them and it was as good as a personal affront; the province would be suddenly and hotly advertised of Mackenzie's existence, and roused by the cry of treason.

The sinner against the light during the autumn of Mackenzie's return was none other than the most influential Methodist in the province and hitherto counted as one of the Reformers' strongest allies.

Egerton Ryerson we have already met as the youthful Methodist preacher whose sermon Mackenzie reviewed in the *Colonial Advocate*, and whose vigorous discussion of the problem of Church and State, published in the same journal, formed the most effective attack ever made upon the Erastian intentions of Archdeacon Strachan. That single work made Ryerson, at twenty-three, the intellectual leader of Upper Canadian Methodism. Now, seven years later, he was one of the best known public figures in the province and editor of the powerful Methodist paper, the *Christian Guardian*.

In those days the word "Methodist" was not blessed with the connotations of solid respectability and financial solvency which it has accumulated with the years. Quite the contrary. In the mouths of the aristocracy it was little better than a term of abuse, associated with vulgarity, displays of enthusiasm, and the lower classes, and in Upper Canada, with the worst dangers of radicalism as well. Our Lord was not at all like the Methodists, said the fastidious, sweetly-reasonable voice of the eighteenth century, but rather "a person of moderation and soundness of judgment".

Methodism in early Upper Canada was marked by the

travelling preacher, riding his circuit from one outpost in the wilderness to the next, bearing the fire of the living word to a congregation grouped around a stump in the open air or packed into a one-room log cabin or primitive meeting house. It was still possessed by the intense spiritual enthusiasm of the Great Awakening, the religious revival in eighteenth century America. Its organization was also originally American and until 1828 the Upper Canadian Conference was linked to its neighbouring Methodist conference in New York State. This connection led persons as intelligent as Sir John Colborne, who should have known better, to believe that the Methodists were potential traitors and republicans. It gave further weight to Archdeacon Strachan's attempt to keep their numbers from growing. But to the ultimate inconvenience of the Archdeacon, such a belief was simply not true. The great majority of Methodists were humble folk, and sympathetic to the Reformers, but scarcely disloyal. Ryerson himself came from a U.E.L. family and his temperament was conservative and thoroughly royalist. Strachan's real and valid objection to Egerton Ryerson and the Methodists was that they stood outside the orthodoxy and order of the main Christian tradition, and, specifically, that they wanted to break the Anglican monopoly of education in Upper Canada and on the public lands set aside for the support of the Protestant religion.

Inevitably these aims brought Ryerson and the Methodists into politics. The Methodists defended their cause in addresses to the Lieutenant-Governor, in the columns of friendly newspapers, and by petitioning the Colonial Office. At election time they voted solidly for Reform. Their most persistent champion in the legislature was Mackenzie himself.

Ryerson did not approve of many of Mackenzie's ideas. Nor did he care for his manner; the agitated style of the *Colonial Advocate* was a far cry from the well modulated, slightly pompous editorial voice of the *Guardian*. Their basic motives were different. Mackenzie attacked Strachan and all his works because he believed in social and political equality, Ryerson because he wanted religious liberty for Protestants in Upper Canada. Nevertheless their immediate cause was the same, and in the minds of the people who supported them there was little difference between them. They were the two chief objects of the Compact's displeasure. They were burned together in effigy at Peterborough. MacNab's Gore *Mercury* berated Mackenzie regularly but reserved its most lurid conceits for the abuse of Ryerson: "a man of profound hyprocrisy and unblushing effrontery who sits blinking on his perch like Satan when he perched on the tree of Life in the shape of a cormorant to meditate the ruin of our first parents in Eden".

In London, the Upper Canadian Methodists naturally looked to Joseph Hume as their spokesman and defender. We have already noticed the Reverend George Ryerson, Egerton's brother, at the Colonial Office in the company of Hume and Mackenzie. When Egerton went to England, however, to negotiate a union between the Upper Canadian Methodists and the British Wesleyans, he discovered that his English brethren took a very different view of Hume and the Philosophical Radicals. Most of them, he was told, were out and out atheists or else Unitarians, which was just as deplorable. The virtuous and religious portion of the nation therefore held strictly aloof from them. Since the Whigs, with their aristocratic eighteenth century indifference to religion, were no great improvement on the Radicals, the English Methodists tended to be moderate Tories. This was unfortunate, Ryerson felt, for the sake of certain necessary reforms, but it obviously could not be helped. He found that, like Mackenzie, the English Radicals wanted religious liberty less for the sake of piety than as another item in the creed of liberal democracy. On that score, the Reverend Jabez Bunting, John Wesley's successor, had already unequivocally enlightened the faithful when he pronounced that "Methodism is opposed to democracy as it is opposed to sin."

On his return to Upper Canada Ryerson undertook, in

a more moderate tone of voice, to say much the same thing
to his Canadian brethren. Not only were the Humes and
the Places virtual democrats and infidels but many of them
made no secret of their wish to see the Empire dissolved
and the monarchy replaced by a republic.

Mackenzie's own views were not discussed, but Ryerson
feared that Mackenzie might already be plotting with the
French Canadian leaders towards the day of Canadian independence. Although he loftily disclaimed the intention in
public, Ryerson's deliberate purpose in writing on English
radicalism was to give warning to his fellow Methodists
of the dangers into which Mackenzie might lead them.
Ryerson's distinction between Methodism and Mackenzie's
doctrines could be planted most clearly in his readers' minds
if there was something of a public quarrel. Ryerson did
not choose to cast the first stone, nor was there need for
him to cast any. Mackenzie could be provoked quite as
easily by the calm, judicious, superior manner in which
Ryerson addressed himself to his subject.

The first of Ryerson's "Impressions of England" appeared
in the *Guardian* of October 30, 1833. Mackenzie's reply
was swift and furious. The very same night a second edition
of the *Colonial Advocate* was published. In Mackenzie's
mind, Ryerson's deprecation of Hume and British Radicalism was an act of treason against the only cause that
mattered. Nor had Mackenzie's zeal ever quite let him
surrender to the idea that Ryerson's previous support was
hedged with reservations and propelled by different and
more pragmatic motives than his own ardent, uncompli-
cated liberalism. To make things doubly bad, this apparent
desertion of a friend came at a dreadful moment in Mackenzie's personal history. That very week his dear little eleven-
months-old boy much longed for, ten years expected, and
wholly adored—took sick and died. It did not improve
Mackenzie's feelings that his baby had been named for the
chief object of Ryerson's criticism, Joseph Hume. Mackenzie burst out in grief and anger:

ANOTHER DESERTER!

The *Christian Guardian* under the management of our reverend neighbour, Egerton Ryerson, has gone over to the enemy, press, types, and all, and hoisted the colours of a cruel, vindictive Tory priesthood. His brother George, when sent to London became an easy convert to the same cause, and it appears that the parent stock were of those who fought to uphold unjust taxation, stamp acts, and Toryism in the United States. [The Ryersons had been Church of England Tories in pre-Revolutionary America.] The contents of the Guardian of to-night tells us in language too plain, too intelligible to be misunderstood that a deadly blow has been struck at the liberties of the people of Upper Canada, by as subtle an adversary in the guise of an old familiar friend as ever crossed the Atlantic. The Americans have their Arnold and the Canadians have their Ryerson.... But he and his allies, the church and state gentry shall now have me in their rear.... Elder Ryan, poor fellow, is in his grave, but I shall remember his telling me, "I have found out the Ryersons and before long the people of Canada will find them out." HE WAS RIGHT.

The Upper Canadian Methodists were thrown into confusion by Ryerson's apparent change of direction. Most of them eventually followed him in his opposition to Reform, especially when doubt was thrown on the Reformers' loyalty to King and Empire. In two later elections (1836 and 1843), before he began his great work of building the Ontario school system, Ryerson called upon the faithful to rally to the governors who took the stump and waved the flag against Reform. Tarred with the brush of disloyalty and ungodliness, the Reformers were beaten. Mackenzie met more than his match when he tackled Ryerson and the Compact together.

Mackenzie's next battle was the climax of an old feud and it followed upon the last, which had scarcely got under way, with indecent haste. While he was overseas Mackenzie had again been expelled from the legislature, *in absentia,* and for the third time was returned in a by-election by the people of County York. Solicitor-General Hagerman said that the returning officer should refuse to accept any votes cast for Mackenzie, and one Tory member even suggested dividing the county as a punishment for its obstinacy. But in the end the House contented itself with the usual procedure of simple expulsion. Mackenzie was back again among his constituents for the next by-election, in December of 1833. He took the opportunity to attack the whole fabric of colonial government.

The county farmers met in great numbers to return him by acclamation, and to carry a series of resolutions attacking the Tory members, the Family Compact, and, for the first time, questioning the secret behaviour in the affair of Governor Colborne himself.

Before he could be expelled following his fourth by-election victory, Mackenzie presented himself to the House to be sworn in. A large crowd of his electors came with him. They squeezed themselves into the galleries and the lobby. In spite of Mackenzie's instructions to remain quiet, they hissed Allan MacNab as he led the attack on Mackenzie. The speaker ordered the galleries and the space below the bar to be cleared of strangers. While the crowds shuffled out, the sergeant-at-arms, Allan MacNab's father, told Mackenzie himself to leave. When Mackenzie stood his ground, he was seized by the scruff of the neck and dragged towards the door. A huge Highlander who was near Mackenzie tried to block the way, and with this the crowd outside in the lobby charged at the entrance way themselves. Honourable members rushed to bolt and hold the door, and by piling their benches into a barricade managed to withstand the siege.

After this incident, more petitions poured into the Assembly demanding justice for Mackenzie. The tax-payers of the York village of King refused to appoint a tax collector on the grounds that they were deprived of one of their representatives. The House had been given fair warning by Jesse Ketchum, but it was in no mood for common sense.

> You have got Mr. Mackenzie very low down. Take
> care you do not end your proceedings by raising him
> higher and higher in the esteem of the province. The
> Canadians are a generous, friendly people. They do not
> like to see a man persecuted. They think, and I think
> your conduct towards him unfair and unlawful. He
> makes some very great blunders, but you cover them
> up by making still greater. Our persecution of him
> may end in placing him, Mr. Speaker, in the chair you
> now fill. [Great laughter.] You may make him governor
> before the game is over. [Increased laughter.]

Sir John Colborne took a more serious view of the affair,
and after two years of being prodded by the Colonial Office,
decided to make some gesture in Mr. Mackenzie's direction.
Since the Assembly would not let Mackenzie qualify by
taking the oath of allegiance, he ordered the clerk of his
Executive Council to tender it.

When this was done, in February 1834, Mackenzie
walked back into the Assembly and for the first time in
three years took his seat. The business of the House came
to an abrupt halt. The low murmur of conversation in the
galleries stopped dead. Mr. MacNab *père*, important in
sword and sash, heaved his embroidered bulk in Mackenzie's
direction and informed the little man that he was a stranger.
Mackenzie said that he was not a stranger. He was a member
duly elected and sworn in and produced a copy of the
oath to prove it. The sergeant managed to pry Mackenzie
loose from his seat and on the third try put him through
the door and out.

The indignity was soon avenged in a manner that could
not have been more distasteful to the MacNabs and the
other Tories. On March 6, 1834, by act of the Governor
and the Assembly, the town of York received its charter to
become the city of Toronto. The Reformers opposed this
move because they were afraid it would mean higher taxes.

(It did.) Mackenzie called the whole scheme a Tory plot and voiced his objections in a jingle:

> Come hither, come hither, my little dog Ponto
> Let's trot down and see where little York's gone to;
> For forty big Tories, assembled in junta
> Have murdered little York in the City of Toronto.

But to make the best of the new and entirely necessary situation, Mackenzie and other Reformers ran for office in Toronto's first civic elections, held on March 27th, 1834. They won.

Scarcely a month after he had left the Assembly with such unbecoming suddenness, His Worship Mayor Mackenzie was presiding over the municipal government of the first city in Upper Canada.

CHAPTER NINE

"HE WHO first fixed upon this spot," wrote a visitor to York in 1820, "as the site of the capital of Upper Canada, whatever predilection he may have had for the roaring of frogs or the effluvia arising from the stagnant water, can certainly have had no very great regard for preserving the lives of His Majesty's subjects. The town is situated upon a piece of low, marshy ground better calculated for a frog pond or a beaver meadow than for the residence of human beings."

Visitors were apt to be told that they did not know the half of it: that one day, for example, "a gentleman walking on King Street espied a good-looking hat in the middle of the road. Curious to see and pick up the hat, he managed to reach it, and on removing it, discovered to his surprise the head of a living man underneath. This individual at once appealed for deliverance, urging as a special plea that if prompt assistance were not rendered, his horse, which was underneath, would certainly perish. The usual mode of extrication by shovels and oxen was soon applied, and man and horse excavated."

Tall stories about the muddiness of York were founded on an uncomfortable quantity of truth. The need for better cart roads has already been suggested by the description of the farmer's detour around the quagmires of Lower Yonge Street on their way to market. One of the few firm footways in town was provided by the fragrant tanbark sidewalks around Jesse Ketchum's tannery near King and Yonge. The lack of sidewalks and street paving, in fact, was one of the reasons that York became Toronto. Its incorporation as a city enabled the community to borrow money to pay for civic improvements and a civic government. There was also a lack of street lighting, drains and sewers, and of any public water supply more bountiful than the hard-won pailfuls drawn from a town pump or carried up from the Bay. A fire alarm consisted of the ringing of St. James' bell, and much shouting. Fires were put out by a general seizure of the leather buckets which hung conspicuously at all front doors, and which were then hustled hand to hand to the Bay and back by files of beady-browed citizens. Police service were of a decrepit sort, and apart from the acts of the county sheriff and of the county magistrates at quarter sessions, there was no municipal government. The general neglect of the public interest, together with the sudden growth in population and the citizens' habit of pitching garbage into the nearest vacant lot and using the street as a sewer, led to Mayor Mackenzie's most serious civic problem.

A dreadful cholera attacked the city. Business came to a complete stop and the streets were deserted. Before the epidemic was over, one person in four had caught the disease and one in ten had died of it. Mackenzie threw himself into the relief work as ferociously as if he were fighting the whole Family Compact single-handed. When no one else could be persuaded to take the sick to the hospital, he went himself to their homes with the cholera cart and helped their families carry them out. He rarely stopped to eat or sleep until in the end he caught the disease himself. His demon of vitality carried him through, and it was not long before he was recovered and back at his post.

Probably his most difficult task as Mayor was to persuade citizens to accept a tax increase in order to pay for the improvements which the city so badly needed. When the council decided that £1000 should be borrowed to put down a two-foot-wide board sidewalk on King Street, a group of indignant citizens protested. Mackenzie called a meeting to explain the council's decision but it was adjourned in an uproar. When they met again the next day,

July 30, in a room over the meat market, another clamour burst out. Whereupon the deity of Progress, Death and Taxes came to the justification of Mackenzie and the undoing of the angry multitudes in a most terrible and sudden judgment. The solid weight of the citizenry and the angry rhythmic stamping of the dissenters brought down the floor, and the whole jeering company sank as suddenly from before the chairman's eyes as if they were a carload of souls bound for nether regions. Eight people were killed by the fall or by being caught on the butchers' meat hooks below, and a dozen others were terribly maimed.

Mackenzie and the council proceeded to levy the taxes and put down the sidewalk. Before their term of office was over they had laid the basis for good city government. Charles Dickens, on his visit to Toronto seven years later, found "the streets well-paved, and lit with gas, and the city full of life and bustle". His only complaint was of Toronto's wild and rabid toryism, which, he said, appalled him.

Mackenzie's duties also involved presiding in municipal court. Difficult as it is to imagine him on the high bench robed in black, his flaming headgear exchanged for a set of formal white curls, he carried out his duties with dignity and a fairness born of a thorough study of every case. His only recorded lapse occurred in the trial of a poor wench who replied to her judge with such choice and contemptuous obscenity as to raise the hackles of his Scottish pride and stir up Calvinist feelings on the need and nature of judgment. Mackenzie put her straightway into the public stocks, and for this severity was much criticized. In spite of this incident, Mackenzie's tenure of office as first Mayor of Toronto can be fairly summed up in the motto "Industry, Intelligence, Integrity" which he placed on the coat of arms he himself designed for the city.

However virtuous Mackenzie's administrative performance, there remained a naughty scrawl on the escutcheon of its respectability. His Worship's *alter ego* was still editor of the *Colonial Advocate*. Editor Mackenzie never allowed the tenure of office to swerve him from the path of good journalism and bad judgment. There are some people, as Mr. LeSueur has said in his unpublished life of Mackenzie, who search for trouble as for hidden treasure. The treasure on this occasion was a personal letter written to Mackenzie by Joseph Hume who had just received news of Mackenzie's fifth scuffle with the Assembly. "Your triumphant election on the 16th and ejection from the Assembly on the 17th," he wrote, "must hasten that crisis which is approaching in the affairs of the Canadas, and which will terminate in independence and freedom from the baneful domination of the Mother Country and the tyrannical conduct of a small and despicable faction in the colonies."

Mackenzie rushed this small ticking package to press on May 22, 1834. Within six hours, 1200 loyal Torontonians had roused themselves to inform the city council and Governor Colborne of their readiness to defend the Empire, and of their abomination of Mackenzie. It was an embarrassing situation for the Reformers. The Tories always have had a habit of winning elections whenever loyalty and the British connection have been the main issues. Eventually the Reformers wriggled out of their difficulty by construing the letter to stress colonial misrule and by disavowing the suggestion of rebellion and republicanism which the Tories, and very likely Joseph Hume himself, had put there.

Exactly what effect Mackenzie intended his explosion to have it is difficult to say. He was certainly not yet planning or even hoping for a rebellion against British rule. He had just recently advised British immigrants that Upper Canada was a better place for them to settle than the American west, in spite of its bad government, and in one of his sanguine moods he expressed the hope that the new Colonial Secretary would carry reform in the direction in which Lord Goderich had pointed. But at the same time he was serving notice that by one means or another the day of social justice and an end of privilege would come in Upper Canada.

To celebrate the approaching provincial elections of

October, 1834, Mackenzie put into print another of those
flaming seizures of the spirit which warmed the hearts of
his rural constituents and caused some of his more careful
Reform colleagues a shudder for fear of what next. The
latest publication was written under the pseudonym of Patrick Swift, Esq., M.P.P., Professor of Astrology (supposed-
ly a nephew of the great master of invective, Jonathan
Swift), and was titled *A New Almanack for the Canadian
True Blues for the Millenial and prophetical year of the
Grand General Election for Upper Canada and the total
and everlasting downfall of Toryism in the British Empire,
1834*.

The usual statistics for every society or institution in
the province were listed in the *Almanack,* and then thickly
frosted with propaganda. Facts cry out for an interpretation and Mackenzie could not forbear from supplying the
right one. The Legislative Council was duly listed as

> The most extraordinary collection of sturdy beggars,
> parsons, priests, pensioners, army people, navy people,
> place-men, bank directors, and stock and land jobbers
> ever established to act as a paltry screen to a rotten
> government. They cost the country about £40,000 a
> year and the good laws by which it might benefit, they
> tomahawk. They don't like to be called a *nuisance.*

The English Methodists' acceptance of a sum of government money for the support of their Canadian missionary
work was a fact which must not only be recorded but named
for what it was—a violation of the eternal rightness of the
principle of the separation of Church and State and of the
"liberty conferred by the Gospel".

> Ye believe these doctrines, so do I. But all at once
> Ryerson and the Canada Conference-join a Tory Con-
> ference in England and accept a part of the people's
> money out of the provincial chest, yearly, saying to the
> Governor and the other gentlemen of the sword and
> surplice who guard it "If we get our small share of
> plunder, you may do with the other hundred thousand
> a year, which you force from the farmers, just what

you please—henceforth 'hush!' is the word with the Methodist conference."

The *Almanack* indulged in praise as well as invective. The founding of the York Mechanics' Institute in 1831 with Doctor Baldwin as its president was celebrated. Its lectures and its library for the working men of the county were welcomed as signs of the dawn of "rational freedom". Universal education was one of Mackenzie's deepest concerns. He was continually at war with the intellectual Philistines of his day. There is, he wrote, "a strong desire in Canada to become rich and powerful; it would be well to unite thereto a wish to cultivate the arts and sciences." He conceived the lack of libraries and schools in the province to be a standing affront to the dignity of the common man, and the founding of Upper Canada College to be part of a plot to set an educated aristocracy firmly upon the people's necks. He returned again and again to the plea for an educated electorate. "The question whether a people should be Educated is the same as whether it should be happy or miserable, liberated or oppressed."

In the *Almanack*'s calendar each day of the year commemorated some anniversary in the history of liberalism— the birth of Sir Isaac Newton, the day the Bostonians dumped the British tea into their harbour, the glorious re-election of William Lyon Mackenzie.

The *Almanack*, like many numbers of the *Advocate*, is a fair indication of the two chief British influences on Mackenzie's thought—the poetry of Robert Burns, and the British periodicals of intelligent commentary and opinion. Robert Burns was the voice, not of the masses, but of the common people on the land, intelligent and sturdily independent, and threatened only by a cruel aristocracy and their rent-gathering factors:

> I've noticed on our laird's court-day
> An' mony a time my heart's been wae
> Poor tenant bodies, scant o' cash
> How they maun thole a factor's snash;
> He'll stamp an' threaten, curse and swear,
> He'll apprehend them, poind their gear;

While they maun stan', wi' aspect humble,
An' hear it a', an' fear an' tremble.

Just as in Scotland, an economic tyranny existed in Upper Canada: "Our farmers are indebted to our country merchants, our country merchants are deeply bound down in the same manner to the Montreal wholesale dealers." And when Mackenzie denounced the commercial tyrants he often added a verse from Burns to drive his point home.

The other British influence, the *Westminster* and *Edinburgh Reviews,* were the chief exponents of the liberal tradition, derived from Locke and Bentham, of cheap rational government, free enterprise, and the prior rights of the individual, which became the prevailing wind in the climate of opinion of later nineteenth century England and twentieth century Canada. Mackenzie was one of the few Canadians who have ever been closely in touch with contemporary British thought, able if not always disposed to criticize it, and who have helped, in a minor way, to shape its development. Mackenzie sorely criticized his fellow legislators for failing to vote money for subscriptions to the intelligent English reviews, including the Tory-minded *Quarterly,* and to the leading American and European periodicals, so that the legislative library might contain something more than "the sweepings of some second-hand London bookshop". The members, he said, "manifested an ultimate unwillingness to put the country in possession of those publications which the spirit of the age requires." He was sufficiently and passionately well-informed to live in his own day and age in the world of ideas. He did not inhabit an intellectual world that was dead and gone. When he did look to the past, it was not to take the ashes but the fire. Most of his countrymen, by contrast, have asserted their colonialism in no stronger way their uncritical acceptance of European ideas long after they have become fashionable and safe, and exciting as cold mutton.

It is true that Mackenzie accepted many liberal ideas somewhat uncritically himself. This, and his lack of intellectual discipline, are two good reasons why he cannot be called a political thinker, as well as why it is difficult, if not foolish, to trace any systematic or consistent development in his thought. He badly needed a circle of kindred spirits whose judgment he could respect, and whose reading was done with something of his own sense of relevance and urgency. They would have never tamed, but might have tempered, the wildness of his expression and the jungle-like proliferation of his style. He needed, too, more opponents capable of countering his dogmatic liberalism with argument rather than abuse.

The liberal tradition of which the *Westminster Review* was the best contemporary expression, included not only the Reform Bill of 1832 but also the American Revolution. Of that fact, above all others, Englishmen at home and overseas were all too keenly aware. Mackenzie often reminded his readers of the consequences of a similar event in Canada. "The loss of the North American provinces would afflict a heavy blow on England, but on them the separation would fall lightly, and they would soon be strong and independent states."

It was not, of course, revolution itself that Mackenzie wanted, but rather that element in American government which appeared to him the great consequence of the Revolution. The heart of the matter, as it was later put by a young lawyer then building his practice in frontier Illinois, lay in government of, for, and by the people. In Mackenzie's day the Upper Canadian government was apparently conducted neither for nor by the people. So it was to American democracy where direct popular control was the theory, and almost the fact, of government that Mackenzie looked for an example. "The road to honour, power and preferment in the United States is public opinion," not the courted favours of "a mushroom aristocracy" and their captive governor.

He had experienced for years the exasperation of seeing the upper house destroy a greater part of the session's work in the Assembly. The obvious remedy was that the people should elect their own Legislative Councillors. In the executive branch of government too, election should replace appointment. Governor and councillors, land registrars and justices of the peace, should each be made directly responsible to the people for their acts.

If the people elected each other to office, not only would government be carried on in their interests but it would be cheaper. There would be no need to provide officials with the income of an English gentleman of leisure nor to supply a princely pension to furnish those who would return to their jobs when their term of office was over. Mackenzie noted that the governor of Vermont, an agricultural state with the same population as Upper Canada, received seven hundred dollars a year while the governor of Upper Canada was supplied with over twenty times that amount, and that there was a similar disproportion between the two government's tax rates, judicial fees, and public debt.

To expect the ordinary man to be capable of making an intelligent choice of several dozen different officials, from a list as tall as himself, and to expect him to keep a close critical eye on the activities of his representatives in the legislature, was to expect a good deal. But Mackenzie always did, just as he expected the farmers of Upper Canada to follow the debates in fine print and the foreign newspaper articles that he published in the *Advocate*. That expectation was based on two assumptions of America's great spokesman of the Enlightenment, Thomas Jefferson: that man was by nature rational, and that this natural virtue only showed to best advantage in a society of simple, self-governing independent people living on the land.

On his return visit to England he had been alarmed at the growth of the new industrial towns. He saw workers who had no means of protecting themselves against the hazards of the hundred-hour week, against starvation wages, and jerry-built slums. The brute fact was brought home to him by the sight of new spinning mills in his native Dundee.

> The smoke of their steam-engines darkens the heavens, and many a poor and miserable boy and girl eke out a wretched existence by long and incessant toil in these ever-to-be detested establishments—the graves of morality, and the parents of vice, deformity, pauperism and crime. Long may Canada be free of all such pests! Let our domestic manufacture be those which our children can easily carry on under the eyes and in the houses and homes of their fathers and mothers.

There was no provision in Mackenzie's political philosophy for the coming industrial order, still a generation away in Upper Canada. Nor would he likely have cared much for the mass political party and the industrial trade unions which were to be the means of bringing a fair share of the new order's benefits to the working masses. The kind of labourers he knew in Upper Canada were employed in small concerns where some knowledge of craftsmanship was required. He was usually of the opinion that their welfare could best be served indirectly, by the general abolition of social privilege and economic and political restriction. Free the small property holder, and the labourer would inevitably benefit. When he spoke of "the people" Mackenzie usually meant the farmers. It was their free judgment that he felt he could trust, if they were but given the chance to exercise it.

"In an agricultural state," wrote Mackenzie, "farmers make the laws and if wrong is done, they have themselves to blame, and can provide a remedy at any time." It was as simple as that. Put the people in control, and if there is any further trouble, it can be remedied by an extra session of the legislature.

War itself can be avoided by a government of farmers. "The truth is, if the *farmers* of the United States see their brethren in Canada happy in the enjoyment of free institutions, all attempts of the place-hunters and manufacturing monopolists will not be able to persuade Congress to interfere. War may be the game of the statesmen but it is the destruction of the peaceful agriculturist. Why should the farmer on one side of the Niagara leave the plough to go to war with the farmer on the other side?"

Mackenzie was fully aware that the United States of his day did not correspond to the Jeffersonian ideal. There were two aspects of American life which he abominated: negro slavery, and the native-born Americans' prejudice against "foreigners" in their midst, who in a host of minor legal and political matters were treated as second class citizens. In a less serious vein, Mackenzie twitted his American friends for withholding the vote from women, who often exercised that prerogative as freeholders in Upper Canada, this almost a century before the suffragettes began their strenuous campaign of leaping from trains and firing pillar-boxes to win the vote in England. "There are certainly several degrees of liberty to which Americans have not attained which are taken for granted in our country. When my friend Col. Baby contested the County of Kent with Messrs. Little and Wilkinson, no less than thirty-five ladies came forward to the hustings—maids and widows—one of them gave Wilkinson a plumper. Which was almost equal to a declaration in form!"

If Mackenzie wished to build an American democracy in Upper Canada, he did not wish to do it by making Upper Canada another state in the Union. He was fully aware, too, of the strong affection, except among settlers born in the United States, for the Old Country, which would work strongly against anyone who attempted to break the British connection:

> Ask a Canadian,—Would you desire an established church; the ministers to be paid by the state? He will reply, No, no; let all denominations be equal. Would you desire the law of primogeniture? No. The election of your own justices of the peace? Yes. The control of your own wild lands and all other revenue? Undoubtedly. Cheap economical government? Yes. The election of your own governors? Ay. Of your legislative councillors? Ay. Well then, would you not also wish to be joined to the United States? No, never!

The whole of Mackenzie's dilemma was contained in that dialogue. How could he sail fair for the "Ayes" without wrecking his craft on the "No, never!"? The only solution he could see was to rouse the farmers with even longer lists of grievances, to excite once more their latent resentment against the state of things and bring its pressure to bear on the authorities. For the present, there was an election to win. But elections had been won before, and speeches made, and bills passed, and petitions signed, and hours waited in the corridors of the Colonial Office. Agitate then —huge meetings in the county towns, mass deputations of farmers marching on York. And what if the authorities chose to ignore them? "If there had been no display of physical force," wrote Mackenzie, quoting an observer of the British crisis of 1832, "there would have been no Reform Bill." But where did the threat of force end and the use of force begin?

In action, and in the minds of angry opponents, those lines which men have drawn in their more deliberate moments between protest and agitation, agitation and rebellion, rebellion and high treason, become blurred. The words melt and crumble. Once embarked upon the course, it is easy to slip from one word to the next, or in one and the same simple act to encompass them all.

The Reformers won the election of October, 1834, and Mackenzie prepared to launch an inquisition of unprecedented thoroughness into the operations of government from his place in the Assembly. What he would do after that he was not certain. He knew it would be something rash. He cried out to the British government to act before it was too late.

CHAPTER TEN

THE SEVENTH Report of the Select Committee of the House of Assembly on Grievances was as thick and thorough a work as the title suggests. It is the record of one of the most remarkable things that Mackenzie ever did. The Grievances Report was his last great arraignment of the Compact from his place in the Assembly. It also proved to be the most important public document on the condition of Upper Canada in the eighteen-thirties, until the publication of the Durham Report. King William read it, and took a hand in the reply. A nervous Colonial Secretary delayed the next session of the Assembly until that reply was ready, and asked Governor Colborne for his resignation. And Egerton Ryerson wrote to confirm the Colonial Secretary's worst fears by telling him that "there is a greater amount of ignorance, vulgar prejudice, and Mackenzie spirit in the present House than has ever been collected in any one House of Assembly in Upper Canada." Such were the fruits of Mackenzie's labour in the spring of 1835.

When the new Assembly met, early in the year, the Reformers put Marshall Spring Bidwell back into the Speaker's chair and discreetly asked the Governor for an Executive Council more in harmony with public opinion. As far as Mackenzie was concerned, a motion was passed to strike from the records those proceedings of the last House which had to do with his expulsion. He was also given the chairmanship of the Committee on Grievances which he wanted.

In the committee Mackenzie directed business as he pleased. Three of his four colleagues were new to the

Assembly, and in any case shared most of his radical opinions. One of them, David Gibson, later had a price put on his head for joining Mackenzie in the Rebellion. Although there was no public scene some of the more moderate Reformers, including Bidwell, were by now soured on Mackenzie and afraid of the extravagances into which he might lead both his followers and their common opponents. They were prepared to avoid the committee and let Mackenzie have his own way there, which was possibly unwise from their point of view, but suited Mackenzie well enough.

Day in and day out the little man held court from behind the long table in the committee room, wearing, as proudly as his large red wig, the full dignity of the House in whose behalf he acted. His porcelain eye fixed the witnesses as they appeared before him and his silent jaw worked nervously while they spoke. When he in turn probed them with his questions it was in a voice so deliberate and quiet that one was apprehensive lest at any moment he shrill out at them, suddenly and wildly.

To conjure him there, with the mind's eye, amid the modest elegance and the snuff-and-tobacco fragrance of the committee room, to observe him at the centre of the long table leaning intently into the thrust and parry of the dialogue, is to see Mackenzie clearly, suddenly, almost as if for the first time, in the role he has really been playing since the day in Queenston when he gave up his profitable business for publishing. He sits there in the tall chair, as judge and jury and prosecuting attorney, a grand inquisitor in the act of putting a whole generation on trial. But there is something else about him, something that brings to mind a fleeting impression we have had of him before. An observer of the eye, the mouth, and the twisting hands might well be tempted to say that the man in the inquisitor's seat was more than a little mad.

We have seen him already working himself towards delirium on his farmcart podium, until the Protestant boys rudely hustled him, cart and all, out of earshot of his audience. He has annoyed more than one British gentleman of rank by using an interview as the occasion for monologous shouting into the teacups. His acid-throwing attacks on the persons of political opponents, and his pursuit of the details of scandal have been, to say the least, compulsive. We shall see him soon burning houses to no apparent purpose, and wearing several greatcoats on the day of the Rebellion to keep the bullets out. In his old age he haunted the era of responsible government, an irrelevant nuisance, with his capering gestures of protest, amid the church parade of progress. A few more sporadic speeches and editorial outbursts, by then the work of a man given over wholly to crankiness and visions, and he died shabbily, of what the Victorians chose to call softening of the brain, his poor mind sliding slowly off into separate schemes of reference.

It often seems that when the occasion demanded of him something sensible, or inspiring, Mackenzie responded with the inappropriate, the uncalled for, or else like Stephen Leacock's knight jumped furiously onto his stallion and rode off in all directions at once.

And yet in spite of a life of increasing, self-frustrating obsession, it was his ability to discipline a great quantity of chaos in the head into something like order; it was his ability to express in words and acts the demands of that order, until the men who needed disturbing were disturbed, and the men who needed a leader found one in him: it was this that distinguished Mackenzie from the ordinary run of mortals. It marks in him a touch of that which is genius, not because it is mad, but because it has conquered madness yet kept the clarity and the intensity of the madman's vision.

As Mackenzie grew older, circumstances hemmed him in more desperately. The gap widened between the world as he wanted it and the world as he found it. Sometimes the disparity was too much for him. But his use of the Grievances Committee is one instance of success. He here gathered up all his resentment against human affairs for their imperfection, all the centrifugal passions and schizotic ideas strewn about his mind and his speeches and the ancient clutter of his news clippings and his reading notes. He gathered them into one huge, almost coherent, structure of questions and accusations, and relentlessly put them to the enemy.

Like Mackenzie's whole life, the accusation was tinged with crankiness and misanthropy and wounded pride, but it served, just as many of the other things he did, the purpose of prophecy. Mackenzie was recalling men to the solemn truth that even in politics a higher righteousness than they can ever achieve is nonetheless inexorably required of them.

One by one Mackenzie confronted the members of the Compact as they appeared before him: the Receiver-General of Upper Canada, the Inspector-General of Public Accounts, the Surveyor-General, the secretary of the Clergy Corporation, and three members of the Executive and Legislative Councils and several more. Some managed an air of lofty indifference or a tone of ironic helpfulness as they replied to the inquiries of the petty inquisition. Others made little attempt to conceal their annoyance and contempt. One interview is short and uneventful in the written record but must surely have been wonderful to behold. Picture the study in contradictory ferocities when before the little Puritan in the oversize judgment seat there stood that hugely fleshed, ill-bred, well-read, rum-soaked Rabelaisian roughneck, "Tiger" Dunlop, Warden of the Forests to the Canada Company.

Mackenzie's first encounter was with Lieutenant-Colonel Rowan, a slightly pompous young British officer who was confidential secretary to the Lieutenant-Governor. His responses were not always well-advised and Mackenzie tripped and tangled him easily.

1. Whose business is it to make out this return? [The return of the names and the offices held by members of the Legislative Council and Assembly of Upper Canada shown to witness.]

It was made out under my superintendence.

2. The first name of a member holding office is that of Mr. Boulton, the Attorney General. Why are his

salary and allowances set down at £300, when it was well known they amounted to four times that sum?

I would rather not answer that question, without seeing the original returns. . . .

3. If a member of the House of Assembly holding office, makes an incorrect return to the Government, does the Government office correct the error?

Certainly, if known to be incorrect. The case of Mr. Boulton was an error. . . .

Mackenzie then questioned Rowan about a man who serves as a perfect example of the Family Compact in power in a single small locality. William Chisholm's father, George Chisholm, was a United Empire Loyalist, and one of the first settlers and chief landowner in the town of Oakville on Lake Ontario. The son was able to sell small parcels of the land at great profit and, through governmental favour, to retain for his family a monopoly of business and government jobs in the area.

17. Mr. William Chisholm is put down in this return as holding the office of Deputy Post Master; has he not lately been appointed Collector of Customs at a place distant from his post office?

He has lately been appointed Collector of Customs at Oakville.

18. Is he not a merchant trading at that place, and importing goods?

I do not know that he is a merchant.

19. Is it fit that a merchant should be his own Collector of Customs?

I am not prepared to give an opinion on that subject.

20. When appointed Collector, was not Mr. Chisholm a known candidate for the office of member of the Provincial Parliament in conjunction with his Post Office?

I cannot say.

47. In the Blue Book for 1830, the income of Thomas Kirkpatrick, Collector of Customs at Kingston, is set down at £282, and no more. In the account signed by Mr. Kirkpatrick himself, his income is set down at £506, stg. Whence arises this difference?

The mistake can only be accounted for by an error of the Clerk in copying the figures.

52. In the Blue Book, for 1830, Mr. Dunn, the Receiver-General, is reported to the Home Government as being in the receipt of £200 and no more. His own return sent to the Assembly through your office for the same year, is upwards of £1000; why this difference?

This accidental omission . . .

At the very least Mackenzie had turned up evidence of inefficiency in the public accounting system, and shown the need for a better one. More such questions about untidiness in the public accounts were directed to the Honourable George Markland, the Inspector-General, and queries about pensions and salaries of somewhat questionable relevance to the service of the people of Upper Canada:

509. Do you know why the Province is paying £200 sterling a year to England as a pension to Sir D. W. Smith, a Northumbrian baronet?

I take it for granted it is by an order from His Majesty's Government.

And some general questions, heavily loaded with criticism, which reduced Markland to exasperation.

513. Ought not the whole public revenue to be paid into the treasury of the Colony, and the proceeds applied only according to law?

I give no answer.

514. What check has the House of Assembly on the other branches of the Government, as a means of preventing executive usurpation of popular rights?

The constitution is quite as well understood by every person present as by myself.

[The Witness withdrew.]

Mackenzie's quizzing of other witnesses ran the whole gamut from the most minute matter of their income sources to their general opinions of established churches and popular election of government officials. He wanted to know what each of them thought of the principle of responsible government.

If this principle were introduced into Canada it would have meant in 1835 an executive council chosen from the Reform majority in the Assembly. "Would not the British Constitutional system," he asked, "by which the head of the government is obliged to choose his Councillors and principal officers from men possessing the confidence of the popular branch of the Legislature, be more suitable to the wants and wishes of the country, if adopted in Upper Canada, than the present irresponsible mode of government?"

The particular interest in that question stems from the fact that Canadian historians have sometimes assumed Mackenzie had no understanding of the precise meaning of responsible government. But it would surely be difficult to find a better definition of it than the words of Mackenzie just quoted. Certainly he was not, in Cromwell's phrase, "glued or wedded" to the idea with the single-minded chastity of a Robert Baldwin. He often advocated, at the very same time, alternative and even contradictory means of constitutional reform.

The fact is he understood the principle well enough but did not believe it would necessarily assure either popular control of government, or cheap efficient government, in Upper Canada. He lived to see his early suspicions, to his way of thinking, entirely vindicated in the railway deals and the political double shuffles of the eighteen-fifties. And meanwhile he was, like the lawyer, willing to win his case by the simultaneous advocacy of several contradictory pleas, "any one of which will do"; he was prepared to press for an American senate, an elected governor, and responsible government, all at once. Any radical change would do so long as control could be wrested from the wrong people. In any case, it cannot be said too often, Mackenzie was more concerned to bring in a verdict of guilty against the city of things as they were than to provide blueprints for the promised land of things as they should be. What better way to embarrass a Colonial Tory than to point out the contrast between the constitutional practice of the colony and that of the mother country? The latter, in the Tory's scheme of things, is possibly the most he ever wishes for in the way of a political Utopia. Why then, Mackenzie asked the Compact, do we not have the British system here?

There is still one witness for the defence whom we have not mentioned, and he the most important of them. Towards the end of the hearings, on April Fool's Day, A.D. MDCCCXXXV, as if somebody were playing Til Eulenspiegel's Merry Pranks on the Lord of Hosts Himself, there was summoned before the little inquisition in the committee room the most formidable and unbending of all the enemy, the senior Executive and Legislative Councillor, President of King's College, Chairman of the Board of Education, Rector of Toronto, Archdeacon of York, and still domine of the whole tribe, the Honourable and Venerable John Strachan, D.D.

"No man," it was said of Daniel Webster, "is as great as *he* looks." So we might say of Strachan, but that the huge receding brow and the deeply chiselled physiognomy and the cutting edge of the jaw suggest a strength of intelligence and will, a sort of spiritual drill sergeantry, which are palpably there to the very marrow of the man. It is as if one of those medieval peasant-born prince-bishops who built cathedrals and colleges and unmade kings had been dropped into the Upper Canadian wilderness. Nor do Strachan's severe manner and the rough accent of his stonemason father detract one whit from the impression. As for his lifelong habit of whistling huskily to himself, on almost any occasion in any company, it only underlines the palpable, living presence of the man, and confirms the effect of massive self-possession. Of his appearance before the Grievances Committee Thomas Roberton has written that he sat "as a watchful lion might allow his speculative gaze to fall idly on a quartet of mysterious jackals".

Strachan had long since spent any fury he deemed worth spending on the little man who had been blaspheming him in the columns of the *Colonial Advocate* these ten years, and denouncing him in the House of Assembly. He had replied in kind on occasions. Now he regarded his self-constituted judge with a contempt bordering on indifference. He was content to turn Mackenzie's questions with a dour weariness or a mild irony. Mackenzie for his part was not so concerned to ask about the minute details of finance and administration he had demanded from the others. He was digging for richer matter now. He wanted to force on to the record Strachan's unequivocally reactionary opinions of the big political issues of the day. It was as if by his very repetition of those opinions Strachan damned himself the deeper, and this was one of the few satisfactions left open to Mackenzie, who could neither punish nor reform his adversary.

The discrepancy between the official fact-gathering purpose of the committee, and the note of accusation and judgment which now crept into almost every question was not lost upon Strachan. By treating the questions as if they were indeed designed to elicit simple fact rather than a defence of principles he frustrated Mackenzie most effectively. "I refer you to the Constitutional Act," he would reply, or "I cannot answer that question, because I do not understand its object." But soon the temptation to rise to Mackenzie's bait was too much for Strachan.

> 556. The vote by ballot in elections is prayed for in many petitions to the Assembly and to His Majesty; what is your opinion of this mode of voting?
> Nobody would ask for the vote by ballot but from gross ignorance; it is the most corrupt way of using the franchise.
> 557. The exclusive religious privileges granted to certain denominations are much complained of; would it not tend to strengthen good government if they were altogether abolished?
> There should be in every Christian country an established religion, otherwise it is not a Christian but an Infidel country.

Mackenzie dropped all pretense of inquiry and began using his questions as cudgels. But Strachan got the better of the exchange with a direct hit on Mackenzie in his reply:

563. Has not the present irresponsible system of government in Upper Canada a tendency to discourage the emigration of the more wealthy and enterprising class of emigrants into the Province?

Certainly not; the Executive Government does everything to encourage emigration, but the slanderous newspapers make people at a distance believe that there are difficulties in the Province, and produce a contrary effect.

James Strachan, upon his first amazed glimpse of his brother's pro-episcopal palace on the waterfront, had exclaimed with a gasp, "I hope it's a' come by honestly, Jock!" Mackenzie now concocted a question about the Archdeacon's salaries which contained the same implication. Strachan protested the wording of Mackenzie's long question, which appeared to attempt a deception of "the careless and the ignorant". "I am unwilling to believe," he added sarcastically, "that such could be the object of this committee." And with the condescension of a bow, he withdrew.

Mackenzie summoned witnesses for the prosecution as well as witnesses for the defence. His most telling evidence, indeed, came from those who were there to air their grievances about the condition of Upper Canada. It need scarcely now be said that the witnesses themselves were very much cast in the role of accusers or accused. The most conspicuous absentees were the moderates—a Robert Baldwin, a Bidwell or a Ketchum. Mackenzie was concerned with those who were for him or against him.

One of his best witnesses was Colonel Van Egmond. He was a splendid old Dutch soldier, a descendant of the Netherlands' hero, Count Egmont, whose execution by the Council of Blood served as overture to the great eighty-years' war that broke the yoke of Spain. He himself was a son of the French Revolution. He had served with distinction in the Grand Army of Napoleon, and later with the Allies' Army against Napoleon at Waterloo. He came eventually to Western Ontario to settle in the Huron Tract, where the Canada Company was the Family Compact's chosen instrument for the sale and settlement and local government of the land. Van Egmond was not afraid to make a public protest against an injustice to himself and his neighbours, even though the protest might eventually cost him his life. We shall meet him again as the commander of Mackenzie's forces in the rebellion of 1837.

For the present he was concerned with the unjust rule of "Tiger" Dunlop and the Canada Company agents in the Huron Tract. If you listen closely you can almost catch the voices in the committee room across the century that divides us from them: the braid Scots of the questions uttered in that methodical monotone which barely checked a smoulder of concern; the slow unbeautiful Dutch lilt of the responses, a like note of concern audible beneath the surface of its matter-of-fact, military way of putting things.

201. What price did the Canada Company pay for the Huron tract?

I believe it would be equal to about one shilling sterling per acre.

202. What are they selling the lands for?

From 12s 6d. to 13s 9d. per acre.

204. How long have you been settled in the Huron Tract?

Six years this Christmas. I am the oldest settler in that tract.

205. Have the Company taken proper means to encourage and promote the settlement of the tract?

For the first year, in Goderich alone; since then they have taken no pains to assist the settlers.

206. Are the Agents to the Company kind to the settlers?

No, they are, with the exception of Mr. Wilson, very arbitrary; they are very tyrannical.

209. Have any settlers been ejected from their farms?

Yes, they are scared out of the tract and ejected without any form of law or justice. Many persons have been driven out of the Territory; there is no other law there except what the Company's servants make. We must be very polite to the Agents.

210. Are the Company empowered to impose on settlers such terms as they please?

Yes, they are.

212. Do the Company take large sums out of the country?

Their profits in 1833, were £28,000, sterling, after paying all expenses—the Stockholders chiefly reside in England.

214. Are there any Schools?

One in Goderich. The Company do not now support any other school that I know of.

220. How do the Company pay for the work they get done?

For the first five years they paid two-thirds of the labor in land, at 7s 6d. (which cost them not much more than one shilling an acre) and one-third in money.

[The Witness withdrew]

Besides the evidence gathered orally from witnesses, Mackenzie's committee collected a large quantity of information on public expenditure from various departments of the government, all of which was tabled and placed in the Report. He justly complained that access to several important pieces of information, such as the accounts before 1833, was denied to him. In other words, it was denied to the Assembly in whose behalf he was acting. But the very fact that an Assembly committee could summon the witnesses and the documents it did is ample proof that in some measure Upper Canada was a free society, as well as ample warning that the people of Upper Canada would use that freedom one day to gain full control of their government.

In the prologue to the Report, Mackenzie deplored once again the fact that the popular House had so little control over that government. The only effective check a colonial Assembly has ever had upon the executive branch has been the right to refuse to vote supplies until grievances are remedied. But in Upper Canada this check had been effectively diminished by the passage, in the Tory Assembly of 1831, of a bill which provided for the chief officials' salaries to be paid without reference to the Assembly. This "Everlasting Salary Bill", as he caustically called it, Mackenzie attacked once again.

The main theme of Mackenzie's preface, however, and of the Report itself, was a slightly different one. It is well-expressed in the words of the famous old motion of the English House of Commons in which they condemned Lord North and George III during the war of the American Revolution: "The power of the Crown has increased, is increasing and ought to be diminished." As we saw from the questioning of Markland, Mackenzie harped constantly on the note of the Crown's influence in politics through placeman: those members of the Legislature who held government jobs and whose independence was thereby compromised. Worse still, said Mackenzie, the postmasters and the local magistrates, the customs officers and the land agents, the agents of the Bank of Upper Canada, and the Roman and Anglican priests, even when they were not legislators, doubled as Tory canvassers and government spies. They formed another potent source of government control in every community in the province.

He saw the influence of the Crown increasing, too, through the semi-public corporations which built and operated the harbours and canals. Not only did he feel that they were a source of government political influence but they wasted and mismanaged the funds which they were granted from the public purse. The issue was an even bigger one in those days than it would be now because the pioneer community was so completely dependent on travel by water. There were still no railways or bog-free roads. Scarcely a town or hamlet was built far from the reach of navigation. The wilderness was first made livable by the fleet of small steamers and sailboats that penetrated the Upper Canadian rivers and lakes; the whistle of the supply boat was the signal for a whole community to break off from its business and assemble to receive the news and the manufacture of the world beyond the forest. Canal building was quite naturally a major industry. The Rideau tied Ottawa and its river to Lake Ontario; the Welland Canal Company was beginning its tremendous task of climbing the mountain from Ontario to Erie, lifting the ships through the peaceful countryside of the peninsula and safely past the terrors of Niagara.

But the building of the Welland Canal was a long and tiresome job. It was as costly as it was slow. By 1835 the badly kept accounts of the Welland Canal Company had become a chronic complaint with William Lyon Mackenzie. However many other martyred causes he discovered, however many good bills he saw decapitated by the upper house, the Welland Canal Company remained his King Charles' head. He scarcely made a speech without uttering his abhorrence of the Company's bungling of a mighty business.

Before the Grievances Committee's work was completed, Mackenzie decided to devote his spare time to a thorough investigation of the Welland Canal. Since the Canal Company was a semi-public corporation the legislature had the right to nominate directors. The Assembly of 1835 picked Mackenzie, among others. Before the House was prorogued for the summer, it ordered the publication of two thousand copies of the Grievances Committee's report. But Mackenzie was no longer in Toronto to supervise the job. The new canal director had embarked post-haste for the Niagara peninsula to investigate the company's work. He had a commission from the House to report his findings to them during their next session. He discovered an accounting system which was, to put it charitably, vague, and evidence of company land being given to members of the Compact and to the Anglican Church in return for sums of money or other pieces of land entirely disproportionate to their value.

Mackenzie was so excited by his discoveries that he founded a summer newspaper on the spot—right in the Niagara peninsula—to put his findings into print immediately, in spite of an obligation to keep his information to himself until it had been reported back to the Assembly and discussed there.

The reaction of Mr. Merritt, the Tory president of the Canal Company, to his director's unsolicited performance in the field of popular journalism was chiefly expressed in the form of the conventional but indecent epithet. But this was by no means the biggest of the home-made time bombs that Mackenzie exploded. The worst blow was still to come.

Now Mackenzie was as anxious as Merritt to get the canal built. He wanted not only to investigate its operations but to expedite them. One of his tasks, therefore, was to go down to Quebec and there attempt to win the support of the Assembly of Lower Canada for the completion of a general canal system of which the Welland would form part. When he arrived, Mackenzie spoke eloquently in behalf of his company and his mission. Then a French Canadian member interrupted him. Would Mr. Mackenzie, he asked, if he were a member of the Assembly of Lower Canada, want to invest the taxpayers' money in Welland Canal stock? It was an embarrassing question. It called for a brazen "Yes", or, to save honesty, some form of double talk, a hem and a haw to turn the question and bury it. But Mackenzie's answer was swift and simple and entirely uncalled for. "No," he replied, a Lower Canadian should not buy Welland Canal stock, "not with the government of Upper Canada as it is." That finished what slight chance of success the mission from Upper Canada had. The Welland Canal Company would have to manage things on its own without help from down-river.

Possibly the reply is worth a canal or two, however, in a country which is inordinately longer on construction work and self-congratulation than on virtue of the kind that costs money or retards progress. In the history of Canadian political rhetoric, among a host of large spotted hypocrisies and little speckled cautions, the utterance and its author betray themselves with a certain dangerous instinct for the direct home truth. Certainly all Mackenzie's virtues shout through that reply. We need not spoil the incident, provided we move a vote of well-reserved sympathy to the unfortunate Mr. Merritt, by inquiring whether all our hero's faults do not lurk there also.

Before Mackenzie had finished sowing his crop of trouble for the Welland Canal Company, the fruits of his spring labours on the Grievances Committee were ripening for the harvest. By the fall of 1835 one of the 2000 printed copies of the Grievances Report had found its way across the Atlantic, and was in the hands of King William IV and his Secretary of State for the Colonies. Now the latter person, Lord Glenelg, with all due respect to his nobility, his intelligence, and his devotion to duty, may be put down as a ditherer. Worse still he was a ditherer in a difficult spot, difficult enough for the most decisive of men. He was a member of a ministry clinging to power by the barest of margins in the House of Commons, liable to be toppled either by trouble or by measures bold enough to remedy the trouble. Lord Glenelg did indeed summon his resolution for one drastic act. On the strength of Mackenzie's charges, he abruptly dismissed Governor Colborne. And then relapsed into a state of agitated paralysis.

He asked that the next session of the Assembly be delayed until he could reply to certain of Mackenzie's charges. But the reply when it came was a little more than a timid defence of the policy practised by the Colonial Office and governors in the past. It took the form of an Instruction to the new governor, who was not according to this instrument to be allowed to make concessions that would satisfy the Reformers. Nor was he to act firmly in opposing them.

Even so, Lord Glenelg's uncertain and unimaginative policy, had it been effected, might just have managed to enter the history books as another uncanny instance of Imperial muddling through. It might have, but for one unfortunate circumstance. That circumstance was the person who was sent to replace Colborne in Upper Canada.

There were three chief deficiencies in Sir Francis Bond Head as a governor-elect. In the first place, by his own cheerful admission, he knew nothing about colonial affairs nor had any experience in politics. In the second place, he entirely disregarded Glenelg's cautions instructions upon discovering in himself a latent genius for demagoguery which rivalled that of William Lyon Mackenzie. And in the most alarming third place, it is just possible that because of a certain confusion of persons on the part of His Majesty's Colonial Office, the invitation to assume the viceregal power in Upper Canada was delivered to the wrong man.

Under the governorship of Sir Francis Head, the moderates in Upper Canada were driven to despair, and their two soundest heads, Baldwin and Bidwell, to retire from politics. Mackenzie was in a sense driven from politics too, but in the other direction. It was the activity of Governor Head which finally and completely convinced him that the arts of political persuasion must be replaced by those of revolution. One suspects that Lord Glenelg's policy was a matter of too little and too late. One does not suspect, one knows, that Sir Francis Head was altogether too much far too suddenly.

CHAPTER ELEVEN

AT 2 A.M. one stormy November morning in 1835, on the coast of Kent, the patron deities of Imperial destiny effected a piece of business from which the Second British Empire never really recovered. A King's messenger arrived at the inn in which Sir Francis Bond Head was spending the night, and would not be turned away until its guest was awakened and informed of a summons to Whitehall at 8:30 the same morning for the purpose of receiving the governorship of Upper Canada. As Sir Francis later observed, no one during the entire course of his eventful tenure of that office, at any of its several stages of surprise and excitement, was ever more utterly astonished than the man himself upon first being informed of his appointment. That he may appreciate something of Sir Francis' amazement the reader is invited, provided he has had no previously relevant experience in business or war and is entirely innocent of politics, to imagine himself urgently invited to assume the immediate and total responsibility for ruling a country he has never seen, by a person he has scarcely heard of.

There are at least three possible explanations of the mystery. The first suggests that Sir Francis had gained a certain public notoriety in the course of a quixotically adventurous career and that his name was therefore known to Lord Glenelg, the Colonial Secretary. Furthermore he had a distant cousin of pronounced talent and intelligence who was apparently not known to Lord Glenelg. The vexing question of finding a gentleman to exile himself to Upper Canada arose in cabinet meeting. Several refusals had already been received. Someone suggested "young Head", the brilliant thirty-year-old Oxford don, who as Sir Edmund Head, was eventually Governor-General of Canada in the 1850's when the job had ceased to matter much. There was a general mutter of assent to the name of Head, and on the morrow Lord Glenelg urgently sent for Sir Francis.

So runs the only definite attempt to explain the mystery, offered a few years after the event by a contemporary Canadian politician.

Another story is that Sir Francis' elder brother, Sir George Head, a senior military officer, who had written a book about his five years' experience in North America, was the intended appointee. But then according to a third explanation there is some reason to believe that Sir Francis himself was, in fact, the considered, even if not the well-advised, choice of the Whig ministers. He was known personally to at least one of them; his wife's nephew, the Earl of Errol, had married into the royal family; and he had once stimulated the admiration of the King himself by a demonstration of his skill with the lasso.

As to why Sir Francis received the invitation to govern Upper Canada, we are left then, where we began, with a mystery. For certainties we must fall back on the two well-established points, that it was he who was appointed, with shattering results, and that the appointment was a strange one, as Sir Francis himself was the first to recognize.

Francis Bond Head was country gentry by birth, a military engineer by profession, and by avocation an adventurer. As a young lieutenant he built forts in Spain for the Peninsular Campaign, and surveyed some ground at Waterloo. When peacetime duties took him to the Mediterranean, he travelled widely and passionately, *en jeune romantique*. He discovered himself as a Byronesque Childe Francis in the Levant, and, on the plains of Marathon where another Napoleon had been beaten by an unmilitary but gallant people, he records how he was suffused with the emotions of patriotism and loyalty to his King. After leaving the army as a half-pay major he was engaged to manage the mining of silver by a British company speculating in South America. In the course of duty he became the first Englishman to gallop clear across the pampas of Argentina to the Andes and back in the space of a week. But the total loss of the investment and a quarrel with his employers finished the venture. He settled down in his native Kent where he paid his debt to society by becoming Assistant Poor Law Commissioner. The military authorities declined to act upon his suggestion, born of an admiration for gauchos, that the lasso be introduced into the British army, in spite of a demonstration so authentic as to move King William to grant him a knighthood. But then the British army's self-esteem, in the period between Waterloo and Balaclava, was such that the donor of a fully equipped machine gun company would have been most uncivilly treated had he been there to offer his services. The use of Sir Francis' South American experience was therefore confined to a series of personal adventure books from which he earned considerable notoriety and the title of "Galloping Head".

It may be apparent from this account why Sir Francis quickly decided it prudent to refuse the offer of a position for which he was almost uniquely unqualified. And why his penchant for adventure and his sense of loyalty caused him to change his mind. Within a matter of hours, he was riding towards the pleasure resort of Brighton to kiss the King's hand and receive the viceregal office.

He sailed almost immediately, but not without complaining of a reduction in salary and the lack of an aide-de-camp. He demanded a baronetcy so that his social position might compensate for a far humbler military rank than that of his predecessor. He got it only after much waiting, much later on. He remarked with some indignation, that

> The government were so intoxicated with the insane theory of conciliating democracy that they actually believed the people of Upper Canada would throw up their hats and be delighted at the vulgarity of seeing the representative of their sovereign arrive among them as actor of all work, without dignity or demeanour.

He prepared himself for office by reading, *en route*, his official instructions from Glenelg, and Mackenzie's Grievances Report. "With Mr. Mackenzie's heavy book of lamentations in my portmanteau, and with my remedial instructions in my writing case, I considered myself as a political physician who, whether regularly educated or not, was about to effect a surprising cure; for as I never doubted for a moment either the existence of the 533 pages of grievances, nor that I would mercilessly destroy them root and branch, I felt perfectly confident that I should soon be able proudly to report that the grievances of Upper Canada were defunct—in short that I had veni-ed, vidi-ed, and vici-ed them." With the ghost of mighty Julius to lead him on, Sir Francis prepared to transform the Upper Canadians into loyal and contented subjects.

Even a man so used to surprises as Sir Francis was scarcely prepared for his astonishing reception. As he rode into Toronto, the Radical portion of the population was out to greet him with cheers and placards of welcome. He suddenly found himself the centre of a raggedy triumphal procession of printers' apprentices and men wearing tanners' aprons. King Street was dotted with gaping shop assistants and clumps of tobacco-chewing farmers, and the banners read "Sir Francis Bond Head, A Tried Reformer".

Mackenzie hoped that the appointee of a Whig government would take the Reformers' part against the Compact. His hopes were reinforced by a letter praising Head from his friend, Joseph Hume, who, in fact, knew as little about Head as Glenelg did. By the time the Reformers were ready to receive him they had convinced themselves and their enemies that the man who was innocent of so much as having cast a vote in his life was an experienced Radical politician. Sir Francis conveyed the incongruity of the affair to his diary in his usual picturesque style: "I was no more connected with human politics than the horses which were drawing me."

The Reformers' spirits were further heightened by the departure of Sir John Colborne, who left amid an orage of popular displeasure after committing the most forceful and politically questionable act of his Canadian career. Archdeacon Strachan and Chief Justice Robinson were as apprehensive about the prospects of a "Reform" governor as their opponents were hopeful. They persuaded Colborne that this might be their last opportunity to strike a blow for Church and King in Upper Canada. Literally on the eve of his departure Colborne agreed to grant out of the public lands an endowment of 77,000 acres for forty-four new rectories of the Church of England in Canada. Such action was in accord with the British Parliament's Act of 1791 for the support of a Protestant clergy but was in direct defiance of Upper Canadian Assemblies, past and present, Tory and Reform alike, and it nullified a recent intimation from the Colonial Office that there would be no new imperial action on the subject without a consultation of colonial opinion.

The Methodist newspapers cried out in pain. Moderates sorrowed that a good man was taking leave not only of his position but of his senses. Even the Tories must have shuddered for the wrath to come, with the exception of Strachan himself who received the gift as nothing more than a long overdue act of justice, and the first step to better things, and was ready to spit in the jaws of hell if it were otherwise.

Meanwhile Sir Francis was sufficiently flattered to attempt the part expected of him. After unwisely and without permission from home delivering the full text of his Instruction to the Assembly, and appearing there in person, he granted interviews with certain leading Reformers, Mackenzie among them.

We are by now accustomed to have apprehensions about Mackenzie and his interviews with distinguished persons. We have the uneasy feeling that he will raise his voice in an ungentlemanly manner, albeit with the most cordial intent of sharing his passions with his interlocutor; that he will, in fact, before the thing is over, shout. But when we learn that Sir Francis Head had already received the discreet and judicious Mr. Bidwell, and had discovered him, within the space of thirty minutes, to be both tiresome and utterly disloyal, and when we reflect that Sir Francis was an eccentric with a privately inflated opinion of himself quite as much as Mackenzie was an eccentric wholly seized with a public passion, we no longer apprehend, we are certain of, the worst. That the ensuing interview did not effect a meeting of hearts and minds may be gathered from Sir Francis' description of it.

> Mr. Mackenzie's mind seemed to nauseate its subjects even more than Mr. Bidwell's. Afraid to look me in the face, he sat, with his feet not reaching the ground and with his countenance averted from me, at an angle of seventy degrees; while, with the eccentricity, the volubility, and indeed the appearance of a madman, the tiny creature raved.

If Head in his miniature cartoon of the interview with Mackenzie has supplied us with no mean treasure for the national portrait gallery, we are also fortunate in having a companion piece to it. Robina Lizars, in her *Humours of '37*, recalls an eye witness' description of Head's first official appearance, when he assumed the throne in the Legislative Council to open the 1836 session of Parliament.

> Although too small to fill the chair, his shoulders and the poise of his head did much to counterbalance the lack of nether proportions. His feet, though unable to touch the floor, were not allowed to dangle but were thrust out stiffly in front and kept there throughout the opening. An American visitor pointed to the feet and whispered to a friend "That is a man of determination." He owed much to a personal magnetism; old and young alike loved him—when they did not hate him.

Mackenzie was now no longer the only person in Upper Canada capable of rousing intense political passion; nor the only one whose feet did not reach the ground.

It took Governor Head very little time to amend his first view of the political situation in Upper Canada and divide his subjects into two categories, this time of his own making. There were the loyal, and socially pleasant; of these he quickly found Chief Justice Robinson the most distinguished example. And there were the disloyal, and tiresome. To this latter company Head had already consigned almost every species of Reformer from Bidwell to Mackenzie. He was next to cross swords with the most moderate and sober man in the province, Robert Baldwin. The consequences of that quarrel, with due help from Mackenzie, led straight towards the final crisis of 1837.

Young Baldwin withdrew from political life in the early 1830's almost as soon as he entered upon it. He despaired of any good coming from the recklessness and extremes of the two existing political factions and his withdrawal suited well his own publicity-shy and retiring nature.

Governor Head wished to make himself politically independent of any group in the colony, and so sought out three moderates to join the three Tories already on the Executive Council. Baldwin was the most obvious choice, but was only with great difficulty persuaded to accept office.

Once he became an Executive Councillor, however, he quickly set to work to convert his three Tory colleagues to his own belief that the Executive Council should be consulted on all matters of administration and policy. If this principle was once accepted responsible government would be possible. It would be but one further step to the Council's full responsibility to the Assembly for all acts of government. The six Councillors presented Head with a paper embodying Baldwin's views and offered to resign if he could not agree with them. The resignations were immediately accepted.

Throughout his tenure of office Head clearly fixed his mind upon the simple basic notion that it was the business of the governor to govern; that he and no one else was solely responsible for everything that was done. The Council, like the two Houses, might recommend but it was for him to decide whether recommendations should be accepted or refused. He demonstrated brilliantly in his reply, doubtless with Robinson's help over the details, that this had always been the practice in Upper Canada and expressed the clear intent of the Constitutional Act of 1791.

Baldwin himself made no further effort to defend his principles publicly. He preferred the course of quiet negotiation, and he set out for England to lay his case for responsible government before the Colonial Secretary. At the request of Head, who described him as a revolutionary agent, Glenelg refused to see him during his stay in London.

Meanwhile there were others who did not take the Governor's assertions with such restraint. A deputation of leading Toronto Reformers, including the Mayor, presented Sir Francis with the request for responsible government adopted at a public meeting. He treated them in the condescending manner apparently reserved for members of "the industrious classes" who have failed to act with due regard to their humble station in life. He promised them an answer suited to their understandings, "in plainer and more homely language" than he used with the Assembly. The Reformers' bitterly sarcastic reply to this was taken back to Government House by Jesse Ketchum, and almost before Head could lay eyes on it, it was in print and much talked of in the city.

The Assembly itself was in an uproar. The Reformers began a series of vicious attacks on the government and the new Council Head found to replace Baldwin's converts.

The Tories in the House, for their part, stood by Governor Head. "The moment we establish the doctrine [of responsible government] in practice we are free from the Mother Country," said one of them. Of all thoughts perish that one. Here they were on to home ground and their favourite issue. Solicitor-General Hagerman turned a menacing red and threatened the Reformers with "the vengeance of 150,000 men loyal and true". The imperial pennons were out and fluttering, ready for the next election campaign; or a bigger fight if necessary, for such remarks were not merely the common coin of political rhetoric. The Hagermans meant what they said, so far as their words were more than expletive and meant anything at all.

But no one was better at ringing the changes on the old familiar hymns of imperial loyalty than Sir Francis Head, if only because of the utter abandon with which he performed and the fact that he had hummed them to himself on all his travels. The issues had reduced themselves to that level of simplicity which suited him perfectly. "The people of Upper Canada detest Democracy; they revere the Constitutional Charter and are staunch in allegiance to their King." He spoke of unnamed persons who, he warned, were inciting invasion by foreigners and foreign principles, and concluded: "In the name of every regiment of militia in Upper Canada, I publicly promulgate—Let them come if they dare!"

In April of 1836 the Assembly wielded the biggest weapon at its disposal. For once stirred to drastic action by Mackenzie's exhortations, and by a cordial dislike of the Governor, the Reformers put the axe to the supply bill, the first time this had actually ever happened in Upper Canada. All the lesser government salaries and pensions not covered by the civil list were thus cut off at one blow. The Reformers accompanied their refusal with an Address to be presented to His Majesty the King and another to the English House of Commons, formally denouncing Sir Francis' arbitrary acts and manner. It was signed by Mr. Speaker Bidwell. But for once in Bidwell's life it could have been a product of Mackenzie's pen. Sir Francis had driven the two wings of the party to speak the same language. But he saw to it that it did them no good. He countered with a refusal to sign the bills sent up to him in that session which embodied an ambitious programme for the building of roads and schools and other public works. A minor economic crisis followed immediately; widespread unemployment, a brief trade slump, and the refusal of bankers to take merchants' credit notes. Many workers left the country to look for jobs in the United States.

For all this Head laid the blame squarely on the Reformers, because they had taken the initiative in blocking the operations of government. To a group of Torontonians he said:

Gentlemen:—No one can be more sensible than I am that the stoppage of the supplies has caused a general stagnation of business which will probably end in the ruin of many inhabitants of this city; and in proportion as the metropolis of the province is impoverished, the farmers' market must be lowered.

My plans and projects are all contained and published in the instructions which I received from the king. They desire me to correct, without impartiality, the grievances of this country; and it is because the agitators see I am determined to do so, that they are endeavouring to obstruct me by every artifice in their power. They declare me to be their enemy, and the truth is, I really am.

The mercantile community rallied to Head's side against the Reformers. So did thousands of recent immigrants, most of whom were now not Americans but British. They were ready to believe the Governor when he told them that the "republicans" in the Assembly, by their irresponsible action, were to blame for bad times. Worse than that, it seemed to be but the first step towards the dissolution of colonial society and the establishment of an American democracy.

Head felt he was now ready to administer the *coup de grace*. In a dispatch home he pictured himself locked with the Reformers in a death struggle about whose outcome he had no fears. "Do you know why a little weasel always kills a rat?" he asked (his choice of language in writing to his superiors managed to combine the didactic with the melodramatic). "I do not think you do, and therefore I will explain it to you. The rat is the strongest animal of the two, and his teeth are the longest, but he bites his enemy anywhere, whereas the weasel waits for an opportunity to fix his teeth in the rat's jugular vein, and when he has done so he never changes his plan or lets go until the rat is dead. Now I have been following the weasel's plan, for when I came out here, Bidwell and the republican party were much too strong for me, and were haughty and arrogant in their success. They did many things to offend me but I took no notice till the party got on the rotten argument about the Executive

Council and then I pounced upon them and have never for a moment deserted the point."

Sir Francis was capable of speaking with a lusty satisfaction of his own part in the raw struggle for power. Yet at the same time he possessed a marvellously innocent confidence that his own actions, the governor's position, and the Empire's survival, were each as sacred as the Persons of the Holy Trinity, and as con-substantial. "In South America truth and justice carried me through difficulties even greater than those I have now to contend with, and I have the firmest reliance that they will again be triumphant."

Sir Francis for all his stiff little mannequin's haughty manner fairly crackled with that political electricity called righteous indignation. His plea for the humble clerk, the immigrant, the labourer, done out of a job by a factious Assembly, his call for loyal subjects to defend their Governor from those who would rob him of his power to govern, these, when Sir Francis uttered them, aroused the emotion of conviction. "The Governor is such a masterly hand at the pen," wrote a correspondent of Egerton Ryerson, "and gave the Assembly such a castigation in his prorogation speech as ever an Assembly got before on this side of the Atlantic, or on the other side since the days of Cromwell." When the Reformers tried to pull Sir Francis into the pen of responsible government, "as Peter Perry would say, 'they got the wrong pig by the ear.'"

Head's appeal to the people in the spring of 1836 was the most successful pre-election campaign ever conducted in Upper Canada. The irony of the thing was that it was fought by a man who did not believe in democracy, and who took every opportunity of saying so. "To put the multitude at the top and the few at the bottom," he wrote, "is a radical reversion of the pyramid of society which can only end by its downfall."

He made no attempt to identify himself with the common man, or indulge in one of those log cabin campaigns which were about to become a prominent feature of the American political scene. He simply appeared before the

Upper Canadians in that which of all the parts he had tried in life was his favourite: Lieutenant-Governor Sir Francis Bond Head, deputy incarnation of the Crown and of the English ruling classes. The first impact at least was definitely effective: "The people appeared quite as anxious that I should ride good horses as I was myself," he wrote in his memoirs. "They liked to see a well appointed carriage, and it is a vulgar error to believe that if I had ridden about in a shooting jacket, distributing stunted nods and talking through my nose, I should have prevented the rebellion."

Sir Francis made it plain that other interests besides those of the Crown, aristocracy, and the British connection depended upon a decision in his favour.

> Can you do as much for yourselves as I can do for you? It is my opinion that you cannot! It is my opinion that if you choose to dispute with me, and live on bad terms with the mother country, you will, to use a homely phrase, "only quarrel with your bread and butter." If you like to try the experiment by electing members who will stop the supplies, do so, for I can have no objection whatever: on the other hand, if you choose fearlessly to embark your interests with my character, depend upon it I will take paternal care of them both.

With his case and his person placed squarely before the public eye, Sir Francis dissolved Parliament at the end of May, and proclamations went out for a general election. The Reformers were a little shaken by the genie they had raised from what had looked like an innocuous bottle. The "tried Reformer" they had welcomed to Upper Canada only a few weeks before had turned out to be an even greater contrast to Sir John Colborne than they had bargained for, but on the farther side of the political spectrum.

Mackenzie still placed his confidence in the intelligence of his farmer constituents. He clung to the belief in the incorruptibility of the people as to an article of faith. He made no effort during the campaign to counter Head's highly charged popular appeal which in any event he could scarcely have surpassed.

The elections themselves saw a greater amount of government influence than usual:

> All along we expected to straighten things out at the polls [said one Reformer, telling of what led to the rebellion] until Sir Francis and his crowd swamped us out at the election in the summer of 1836. Why, his men distributed tickets giving titles to farms on the shore road and the bush that no one ever knew were farms. With these tickets in their hands the hired men would go to the polls and swear that they got four dollars a year out of farms they did not own nor no one else ever did own. But these ticket holders swore enough votes through to beat us Reformers who had property in the country, and after that we saw that there was nothing before us but a fight.

Mackenzie later told the same kind of tale about the good-hearted blacksmith, Samuel Lount, Reform member for Simcoe, who was soon to be hanged for leading his constituents in the 1837 rebellion:

> Samuel Lount called at my house accompanied by Thrift Meldrum, merchant and innkeeper at Barrie, and stated that Meldrum had been requested to open his tavern for the Tories at the time of the late election, and that he did so; the government agent from Toronto called Meldrum to one side at Crew's tavern, where the stage stopped, and told him that Sir Francis wanted him to assist in turning Lount out. Meldrum agreed to do his best, opened his house, and says that they paid him faithfully for his liquor.

There were more threats of violence than in normal elections and the Orange mobs were at their worst:

> If you had been in London at the last election, you would have seen a set of government tools called Orange men running up and down the streets crying five pounds for a liberal; and if a man said contrary to their opinion he was knocked down. Many were knocked down in this way and others were threatened; and all this in the presence of magistrates, Church of England ministers

and judges, who made use of no means to prevent such outrages.

One of the most blatant pieces of Tory propaganda was re-printed in the St. Thomas *Liberal.* Though it applies to a meeting of Reformers which took place earlier than this particular campaign, it is thoroughly typical of the spirit of '36.

NOTICE

The Ripstavers, Gallbursters, etc. with their friends are requested to meet at St. Thomas on the 17th of January at 12 o'clock, as there will be work for them on that day. The Doctors are requested to be in readiness to heal the sick and to care for the broken-headed. Let no rotten eggs be wanting.

The object of the nasty republicans in their intended meeting is to wheadle weak and simple souls so far into the paths of rebellion, that they cannot afterwards retreat even if they want to do so. Therefore, most noble Ripstavers, check the evil in the beginning, that is, hoe them out—sugar them off—in short sew them up. The dastards may think to screen themselves from the public fury by holding their meetings at a private house; but public or private, put yourselves in the midst of them. You have a right to be there. It is a public meeting.

One other decisive factor in the government's favour was the Church vote. The support of the Anglicans could always be counted upon. Such a Canadian Barchester Towers as Kingston, for instance, returned Christopher Hagerman unopposed. Bishop Macdonell's vigorous political campaigning enabled him to deliver a goodly portion of the Roman Catholic vote. The most effective intervention from a Church leader in the campaign came however from across the Atlantic. Egerton Ryerson's letters to the *Christian Guardian* included praise for Sir Francis Head, and attacks upon Peter Perry and upon Mackenzie's Grievances Report. These were widely circulated during the election, and for the first time since the Mackenzie-Ryerson quarrel Methodist votes apparently swung strongly against the Reformers.

Beneath all the factors that told against the Reformers, whether Orangeman's big stick, Methodist's fear of a God-less republic, or Tory ingenuity in manipulating the electoral machinery—there lay the inspiration of one man and one idea. Those people in Upper Canada who prized the British connection, for whatever reason, above all other political values, were stirred to action by the call of Governor Head.

The news from the returning officers early in July was sweet music to Tory ears. The Reformers went down to defeat in numbers that only the Governor himself really expected. Mr. Speaker Bidwell came at the foot of the poll in Lennox and Addington. Peter Perry was handily trounced. And in the most radical riding in the province, a man who passed for a moderate, by a margin of one hundred votes, had beaten William Lyon Mackenzie.

Among the romantic adventures of Sir Francis Head, it was an accomplishment more important than his transcontinental gallop over the pampas, and it meant the introduction of something more remarkable than the lasso into Canadian politics. Governments which valued their lives would in the future stump the country to hold on to them. A new practice in the politics of democracy had come to Canada.

CHAPTER TWELVE

HIS FIRST and only defeat at the polls rocked Mackenzie to the foundations. He went to a neighbour's home where a small group of supporters attended him, and wept inconsolably. It was as if he had lost, along with his vocation, his religion and half his friends. He was a visibly different man when he recovered and returned to politics. There was a fixed look, a grimness about him, as if he were a determined force, a public statue in action, or rather as if the private man had turned to living stone. He had always felt the pressure of obsession, and his mind, like an objective observer, watched and permitted while it gripped a part of him.

Only a few months earlier, in November of 1835, he wrote to his friend John Neilson in Quebec: "I am hot and fiery and age has not yet tempered as much as I could wish my political conduct and opinions, but *you* might do much good by casting oil upon the waters and waiting for the tide of human affairs in Canada." And to another correspondent: "Try to moderate parties rather than irritate, and exhibit the noble qualities of your nature; *I cannot*. . . . Why are you so bitter? Such bitterness were in character with me —a sort of misanthrope—but with you I hope it will be like the winter apple, ungrateful to the taste until the latter time, and then most sweet and mellow when most to be desired."

Mackenzie now embraced his fate. He became a sort of political trajectory, and aimed himself at his target. "I turn to the dark," he told his friend, and the words conjure Captain Ahab's terrible act of will as he closed at last his fixed purpose upon his enemy the white whale: "I turn my body from the sun."

Mackenzie returned to public life as an agitator. He had handed over the *Advocate* to another publisher before the first meeting of the 1835 Parliament. He now became a full-time journalist again. On the sixtieth anniversary of the American Declaration of Independence, July 4, 1836, he founded a paper called *The Constitution*. In its columns he invited patriots to join him in "this bold, dangerous but delightful course" and in "preparing the public mind for nobler actions than our tyrants dream of."

He now surpassed all his diatribes in the *Advocate,* with his new expletives and cries of pain: "Tories! Pensioners! Placemen! Profligates! Orangemen! Churchmen! Brokers! Gamblers! Parasites! allow me to congratulate you. Your feet at last are on the people's necks." He still fumed at the same members of the Family Compact. He still attacked "the priests of the leading denominations who have swallowed bribes like sweet morsels". And he had special words for the Methodists whose vote had just swung several constituencies to the Compact's side: "God sent down fire and brimstone on Sodom and Gomorrah four thousand years ago and it is to us a matter of surprise how your conference escapes." Now, however, behind these familiar local enemies he discerned a sinister imperial government. Like the American colonists, he asked if the power that had oppressed Ireland for centuries had not forfeited all claim upon the loyalties of free men.

Mackenzie called forth the ghosts of his rebel grandfathers and the Highlanders who had fought in the '45 for Prince Charlie, and he pressed them into service once more against the same line of Guelphic kings and their hired Lowland minions. The clan Mackenzie was at war again with England:

> Small cause have Highlanders and the descendants of Highlanders to feel a friendship for the Guelphic family. If the Stuarts had their faults, they never enforced loyalty in the glens and valleys of the north by banishing and extirpating the people. I am proud of my

descent from a rebel race who held borrowed chieftains in abomination. Words cannot express my contempt at witnessing the servile, crouching attitude of the country of my choice. If the people felt as I feel, there is never a Glenelg who crossed the Tay and Tweed to exchange highborn Highland poverty for substantial Lowland wealth, who would dare to insult Upper Canada with the official presence of such an equivocal character of this Mr. what do they call him—Francis Bond Head.

Glenelg, meanwhile, was in an ineffective way attempting to persuade Governor Head of the wisdom of conciliation. But Head was exultant in victory, and pointed to the elections as the clear vindication of his refusal to concede anything to the Reformers. Conciliate them and you will have an Assembly full of disloyal republicans. Attack and the vast loyal majority of the population will follow your lead. Glenelg himself was half convinced for a time, and in any case he was obliged to forward to Head the personal congratulations of King William.

Head celebrated by dismissing certain prominent holders of judicial office. They had attended early in July a meeting of the Constitutional Reform Society which issued a circular attacking the Governor. Of these, Dr. Baldwin, the society's president, made no protest. But another of them, Judge Ridout, complained to Glenelg that he took no part in approving the circular, gave good evidence, and asked for his job back. Glenelg told Head to reinstate him or else substantiate his charges. Head refused to do either and Glenelg lamely backed down.

Head next began lecturing the Colonial Office upon the conciliatory course which they and the new Governor-in-Chief, Lord Gosford, were attempting to pursue in Lower Canada and New Brunswick. For all that these prescriptions of imperial policy were scarcely in keeping with his rank and position, Head was right about the state of things in Quebec. It is hard to see what could have solved the permanent crisis there but the effective coercion of a whole people, or else a complete capitulation to Papineau and his party. Glenelg and Gosford offered no acceptable concessions and Lower Canada drifted toward armed rebellion.

In Upper Canada Sir Francis continued to defy his superiors. There would clearly be no surrender here while he was Governor. He ignored Glenelg's advice to give a judgeship to Bidwell, now despondently retired from politics. He filled the vacancies with men who he agreed were inferior in their legal capacities but had the advantage, he said, of supporting the constitution rather than "the low grovelling principles of democracy".

Sir Francis' loyal "bread-and-butter" Assembly met in November of 1836. They duly voted supplies and passed a number of bills for public improvements. In spite of their huge majority the Tories showed signs of nervousness, as if they could not quite believe in the enemy's rout, or that the country was as tranquil as Sir Francis said it was.

They took out an insurance policy on their places by passing a bill to obviate the usual custom of fresh elections in case of the death of the king. They failed to give the leading Reformer in the House, Dr. Rolph, an adequate hearing. On a technical point they denied Mackenzie's right to petition for a recount of the votes in his constituency. He took seriously ill late in the year, and, although he recovered rapidly, he was unable to meet the deadline for gathering and presenting the evidence to support his case. He was granted extra time, but when he was actually ready within the prescribed period, the Assembly reversed its decision and refused to hear him.

By the following spring there was real unrest in the country. The crushing defeat of the Reformers and the failure of the economic situation to improve sent a steady flow of emigrants to the United States during the rest of 1836. The situation was greatly aggravated for those who remained by the effect of a serious general depression early in 1837 which began with a series of failures among small banks in the United States.

As usual, it was the farmers—living closest to margin

and the ultimate debtors—who felt the depression most keenly. Upper Canada was ripe for an agrarian revolt. Mackenzie did not spare the bellows in fanning the latent fear of big commercial interests. He accused them of oppressing the people, and he warned the farmers that "the days of brass money and wooden shoes" would return. Like Francis Place and his "Go for Gold" he urged those of his readers who had anything in the bank to get their money while the getting was good, and so do their bit towards breaking the banks and embarrassing the Compact. The Bank of Upper Canada met the flood tide with shorter hours and, as Mackenzie complained, by putting a single slow man at the till. *The Constitution* returned to the attack with headlines:

☞ EXCHANGE YOUR BANK NOTES
FOR GOLD AND SILVER

And with slogans: "Labour is the true source of all wealth."

Mackenzie watched in hopeful anxiety as the news came in from down-river. In Lower Canada the issues were far more clear-cut. The most vocal part of the population was solidly behind Papineau and Dr. Wolfred Nelson and the other *Patriote* leaders, and they were preparing the province for rebellion. Gosford, sent over to bring peace, could do little more than issue proclamations against agitators and sent out warrants for the worst of them. Sir John Colborne, now the military commander-in-chief in British North America, deployed his troops for action.

Mackenzie speculated in *The Constitution* about the quality of the French Canadians as soldiers and their ability to fight their way to independence. He kept closely in touch with Papineau through the summer and fall. He had been the first English-speaking Canadian from his province to preach and practise the idea of the two nations co-operating in the cause of reform. He now determined that if he could help it they would take more drastic action together. Early in the summer of 1837 he decided to make plans for a rebellion in Upper Canada.

The first step was to take his fellow radicals with him as close to the brink as he could. At Mackenzie's instigation a group of them met on the 28th and again on the 31st of July in John Doel's brewery at the back of his house on Bay and Adelaide Streets. The document they signed stopped just short of being a declaration of independence: a list of grievances was recited; sympathy and admiration for the *Patriotes'* opposition to British tyranny. in Lower Canada were expressed; public meetings and political unions were urged upon every community in the province; and a congress of delegates (which never met) was called to Toronto to meet representatives from Lower Canada and "to seek an effectual remedy for the grievances of the colonists". The signatories constituted themselves into a Committee of Vigilance for the city of Toronto and appointed Mackenzie as their Agent and Corresponding Secretary.

Mackenzie interpreted his powers liberally and used his title to add new force to the agitation he had already begun among the farmers beyond the ridges. He published the whole of the declaration in *The Constitution* on August 2nd and then moved north again. In most cases he managed to organize vigilance committees and to pass resolutions like those in the Toronto declaration. Sometimes, when he sensed the meeting was ready, Mackenzie went beyond anything he said at Toronto. In the township of Caledon, he gave his audience a lesson in Locke and the legal right of rebellion:

> When a government is engaged in systematically oppressing a people it commits the same species of wrong to them that warrants an appeal to force against a foreign enemy. . . . The glorious revolutions of 1688 on one continent, and of 1776 on another, may serve to remind those rulers that they are placing themselves in a state of hostility against the governed. . . . A magistrate who shuts the gates of justice on the public restores them to their original right of defending themselves.

These words and many more did the farmers of the village

of Chinguacousy declare to be their solemn opinion and resolve.

Mackenzie went first straight up Yonge Street to Newmarket on August 3rd. He then moved across to Lloydtown, where banners on either side of the main thoroughfare posed the drastic choices of LIBERTY OR DEATH. An escort of fifty farmers, armed and mounted, took him on to Boltontown still in his own home constituency. "We all separated," wrote a Vaughan man to *The Constitution,* "with the understanding that to produce good order there must be hickory sticks, pikes and rifles at our future meetings. For Orange ruffians and Tory squires stand in need of such special constables, and with them are as meek as lambs."

There was only one notable outbreak of violence in connection with the meetings. It happened when a mounted party of twenty-six Mackenzie men were crossing the Humber River. A group of the enemy came up from behind and tried to pull the last pair of Patriots into the water. The Mackenzie men bridled and slid off their mounts, and set upon their assailants, with the most satisfactory results.

Some of the Tory papers threatened Mackenzie with assassination if the meetings continued. The answer to that was to increase the bodyguard. Mackenzie's procession from village to village took the shape of a rustic triumphal procession, with its carriages and ox-carts and motley unmilitary collection of mounts and riders.

They had everything to lose by violence or public disturbance at the meetings, however, and the Tories had everything to gain. Charges could be laid and the meetings stopped. In Esquesing on August 12th, the magistrates were primed and ready to read the riot act, and the Orangemen primed and ready to create the riot. So the meeting was adjourned to a private house where unwelcome visitors could be squeezed out.

At other points Mackenzie's friends quietly blocked off the entrances to a village square, or scattered themselves heavily into what looked like the Orange section of the crowd. On through the hot dusty afternoons Mackenzie's highland tongue and flinging arms declaimed and questioned and warned from his little stage atop cart or wagon, above the small field of rural headgear and leathery sunburnt necks and intent, immobile faces.

Here at last Mackenzie was in his truest element. The journalist's art was caught up into the eloquent fury of the word spoken and declaimed. The tirades in *The Constitution* with their baroque convolutions of style and their harsh jumble of book learning are really not for the printed page. They are written for the stump or the barn theatre and to be convincing or credible at all require a Mackenzie to deliver them. The ear is more credulous than the eye, especially when it listens in the hypnotic presence of an orator and the latent mute passion of a crowd. The farmers listened, and believed.

"There is discontent, vengeance and rage in men's minds." wrote Mackenzie. "No one can have any idea of the public feeling who has not taken the means I have to ascertain it." It almost seems as if he should have said "to create it". Not quite. For the feeling was neither a thing there and fully grown in the public mind, nor was it the mere creation of Mackenzie's eloquence, but that which was generated from the two. Rub them together and they would ignite something.

Times continued bad through the summer and fall of 1837. Jobs were scarce and money scarcer. The bills of the bread-and-butter Assembly had not improved the economic prospect, while the refusal to hear the Reformers' charges of electoral fraud had clearly made a bad public impression. And these things came to many men as the reward for years of heartbreaking struggle against the wilderness, with scarcely any help and considerable hindrance, from their governors. A Western Ontario farmer wrote a little apology for his life in a book published in 1837, several months before he joined a party of Patriot raiders at Amherstburg and died from wounds received there. Here, in part, is what he said:

The author has been in Canada since he was a little boy, and he has not had the advantage of a classical education at the King's College, or the less advantages derived from a District School. The greater part of his time has been spent watching over and providing for an increasing and tender family. He had in most instances to make his own roads and bridges, clear his own farm, educate himself and his children, be his own mechanic, and except now and then, he had no society but his own family. He had his bones broken by the fall of trees, his feet lacerated by the axe, and suffered almost everything except death. He waited year after year in hope of better days, expecting that the government would care less for themselves and more for the people. But every year he has been disappointed.

The lives of the men who came to hear Mackenzie had been often but little different from this. And they saw in him, more clearly now than ever, a projection of themselves, and of their own rage and hope. He was as wild and reckless and voluble as they were taciturn and cautious, but like themselves, he was abused, the underdog, the victim of injustice.

The hoax in Head's panic campaign had become plainer after the event. Or was it after all that Head was completely right? That the only way to democracy and social equality lay by the path of disloyalty?

The vigilance committees that Mackenzie left in his wake met again for other business than discussion. Ancient muskets and weird wonderful varieties of rifle were brought out, and desultory target practice began. The more cautious practised their marksmanship at organized turkey shoots which Bidwell (though not a participant himself) laconically told them was a legal form of recreation. Forges in the home district were busy casting bullets, and Samuel Lount's blacksmith shop in County Simcoe rang with the beating of new pike heads.

A young Reformer by the name of Thomas Sheppard who later fought in the rebellion recalled how he and his brother spent the fall getting ready: "Mike and I then lived at the mill back of Lansing, up Yonge Street. We would take our muskets and join the other Reformers who were drilled by an old soldier who worked I think in Mackenzie's printing office. We drilled at Uncle Jake Fisher's Farm in Vaughan. Mackenzie used to ride from the city (with his brace of pocket pistols under his belt) to watch the old soldier put the farmers through their facings."

Most of the formal drilling, however, left almost everything to be desired. An observer of one meeting saw "three or four hundred men and boys marshalled or rather scattered in picturesque fashion hither and thither. A few mounted lancers—well-appointed but with a great variety of uniform, others having only a carving knife at the end of a fishing pole." The rifle drill, often a matter of manipulating walking sticks and umbrellas to the shoulder or the port, was scarcely a display of arrant militarism. Nor was the routine of civilian life much impinged upon even by the grandest of military exercises: "The captain of lancers was proprietor of the village store and might be seen shortly after the military display, plumed helmet in hand, vaulting over the counter to serve one customer a penn'orth of tobacco and another a yard of check cloth." Sometimes a vigilance meeting, as the evening progressed, acquired the chief characteristic of a wake: "One invention of '37 was the fuddle-o-meter, an instrument designed to tell a man when he had taken his innermost utmost."

For all its ludicrous manner and sometimes diverted purposes, the activity of the Patriots was a serious attempt to follow the lesson Mackenzie learned from Joseph Hume and the Reform Bill crisis—"without a display of physical force there would have been no Reform Bill." The Patriots were at heart determined men. They knew they risked arrest at the very least. And there were a few among them, like Samuel Lount of Holland Landing, capable of leadership and responsibility, as well as zeal for the cause.

Sir Francis Head did not deem their activity worthy of notice. He discounted much of the reports of it as fiction or simply as evidence that there must exist in any society the posturing bravado of a few lunatics. He knew the country was loyal and contented. He would be content to let Mackenzie "speak and stamp and foam" until he could catch him on a treason charge with a certainty of conviction. With an incredible gesture of confidence, in October of 1837, he emptied Fork York and Fort Henry in Kingston of all his troops, and sent them to bolster Sir John Colborne against the hotheads in Lower Canada. They left behind them several thousand stand of arms, with ammunition, which Sir Francis stowed in the City Hall in the care of two constables.

This was an open invitation to mischief and Mackenzie jumped to accept.

CHAPTER THIRTEEN

ON MONDAY morning, October 9, 1837, a gentleman who
looked as if he had spent the night travelling entered Mr.
Mackenzie's Toronto bookshop short of breath and clearly
agitated about something, and asked for the master. It was
believed that the master was somewhere in the northern part
of county York. The gentleman disappeared up Yonge
Street.

After more enquiries the gentleman, Jesse Lloyd by name,
and by way of present occupation Mackenzie's ambassador
to Papineau, discovered the object of his search, and relayed his message from Lower Canada. The word from the
Patriotes was that the hour "for a brave stroke of liberty"
had arrived. Mackenzie was urgently invited to strike with
them. Mr. Lloyd added his own plea to Papineau's.

Mackenzie needed no coaxing to put the most precise
interpretation upon the rather vague rhetoric of Papineau's
message. He had already decided that "those who persuaded Head to place four thousand stand of arms in the
midst of an unarmed people seemed evidently not opposed
to their being used." They would have their way presently,
he decided. A few discreet inquiries, a word passed here,
messages there, and the thing could be done tonight. No
need to wait upon the vigilance committees. It could be
done by a handful of Torontonians; and the farmers, and
Patriots in the city would rise the quicker after the event.

Mackenzie rode for Toronto at a headlong gallop. He
packed off two persons, separately, to Fort York to make
sure it was empty, and another pair to discover the present

whereabouts of Governor Head. He called together a small caucus of Toronto radicals for the same evening.

It was dark early, and there was an exhilarating tang of frost in the autumn air. The radicals gathered in the grate-and-candlelit room at the back of John Doel's brewery. The firelight gave a high gloss to the expanse of Mackenzie's brow as he spoke, and the faint shadows rose and subsided at the same darting hushed pace of his voice.

Mackenzie talked first in familiar generalities—Ireland, the Thirteen Colonies, the Glorious Revolution of 1688, and the state of things in Lower Canada—and the group listened approvingly though with a measure of long-sufferance. Mackenzie, as usual, was taking a long rhetorical run at his subject. Then suddenly he was applying it all to them, to Upper Canada, to tonight: he was asking them to do something, something drastic. "I said that the troops had left . . . that Fort Henry was open and empty, and a steamer had only to sail down to the wharf and take possession; that I had sent two trusty persons to the garrison that day, and it was also 'to let'; that the Lieutenant-Governor had just come in from his ride, and was now at home, guarded by one sentinel; and that my judgement was that we should instantly send for Dutcher's foundry-men and Armstrong's axe-makers, all of whom could be depended on, and, with them, go promptly to the Government House, seize Sir Francis, carry him to the City Hall, a fortress in itself, seize the arms and ammunition there, and the artillery, etc., in the old garrison; rouse our innumerable friends in town and country, proclaim a provisional government, send off the steamer of that evening to secure Fort Henry, and either induce Sir Francis to give the country an Executive Council responsible to a new and fairly chosen Assembly to be forthwith elected, after packing off the usurpers in the 'Bread and Butter' Parliament; or if he refused to comply, go at once for Independence, and take the proper steps to obtain it."

Mackenzie's audience was scarcely prepared for this. Of course they were radicals by conviction. Of course they held all the right liberal principles. They believed fervently in an oppressed people's right to rebel. Then even believed that it might happen here. But to do something now, to go act out the meaning of their beliefs tonight! One does not just begin a revolution without going home to think about it, without checking one's will or changing one's clothes. Their convictions were as radical as any man's, but they were solid citizens too, well-off, and with businesses to think of, and families. The thing sounded too easy to be true. More precautions should be taken. The matter should be more fully discussed. Prudent men know that big decisions should be slept on.

One of them, Dr. Morrison, M.L.A. and ex-mayor of Toronto, shifted nervously when Mackenzie got on to the part about seizing the arms and the forts and began to mutter his disapproval. When Mackenzie was finished, Morrison indignantly proclaimed that this was treason and he was not their man. He explained later, after finally agreeing to another of Mackenzie's schemes, that his vehemence arose from the suspicion that an informer was among them. He may have suspected the Englishman, Mr. Attorney Elliott; the rest apart from Parsons, the drygoods man, and Doel, the brewer, were Scots. Whether this was so or not, both Morrison and the others were ready enough to demur and postpone—anything but walk right out into the cold October air, and without so much as telling their wives, go slug the guard at the City Hall and pull His Excellency out of bed at gunpoint. The meeting broke up without any decision. Mackenzie went home exasperated.

As it happened, such a golden opportunity for success never presented itself again.

The men whom Mackenzie had invited were all in principle committed to the same goal: reform if possible, rebellion if not. Yet when the one clear chance to achieve the goal came, they were incapable of seizing it. Sound and shrewd, men of affairs, they were schooled in the calculation of the small risk and the limited liability. Their system of accounting had no trusty measure for the longer sums and they fell back, not on rational calculation but on instinct. It was not the practical men who were capable of the practical now, but the unstable irresponsible visionary. Mackenzie thought and dealt in the shortest ways and means to the absolute. In his scheme of values, he had long since given up, dearly as he loved them, worldly goods, wife, children, all, to the pursuit of the One Necessary Thing. When the pilgrim saw the way at last to the Delectable Mountains, he was ready to set out on the instant. The others with one accord made their excuses.

The most substantial and respected of the radical leaders, Dr. John Rolph, M.L.A., had been invited to the meeting at Doel's brewery but did not appear. Mackenzie reached him the following evening and by submitting himself to a long cross-examination, persuaded Rolph that a bloodless and successful *coup d'état* was perfectly feasible. Not only were there no troops in Upper Canada but the Governor refused to allow the militia to be organized, so loyal and contented did he deem His Majesty's Canadians. Clearly there would have been a good response if Head had gone out and recruited, though even the Tories had now no illusions about his capacity as governor. But this was a course he would not remotely have considered. On the other hand, any spontaneous rising of loyalists after the rebellion to rescue the Governor from the clutches of a fully armed rebel government was unlikely to succeed. It might not occur at all if that government were headed by solid men like Doctors Rolph and Morrison, both members of that profession which has enjoyed in Canada something of the prestige of the Godhead Itself.

In the course of the week, Rolph convinced Dr. Morrison that the thing could be done without serious risk. But they wanted further assurances from Mackenzie about the state of opinion in the countryside. Were there really two or three thousand men willing to march on Toronto? Better for Mackenzie to go back to the vigilance committees, get more lists, put his specific plan to them for discussion. If they agreed, Mackenzie could report back to Rolph and

Morrison for final consideration. Then in due course their date for the attack on the City Hall might be set. That done, and the Governor captured, the rebels would invite Dr. Rolph to become head of a provisional government. Should this point be reached, Dr. Rolph said he could scarcely decline the invitation. Dr. Morrison said that he too would subscribe under such circumstances. What else, after all, would they be doing but complying with the wishes of a people who had obviously been burdened past bearing? A revolution carried out this way could acquire quickly all the respectability of 1688. The British would scarcely have the stomach for outright coercion. Anything but the sudden and ignoble business of packing Mackenzie and a mob of rude mechanics post-haste out the door to do the thing secretly and immediately. Mackenzie had, of necessity, to comply with his colleagues' more leisurely plans and higher wisdom. He knew better than to attempt the *coup* alone. If the rebel government was to command sufficient general respect to prevent a loyalist insurrection and to deal with the British, it must contain men like Rolph and Morrison.

Mackenzie returned cheerfully enough to the original, more cumbersome plan. After another series of meetings with the two worthy doctors, and after wringing permission to use their names in the Home District Committees (though to make no commitments), Mackenzie headed north again at the beginning of November with the ostensible mission of sounding out radical opinion on the plan.

Before long rumours reached Rolph that Mackenzie had done far more than gather opinion. He and Jesse Lloyd, together with Samuel Lount of County Simcoe and several other radical leaders, had met and apparently gone so far as to set a date for the uprising: Thursday December 7th. Five thousand men would assemble at Montgomery's tavern at the Eglinton crossroad, arriving in small groups the night and day before. Lount and Captain Anthony Anderson, a soldier of "great courage and firmness", who had spent the autumn drilling the farmers of North York "into a state of comparative efficiency" were to take charge.

Presented with this *fait accompli*, the truth of which was confirmed by Mackenzie on his return to Toronto in mid-November, Rolph and Morrison reluctantly concurred. To satisfy their concern that there be a man of more professional military experience in supreme command, Mackenzie sent a messenger off to the Huron tract in the far west of the province to summon Colonel Anthony Van Egmond.

Rumours, like comet tails, started by Mackenzie's last blazing trip north, began descending upon Toronto. Most of the Tories, however, were of the opinion that only the superstitious would heed them, and they persisted, like Sir Francis, in ignoring them. Not so Colonel James Fitzgibbon of the militia, who had captured a whole battalion of Americans in the War of 1812 with only a platoon to help him. When he saw the last thirty British soldiers coming through Toronto on their way from Penetang to Montreal, he went to Governor Head and pleaded with him to keep them. Failing that, he asked the Governor to arm the militia. "No," was the reply, "I do not apprehend rebellion in Upper Canada." Poor Fitzgibbon even arranged for his own small rifle corps to volunteer a corporal's guard for nightly watch over the City Hall and to post two sentries close to Government House, for all of which Sir Francis Head graciously refused any permission whatsoever. Sir Francis simply would not admit to himself and "the British people" that his rule had aroused anything but the beat of loyal hearts in the breasts of Upper Canadians.

On the evening of November 24, Mackenzie left Dr. Rolph's house and moved up Yonge Street for the last time, to speed the recruiting and set the final plans for the meeting at Montgomery's on December 7th. Before he left he put the finishing touches on an issue of *The Constitution* which was literally just that: a small draft constitution declared to be law by "we the people of the State of Upper Canada". Governor, Senate, and House were all to be elected by free secret ballot. Religious and legal discrimination of every sort was to be abolished. It was a thoroughly American document, except for such items as the declaration against slavery, and certain of Mackenzie's own ideas on the hawk-eyed supervision of the public purse. This constitution was to be submitted to a proposed Reform convention for which the radicals had rather vaguely arranged to meet in Toronto. The last few numbers of *The Constitution* also urged every man to provide himself with a musket because the crisis of liberty was approaching. But the government still refused to take Mackenzie seriously. A few irresponsible Tories contented themselves with the old trick of throwing stones at Mackenzie's windows. One big rock smashed through the children's pane as they were asleep one Friday night in November and just missed their bed.

Near the end of November alarming news reached the government from down-river. The *Patriotes* were in arms and on November 23 under Dr. Wolfred Nelson had fought a seven-hour pitched battle against several companies of British troops at St. Denis and driven them off with heavy losses.

Colonel Fitzgibbon decided to take matters into his own hands by preparing a list of dependable men in Toronto and on lower Yonge Street. He determined to call upon them personally with the warning to keep their firearms ready to hand. He wanted the mayor to arrange for the ringing of the Upper Canada College bell as a warning, should the rising take place, and this in turn to be the signal for all the bells in the city to sound a general alarm. The mayor felt that this was rank interference with the prerogatives of his office and refused to do anything. When Fitzgibbon called on John Beverley Robinson, he was told, "I am sorry to see you alarming the people in this way." Robinson was opposed to fanaticism in all its forms and the sight of this zealot in the cause of imperial defence undertaking a house-to-house canvass for the loading of guns quite understandably offended his sense of proportion and good breeding. Meanwhile, beyond the ridges, a handbill of Mackenzie's struck by the printer on the little press Mackenzie had taken north with him was being distributed to the rural population.

INDEPENDENCE!

There have been Nineteen Strikes for Independence from European Tyranny on the Continent of America. *They were all successful!*

BRAVE CANADIANS! Do you love freedom? I know you do. Do you hate oppression? Who dare deny it? Do you wish perpetual peace, and a government founded upon the eternal heaven-born principle of the Lord Jesus Christ? Then buckle on your armour, and put down the villains who oppress and enslave our country—put them down in the name of that God who goes forth with the armies of his people.

Bishops and Archdeacons are bribed to instruct their flocks that they should be obedient to a government which defies the law; yet God has opened the eyes of the people to the wickedness of these reverend sinners, just as God's prophet Elijah did the priests of Baal of old. Is there any one afraid to fight for freedom, let him remember, that,

> God sees with equal eye, as Lord of all,
> A hero perish, or a sparrow fall:

The power that protected ourselves and our forefathers in the deserts of Canada—that preserved from cholera those whom he would—that brought us safely to this continent through the dangers of the Atlantic waves— aye, and who has watched over us from infancy to manhood, will be in the midst of us in the day of our struggle for our liberties.

We have given Head and his employers a trial of forty-five years—five years longer than the Israelites were detained in the wilderness. The promised land is now before us—up then and take it—but set not the torch to one house in Toronto, unless we are fired at.

We cannot be reconciled to Britain—we have humbled ourselves to the Pharaoh of England, to the Ministers and great people, and they will neither rule us justly or let us go. Up then, brave Canadians! Get

ready your rifles, and make short work of it. Woe
be to those that oppose us, for "In God is our trust."

Mackenzie left the printer near Hogg's Hollow with
instructions to distribute copies of the handbill. The poor
man got mobbed when he attempted to leave samples of his
handiwork among a group of Tories. One of the latter,
after the types and cases were found and deposited piece-
meal in the nearest well, bore copies to the city and showed
them to the authorities. Chief Justice Robinson had long
ago written off Mackenzie as a candidate for Bedlam, and
remained blithely undisturbed. The prophet's cry was meant
for less sophisticated minds than that of an Anglican gentleman, however. We may conjecture that there was more than
one simple, peaceable yeoman, quaking at the deed he was
about to do, but heartened to it by a good swig of Mackenzie's Biblical comfort chased down with a chest-burning
swallow of twenty-cent John Barleycorn.

Warnings now poured into the city; the very day of the
intended rising was even included among them. On Saturday
December 2nd a meeting of leading official personages
gathered in Government House. Besides the Governor and
part of his Executive Council there was present Chief Justice Robinson, Attorney-General Hagerman and Colonel
Allan MacNab, Speaker of the Assembly, and several others.
Their chief concern was apparently to decide whether any
action on their part could put a stop to the idle rumours
flying about the city. It was still obvious to them that there
would be no rebellion. Sir Francis, in fact, was to remain
adamant in his refusal to admit the existence of rebels until
the first report of actual bloodshed reached him. Hagerman
declared loudly that "Not fifty people in the Province could
be got to take arms against the Government." Various
masculine rumbles and groans signalled the room's general
agreement with Hagerman.

At this point, poor Fitzgibbon burst in upon them, flushed
and breathless. A magistrate from the north had just
brought him certain word of the secret manufacture of a
large number of pikes. "You do not mean to say," asked

Judge Jonas Jones, contemptuously, "that these people are going to use them?" "Most distinctly I do," said Fitzgibbon. "Pugh! pugh!" said the Judge, with a knowing leer at Sir Francis Head. Fitzgibbon was by now a standing joke. And in all fairness to the Governor's advisers, one must admit that he was of that breed of alarmist defenders of the *status quo* who chronically interpret the least irregularity as sure evidence that the Omniscient Power of Evil, which peer with eyes of unceasing malevolence into every corner of civilized society, have now matured their wicked plans and will presently do a dishonour upon all flags, women and children, should brave men not act to stop them.

Tolerant smiles were exchanged, and Fitzgibbon's magistrate friend was summoned for questioning. His evidence was dismissed as "third hand" by all but one of the officials present. Fitzgibbon was appeased by an appointment as Acting Adjutant General of the Militia, and, as a means of calming the city, it was decided to issue on the following Monday an order for the organization of two militia regiments. For an added measure of precaution, a warrant was to be sent out for William Lyon Mackenzie.

That Saturday afternoon there was more excited gossip in the city. Everyone knew of the conclave at Government House, but not its results at first hand. Allan MacNab dropped a remark about organizing the Gore militia as he boarded the evening steamer for Hamilton. This and other hints gleaned from those who had been present led to rather exaggerated views of the government's safety measures: "the Orangemen are to be given the guns from City Hall." "The government has found the radicals' plans and little Mac's for it now—high treason—it's the rope for him!"

It was now Rolph's turn to be alarmed. He sent a message to Mackenzie via David Gibson's place above Yonge and Eglinton that the alarm was out, and a warrant for Mackenzie's arrest; but that if he could get as many as three hundred men together by Monday, four days sooner than the date for the grand reunion, it would still be quite possible to take the City Hall. The scheme appears strangely familiar:

it was indeed almost the twin of Mackenzie's proposal on
that October evening at Doel's brewery before even the
Fitzgibbons were seriously alarmed.

Mackenzie was not to be found anywhere, and eventually
the message was delivered to Mrs. Lount in Holland Landing. One can understand her husband's concern when he
returned home that Sunday night after sending two men
to arrange for the victualling of the rebels at Montgomery's
on Thursday. He took the message as an order to jump the
deadline and march south on Monday. Lount sent for
Captain Anthony Anderson who was staying nearby and
early on Monday they assembled such bodies as they could
get hold of for the march. All through the afternoon and
on into the bitter cold of a December dusk, small clusters
of men, bearing staves and pitchforks and rifles, were to be
seen moving south on Yonge Street or tramping the nearby
sideroads. They picked up reinforcements on the way and
made prisoners of all known Tories they encountered, bringing them along with them.

Mackenzie meanwhile arrived at Gibson's house Sunday
night, got the news, and dispatched one of the servants to
Lount to tell him to stick to the original plan: rising on
Thursday. He sent also for Rolph, and on Monday morning
they met at a friend's house near Montgomery's but closer
to the city. Rolph was thoroughly depressed by the late
news from Lower Canada. The rebels there had been de-
cisively defeated and the affair was practically finished. (It
later proved to have been hopelessly sporadic and unorganized, and in spite of the great courage of the *Patriotes*
under Nelson, it had none of the real chances of success
which Mackenzie's small measure of planning and Sir Francis Head's incredulity afforded the Upper Canadian rising.)
Rolph urged Mackenzie to call the whole scheme off. Victory
would only last as long as it took General Colborne to
march his troops to Toronto, several weeks at the most.
Mackenzie refused, and with Rolph's reluctant consent to
proceed, they parted.

Mackenzie and Gibson made for an old building back

of Gibson's farm where they found, as expected, several local mechanics casting bullets. Here Gibson's servant, back from Holland Landing, found them towards noon. The word from Lount was that the rising was now public knowledge in the north. It was too late to turn back. The first companies would be at Montgomery's by nightfall.

Mackenzie accepted this with a sort of grim exultation and rushed to place a guard on Yonge Street to prevent anyone moving into the city. To add to his troubles the tavern had just changed hands in the last few days and was now owned by a man called Lingfoot, who would have nothing to do with victualling the likes of Mackenzie and his friends until he saw his way clear to a cash return. Mackenzie raved at him, shook him by the collar, threatened him with far worse than a shaking, but Lingfoot would not budge.

The first files of weary rebels arrived about eight o'clock in the evening, aching to heat their bones by a good fire, mouths set and bellies cramped for a good hot dinner. They found instead a sullen innkeeper, Mackenzie in a raving fit of temper, and the sorry news from the Yonge Street guards that there were no muskets at all stored ready for them at the tavern. To season this supper of gall, they were plied with the dismal news of the disaster to the *Patriote* cause, which was the first most of them had heard from Lower Canada since the glowing report of Nelson's defence of St. Denis. Some of the men lit out for home then and there.

Spirits picked up a bit by nine o'clock when supplies for a meagre supper had been scavenged from the neighbourhood, and their trusty leaders Lount and Captain Anderson arrived.

Some of the later arrivals had taken the precaution of calling in for victuals at friendly households on their way down Yonge Street, and their outlook was somewhat more sanguine. "The Monday night before the fight I was sitting by the fire at mother's getting ready to join the rebels, when we heard a knock at the door. My mother hurried across the floor to open it and there stood Samuel Lount with fifty Reformers from up Lloydtown way. They had marched thirty miles and were tired and cold and hungry. Poor mother couldn't do enough for them when she saw who they were. They crowded around the fire, and after getting all they could eat Lount ordered them to fall in and away they marched to Montgomery's."

Once Lount had arrived, he, Anderson, Lloyd, and others held conference with Mackenzie, who urged an immediate attack upon the city. The rest refused. Their men were tired, reinforcements were expected, and Rolph had failed to send up any message as to the present state of the city. Without this there was no way of stopping talk among the men about the militia being armed and Orangemen arriving in Toronto by the shipload. For that matter some of the talk might be true. They would wait and march in daylight, refreshed and with a fuller muster of men.

Mackenzie was beside himself with restlessness. But the most he could get was a mounted patrol of five led by Captain Anderson and himself to approach the city and reconnoitre.

As things actually stood, the five men themselves would have been enough to capture the Governor, who had retired early and was sleeping peacefully in his bed. With a few calls, on Rolph, on Morrison, and the axe-maker's men, they could still have effected Mackenzie's October plan, although now with the risk of some opposition.

Colonel Fitzgibbon had spent an exhausting day discovering that his new title did him no good whatsoever as a means of persuading the friends of the government to arm themselves and defend the city. He now feared a general uprising that night or at the very least an attempt by the radicals to assassinate him. He decided to watch in the Parliament Buildings, and persuaded a few friends to accompany him. They were ready enough to do so for, as one of them said, he feared the man's mind was on the point of giving way.

About ten o'clock Fitzgibbon decided he must rouse the Governor. After some protest, the women of the house were won over by Fitzgibbon's harassed looks and fervent pleas and went to waken Sir Francis. His Excellency appeared at length in his dressing gown, considerably irritated. Fitzgibbon told him he was now certain of his premonition that the rising would take place that very night. Sir Francis heard him out, dismissed him, and went back to bed. Directly after this, a horseman who had ridden into the city by a sideroad found Fitzgibbon at his vigil in the Parliament Buildings and confirmed his worst fears: the rebels had been sighted on their way down Yonge Street. Fitzgibbon and his friends galloped off to warn the leading citizens of Toronto. But it was late now and most of them refused to budge. Nightcap tassel bobbing, Judge Jones peered out of his window in startled response to the messengers clattering at the door. When told the source of the warning, he was heard to make an uncomplimentary remark about Fitzgibbon and with that withdrew his neck, talking quietly to himself, and slammed down the window sash. Fitzgibbon sent young John Cameron, a barrister's apprentice and recently a pupil at Upper Canada College, to ring the College bell. A vigilant housemaster seized and silenced him after the first half dozen strokes.

Back at Montgomery's at the same moment three horsemen came flying down the little rise north of Eglinton and charged straight at the guards who were blocking the road. The guards shouted for them to halt but they went on through at full tilt, making for Toronto. Rifles cracked out and Colonel Moodie, a formidable Tory from Richmond Hill, reared back over his mount and fell mortally wounded to the ground. One of his companions was caught, but the other raced on towards the city. His pursuer's carthorse quickly crumpled at the fast clip and the rider disappeared into the night.

Farther down Yonge Street, Fitzgibbon decided to set out and reconnoitre for himself. He found everything so quiet that for the first time that evening he began to lose faith in his premonition. He fell in with Alderman Powell and a friend, who had heard the same report as he, and when he learned that Powell was going as far as Montgomery's tavern, he turned back to Toronto to see what more could be done there and to await the report of Powell's reconnaissance.

Powell had no sooner climbed Gallows Hill than he met Mackenzie's patrol. Mackenzie called on Powell and his friend to halt, charged up to them pistol first, and took them prisoner. Although they were obviously out on a dangerous mission, he accepted their word "as men of honour and my townsmen", that they were unarmed, and did not search them. It was one of those extravagant gestures which Mackenzie expected of himself. He would show the local aristocracy that for all their contempt, he was as good a gentleman as any of them. Indeed, in questions of honour and of generosity, a Mackenzie and a highlander could outdo them all. We have seen him act in a similar way when Mr. Justice Kerr called on him the night he was nearly assassinated in Hamilton. The gesture on this occasion, it soon proved, was made at a more dreadful cost.

The patrol split, Anderson taking the prisoners north to Montgomery's and Mackenzie moving on farther towards the city. Anderson's party soon encountered the escaped companion of Colonel Moodie. Powell cried out for help. Moodie's companion recognized his voice and shouted "The rebels have shot poor Colonel Moodie and are advancing on the city!" With that the rider swerved past Anderson and continued towards the city, which he apparently reached by a round about way much later. Anderson moved on north forcing Powell to stay ahead of him. As they approached the tavern, Powell slipped out one of his hidden pistols, swung his horse violently around and caught Anderson in the neck with his first shot. He dropped dead to the ground: the rebels had lost the man who was to have led them into Toronto, and the only military leader among them in whom all the troops placed their entire confidence.

Powell and his companion charged back down Gallows Hill, and overtook Mackenzie. He fired point blank in Mackenzie's face, but the priming flashed in the pan and the bullet did not discharge. When he reached Davenport

Road, Powell turned off Yonge Street and leapt from his horse. He hid behind a log in a nearby thicket until he decided he was not being chased. On his feet again, he stumbled across into Queen's Park, and with all two hundred and more pounds of him wheezing and puffing mightily, jogged at his utmost, if still stately, pace down what is now University Avenue towards Government House.

Sir Francis had been roused again to no purpose at the few strokes of the College bell which had escaped the house-master's vigilance, and this time his family was determined to protect his slumbers. When Powell arrived in considerable disarray and scarcely coherent, there was a scene. He ended by pushing his way into the Governor's bedroom. His Excellency blinked awake for the third time that evening fairly itching with distemper.

Sir Francis was no fool, however, when it came to reading the signs of adventure. He saw almost before Alderman Powell began speaking that this alarm was the real thing. He dressed immediately and came down, though not before his distraught sister had another encounter with Colonel Fitzgibbon who appeared again, more agitated than ever. Fitzgibbon managed to get past her again and crossed paths with the Alderman who was descending the stairs from His Excellency's bedroom on his way to the City Hall. Sir Francis followed soon after, keenly excited and savouring Danger to the full.

> I walked along King Street. . . . The stars were shining bright as diamonds in the black canopy over my head. The air was intensely cold, and the snow-covered planks that formed the footpaths of the city creaked as I trod upon them. The principal bell of the town was in an agony of fear, and her shrill irregular monotonous little voice, strangely breaking the serene silence of night, was exclaiming to the utmost of its strength— *Murder! Murder! Murder! and much worse!*

At Montgomery's the men were sprawled thickly over the floors, a sea of uneasy sleepers, their brains dreaming on a supper of bad whiskey and biscuit, and filled with

169

heavy forebodings. Mackenzie hopped among them like a little nightmare incarnate, from one room to the next, and out the tavern door and in again a dozen times in an hour, still arguing that they should all rise and head for the city in the dark. More volunteers kept straggling in to be met with the sorry tale of their commander's death, and to hear the muffled sobs of agony from the room where Colonel Moodie lay dying. About midnight a light breeze off the lake brought them firsthand news of the city for the first time since Rolph's conference with Mackenzie that morning: faintly, in short gusts, far down the south side of the night, a strange ice-like tinkling. All the bells of Toronto were ringing.

All through the early hours of the morning and on past daybreak, the rebel leaders frittered their time away in confused conference. Several dozen groups of the men who continued to arrive turned around and went home when they found there were no muskets for them. Mackenzie continually kept bursting out to harangue Montgomery, who was still a lodger at his old inn, into finding provisions. Then a wild urgent remark, half to himself, half to the nearest knot of men, and back he would go again to the council of war. "Once or twice I thought he was going to have a fit," one of the rebels said later. "Little Mac conducted himself like a crazy man all the time we were at Montgomery's. He went about storming and screaming like a lunatic, and many of us felt certain he was not in his right senses. He abused and insulted several of the men without any shadow of cause, and Lount had to go round and pacify them by telling them not to pay any attention to him, as he was hardly responsible for his actions."

Some of the men were for dispersing, the leaders could not agree on tactics, and Lount persisted in refusing to take sole command since he lacked sufficient military experience. Finally Mackenzie said he would take full charge himself and the others agreed. About eleven o'clock that Tuesday morning the rebels, about eight hundred of them in all and gaining in numbers every few minutes, were ordered to assemble outside the tavern. Mackenzie came out, bundled into several greatcoats (a precaution against bullets, some of the men said) with the outer one buttoned right to the chin and ears. He mounted a white pony, like a sort of deranged Yankee Doodle, and from this perch addressed the whole company. He himself would be their commander-in-chief for the day, he proclaimed, and lead them into Toronto. There was another delay, a further hurried conference, and finally, just before noon, the order to fall in and march.

Towards the brow of Gallows Hill the strange army moved, hats pulled down to ear level, rifles, pikes, farm implements shouldered at the cock-eyed slope, heavy clogs treading the ground with wide or lanky gait: for all the world, if you saw them from a distance in an unfamiliar landscape, like some company of clay-footed rustic shades tramping to the aid of Wat Tyler and John Ball.

> There are rich men now [Mackenzie had told them] as there were in Christ's time. A wicked government has trampled the law . . . declared that they will roll their fine carriages, and riot in their palaces at our expense; that we are poor spiritless ignorant peasants who were born to toil for our betters. But the peasants are beginning to open their eyes and to feel their strength.

> *When Adam delved and Eve span*
> *Who was then the gentleman?*

On and on they clogged in their bulging homespun and ill-cut trousers, some last lagging contingent of agrarian democracy, too late to change the world's history as Tyler's peasants had been too early, inconsequential, ludicrous, uncertain of their leaders and of themselves; but still palpably, grossly real in their stubborn intent to drive the one life they had down into the valley of decision and to be numbered among those who were not merely for themselves but for righteousness.

The gentlemen of Toronto were ill-prepared to meet their rural visitors. Sir Francis Head, in the course of making his toilette and walking to the City Hall, had progressed rapidly from complete disbelief in the rebels' existence to a ready acceptance of the worst possible reports of their strength and intentions. In the presence of a small group of advisers he put his head in his hands and cried out in despair that there was nothing to be done—not a single British soldier remained in Upper Canada.

Sturdy Chris Hagerman, who had meant every last bombastic word of his speeches about dying for King and Empire, replied gruffly to this that he was ready to shoulder a musket; he was sure other gentlemen would do the same. With that he went below and helped himself.

Soon all the heads of the Compact families, from Chief Justice Robinson down, were assembled in the market place, muskets in hand, chatting calmly and without the least vulgar display of panic in what many of them suspected— for good reason—would be their last hour. They were two hundred against a rebel force (as they believed) of five thousand. There was little more they could do but wait bravely for the attack.

Young James McGill Strachan, the Archdeacon's son, and John Beverley Robinson, Junior, were appointed aides-de-camp to the Governor, and were dispatched about the city with messages: very dashing, but with results which were not apparent. Riders had already been sent off to MacNab and the men of Gore and to the other loyal militiamen, and to the half-pay officers from Lakefield and the Eastern districts. Judge Jones made recompense for his extravagant skepticism by firing all his Welsh fury into recruiting a picket of thirty loyal men to guard the northern limits of the city. In so doing he deliberately disobeyed orders. Sir Francis told them that not a man was to leave him, that they were all to stick to their posts at the City Hall. Nevertheless a picket under Sheriff Jarvis was kept all the next day as well on either side of Yonge Street at the edge of town, without permission, but with important consequences for the fate of the rebellion.

Toronto, like Sir Francis, spent Tuesday morning in a paralysis of futility. Business stopped dead. Rumours flew:

"they" were five thousand strong; were fully armed; were on their way to fire the city; or worse. And no more than three hundred loyal men could be found, from a male population ten times that number, to take musket and defend the Governor and his capital.

Sir Francis' most decisive act was to place his family abroad a little steamer in the Bay, which was still free of ice. "He had his family out in the bay," wrote Mackenzie later, "as if they were china, while other folks' families, being but brownware, had to run all risks ashore."

Alderman Powell who was soon to be chosen Mayor of Toronto for the bold patriotism he displayed in shooting Captain Anderson and saving the city, now decided to perform the act of higher justice which the law had prevented from taking its course ten years earlier. He organized a raid on Mackenzie's press and bookshop. The pillage was more thorough than before and this time there were no questions asked and no suit for damages.

Mackenzie's house in York Street was put under guard. Search parties tramped through every few minutes, thrusting their swords under the beds and into the mattresses on the chance of sticking a rebel. They hunted several times through all the drawers and cupboards for Mackenzie's papers and correspondence. Most of this material was hanging in files from the ceiling of Mackenzie's bedroom, in full view. While the women watched in considerable suspense the searchers walked back and forth beneath the hanging files. The officers' helmet plumes sometimes brushed against them. Eventually Isabel managed to find an excuse to keep the soldiers out of the house long enough for her daughters to clear the ceiling. The papers were stuffed hurriedly into four wood stoves, and the only glimpse the searchers got of them was in the smoke pouring from the chimney as they returned to the house. Half a dozen men were detailed to remain every night in the dining room, the official reason being to protect the house and its occupants. But the women denounced them for spies. Old Elizabeth Mackenzie, sparser of flesh and stature than ever and nearing her ninetieth year, came downstairs into their midst and declared fiercely that they should be ashamed to force themselves on defence-less women and children. The men abandoned their post and did not return.

The rebel army reached the brow of Gallows Hill early Tuesday afternoon. Here Mackenzie and Lount decided to halt and re-form into two columns half a mile apart for the last stage of the march on the city, which was to begin at two o'clock.

A little before the hour, however, Lount's men, still on the Yonge street slopes of the hill, heard a cry from their advance sentry. In a moment they caught sight of a small party of horsemen riding towards them from the city and bearing a large flag. It was a truce mission from the Governor apparently. As they approached one rider was identified as Robert Baldwin, and another—a startling surprise—was the very man the rebels had been told was their own chief of state, Dr. John Rolph.

The government had decided to gain time, or even peace, by parleying with the rebels. Emissaries whose word the rebels could trust were selected. Bidwell refused to comply, however, and Rolph was invited to take his place. To avoid suspicion and possible arrest, he accepted.

Their message was a promise of full amnesty for the rebels if they would all disperse immediately. Lount and Mackenzie sent the truce mission back for a written document to this effect before conditions for a settlement would even be discussed, but agreed meanwhile to march no farther south than the Red Lion Inn and the Bloor Street toll-gate. This they did. They were now only a mile and a quarter from the edge of the city.

The government meanwhile received news that militia-men were on their way and withdrew their offer. Baldwin and Rolph returned to tell the rebels that the truce was over. Rolph drew Mackenzie aside for a moment and told him the city was still poorly defended and that the rebels should attack as soon as possible.

The delay, however, and the appearance of Rolph as the

Governor's messenger, had an unnerving effect on the rebel forces. Most disturbing of all was their commander's behaviour.

Mackenzie was becoming steadily more excited. A little past noon, near Gallows Hill, he stove in somebody's fence, marched through the property like a little Prussian, and into the neighbouring house. It belonged to Postmaster Howard, and postal mismanagement was one of editor Mackenzie's old sores. He shook a horsewhip in poor Mrs. Howard's face and ordered her cook to prepare dinner immediately for fifty of his men.

Then there was the Bank of Upper Canada; the thought of it, like an old sciatica, made him twinge with pain. Down towards the Bloor Street corner rode Mackenzie, where he made a personal assault upon the home of Dr. Horne of the Bank. He broke in, and after scrimmaging with a dog as large as himself and with as much wool on, he dispatched the beast with a shovel, overturned the kitchen stove, and so burned the house to the ground. Spies were using the place anyway, he was convinced, and if some of them were nesting in the closets, well, a smoking-out would be good for them.

Back at the Howards', the footman had fled in terror, leaving the women and children to fend for themselves. Thither Mackenzie returned, and in such an ugly mood that Lount felt compelled to follow and watch him. Mackenzie finally abandoned his threats, left Lount apologizing to Mrs. Howard, and stamped out to harangue his troops again, who were arguing about the wisdom of any attack on the city that afternoon.

Two hours after the final flag-of-truce mission, Rolph and his friends sent a messenger (one of Rolph's medical students) out from Toronto to look for Mackenzie and urge him to hurry the attack. After much searching, the rebel general was discovered in the early winter dusk, away back at Montgomery's tavern intently cross-questioning an unhappy volunteer of whose loyalty he found cause for suspicion.

175

The intelligence from Rolph, that the Toronto radicals were ready for them and the Tories ill prepared to fight, steadied Mackenzie and snapped him back to the business at hand. It was good tonic too for his army. Most of them by mid-afternoon had been determined to go no nearer Toronto that day. They had decided, by means of rumour, that its citizens were barricaded behind mattresses by their second-storey windows, muskets to hand, and all ready to make blood soup of the first rebel columns that entered the streets.

But the fresh news from Rolph made Mackenzie's next call to battle rather more like a credible promise of success and less like the invitations to immediate martyrdom he had appeared to be issuing earlier. Mackenzie's eloquence, and the steadier portion of the riflemen, prevailed upon the rest, and they all declared themselves ready to go.

In the last of the December twilight, at ten minutes past six, the insurgent army set out south from the Bloor toll-gate. The riflemen made up the van, marching three abreast, with a grim determination in their stride, the stovepipe hats of the more prosperous of them stuck dead on the vertical and transforming the first platoon into a silhouette of moving chimneypots against the last crack of the western sky. Behind them the two hundred pikemen marched, trailing the twenty-foot staves tipped with new-smithied iron, a gesture of respect to the formidable weapon which once had made the Spanish infantry the terror of Europe. The pikes were followed by an oddly assorted crew of musketeers and persons equipped for duckhunting or a turkey shoot. Lastly, by the hundreds, came the shades of the Jacquerie—the great bulk of the army, with their pitchforks and beechroot clubs and thick green willow spears cut from the woods they had come from that day. Around the whole company, shouting orders or breathing out hoarse Gaelic encouragements, a tiny bundled figure on a little white mare darted and hustled and circled, like a sheepdog herding its flock to the fold.

The front ranks had covered over half the mile between the Red Lion and the city edge when they hove into view of Sheriff Jarvis and his advance picket. These had spent the better part of the afternoon crouching, against the Governor's orders and without his knowledge, in the summer vegetable garden of one William Sharpe, Esquire, the back of whose farm figures in twentieth century Canadian history as the site of Maple Leaf Gardens. In the last of the twilight, all the sheriff could see was a group of dark figures led by a horseman, with a little ghost of a pony coming up beside them. But he knew well enough who they were. He had been waiting a long time for this moment. It was eleven years since the day his oldest Jarvis cousin had inspired the fashionable young men of York to give the *Advocate* a ducking in the Bay, and failed to catch Mackenzie.

Sheriff Jarvis sent a whispered order along the snake-rail fence. Twenty-seven muskets poked out, aimed towards the van of the advancing column. In another minute the rebels would be on top of them. They could see, indistinctly, the whole rifle company now, and hear the tramp of more men coming behind. Jarvis stood up, glancing along the row of raised muskets. The ground set up a slight, increasing shudder. He gripped his long pistol and peered out into the dusk at the rebels. A hundred yards off still, but they looked closer. Another long second's wait. Then Jarvis roared out the command.

There was a great flash and blast as the muskets discharged. The rebels were abruptly aware of a thunder and lightning leaping up at them from the roadside ahead.

A scene of dark confusion followed. The Sheriff's twenty-seven musketeers had no sooner fired than they dropped their weapons and began to scatter, forcefully propelled by a sudden certitude of the rebels' keen marksmanship by owl-light.

The Sheriff bugled out curses and commands at his pickets, who were making off every which way into the night, at what was really a dangerous clip, considering the risk of a broken leg from the roughness of terrain and dimness of visibility. But this was clearly no time for considerations of safety or obedience, and the Sheriff failed to hold a single man to the ground.

Lount ordered his front ranks to return the fire, which they did. Then they dropped to the ground to let those behind have a clear shot. But this action was mistaken for the dreadful effects of the enemy's fire. To the riflemen in the rear it appeared that they had lost their bravest comrades at a single blow. For all they could tell, Yonge Street was lined with Tories clear down to Toronto, and another volley would follow directly. Several of the riflemen wheeled and broke the ranks of the pikemen and duckhunters behind. As for the hosts to the rear, it needed nothing more than a few bodies hurtling into their midst, posthaste upon the awful blast, to turn hesitation into panic, and a halt into a rout. Mackenzie chased and screamed at one headlong group after another. He might as well have whistled at a stampede. The general *sauve qui peut* had soon put a mile between the opposing forces.

Lount and a few riflemen held their ground, firing sporadically, until they saw that they had the battlefield to themselves. They could not take Toronto alone, so there was nothing for it but to retire up Yonge Street in search of their army. They discovered most of it, halted at last behind the safety of the Bloor toll-gate, stoutly refusing to be persuaded by Mackenzie and the other leaders to re-form for another attack. The men said they would willingly advance again into the valley of death, but only by daylight, when they could get a good clear squint at who and what might choose to attack them.

Sheriff Jarvis picked himself up off the frozen ground of Mrs. Sharpe's garden, and walked back to Toronto under the total silence of the winter stars. He was not yet aware that he had broken the back of the rebellion.

Through the night Mrs. Sharpe kept watch from her window over the corpse of a cooper from Sharon, a former British soldier, who was the only immediate victim of the picketers' volley. But she saw no more traffic on Yonge Street that evening, and no one returned to break the peace of her garden.

CHAPTER FOURTEEN

IN THE city, Tuesday's condition of confusion and despair was replaced by the increasing confusion, and confidence, of the following day. A spy came down from the tavern, several hours after the battle of Mrs. Sharpe's garden, to report that it had proved to be a victory of decisive proportions, and that the rebels were capable of mounting no further attack for the present. To judge from their state of discouragement and the rate of desertion, the threat would not likely be formidable at any later period. This news in part explains Wednesday's change of mood in Tory Toronto. But the chief source both of new hope and of confusion confounded lay in the various accessions to the city's small company of defenders.

Late Tuesday night the intrepid MacNab arrived by steamer with sixty men of Gore, the district surrounding Hamilton. Sir Francis declared MacNab to be the saviour of his city, and embraced him with an ecstasy which one witness described as hysterical. Sir Francis was the more relieved and overjoyed because of his fond admiration for this virile young favourite. MacNab seemed to share his own very thoughts on the subject of Empire and appeared capable of putting them into action of the most robust and decisive kind, in a way that he envied. Sir Francis named Colonel MacNab his commander-in-chief, and the leader of the attack which must soon be made upon the rebels.

No organizing or planning for this purpose was done, however, either Tuesday night or during the course of the next day, in spite of the need for dealing with the rebels while they were still dispirited and lacking reinforcement. No effort was made, that is, apart from the harried attempts of Colonel Fitzgibbon to arm and reduce to some semblance of military discipline the untrained volunteers who drifted into town all through the day. Fortunately for the state of his mental balance during these exertions, he did not learn until nightfall of MacNab's appointment to a position he thought was his own. His problem was not made easier, even as it was, by the fact that some of the new arrivals had undoubtedly set out from their farms with some notion of joining or watching the rebellion, and upon hearing how things stood at the tavern had decided the most prudent way of avoiding arrest or suspicion was to respond to the government's call to arms. While their lack of training and arms would have lent them dubious value to the morale and power of Mackenzie's company, the presence of their inertia and perfunctory enthusiasm undoubtedly contributed further to the military disorganization of Toronto, and made Colonel Fitzgibbon's task no easier.

The Radicals in the city also decided that the rebellion was, for all practical purposes, finished. Dr. Rolph sent a message to Mackenzie with the advice to disband his army. Then, with little black bag in hand, he set out by foot at a leisurely pace through the town, greeted Chief Justice Robinson in passing, and in the first stretch of open country mounted the colt which one of his students had arranged to bring him, and made good his escape to the American border. Dr. Morrison, who actually was on his professional rounds that morning, was stopped just as he passed the Mackenzie's place in York Street, and arrested on a charge of treason.

Mackenzie himself received Rolph's message, and ignored it; attempted a military review of his remaining five hundred troops, and failed to improve their spirits or their state of preparation; stopped to cut one of Sheriff Jarvis' bullets from between a man's toes, but shook so that he gashed himself instead. Two of the men seriously wounded in Tuesday's skirmish died from loss of blood.

Hope was now chiefly placed in the arrival of reinforcements and the Napoleonic veteran, Colonel Van Egmond, both being expected to appear on Thursday, the day originally set for the rebellion. Mackenzie, meanwhile, continued in a frenzy of business. He dispatched messages to his ally in the west of the province, Dr. Charles Duncombe, who had managed to raise a small rebellion there. Then Mackenzie led a small force of mounted gunmen down to intercept the western mail which was approaching Toronto by Dundas Street. He stepped out of cover as the stage coach pulled up to the Peacock Inn, and brought it to an abrupt halt by waving his pistol at the driver. With the efficiency of a bandit, Mackenzie lined up the passengers at gunpoint, relieved them of their ready cash, which the rebels' exchequer badly needed, and ransacked the mail bags in search of more money, and dispatches on the state of the western militia and the progress of Duncombe's rising.

One poor woman, according to a Tory account, "he robbed of *her all*". The incident in fact amounted to no more than the seizure of the contents of a large portmanteau, over her impassioned protest, but it started the legend, still prevalent, about Mackenzie's flight to the frontier in female disguise. It is probably safe to say that no action of Mackenzie's was ever prompted by motives of personal insurance against total defeat, even if he expected such defeat. His next move was also devoid of any mere prudence or calculation. He had discovered that highway robbery was to his taste; and at the same moment he was sure that it was a necessary part of the strategy of rebellion. He proceeded to attack other travellers and take them prisoner to the inn, where he threatened, robbed and cross-questioned them. The whole performance helped give some credence to Governor Head's accusation that Mackenzie's object in the rebellion was to rob banks and pillage the countryside, an accusation which was entirely false even if, after the bizarre fashion of its maker, entirely sincere.

Mackenzie caused his companions to fear for his sanity, when he began rummaging again among the mailbags to extract private correspondence of no military use whatsoever. He appeared at an upstairs window of the inn, from which he scattered all the newspapers in the postbags broadside upon the gentlemen prisoners in the yard below.

The whole episode is, on a grosser scale, very like one of his earlier outbursts of journalistic invective: the first salvo of words uttered generating a fierce elation, which in turn inspired him to stronger language but less careful aim, and so on until some event intervened or the frenzy subsided. Mackenzie's gratuitous zest for the role of desperado brings to mind the same unspecified, but always "bold, delightful, dangerous course" in which he had once invited the readers of his newspaper to join him.

At dusk, Mackenzie's attention returned to the main business in hand, which was to prepare for the morrow's battle. He and his troop rode back to their headquarters at Montgomery's.

The authorities in Toronto had also decided at last to engage in some definite military planning. A council of war was summoned that Wednesday evening to the Archdeacon's pro-episcopal palace overlooking the Bay. There in the large well-appointed library (the one thing for which Mackenzie deeply envied Dr. Strachan), Governor Head and several of the leading members of the Compact assembled. For obvious reasons, Colonel Fitzgibbon was also invited. But before matters had got very far, the hero of 1812 and the city's most active defender became aware of the unspeakably dismal fact that the upstart MacNab, not he himself, was now the supreme military commander. Still more distressing, MacNab proposed to attack in the middle of the night, with the motley collection of individuals which Fitzgibbon in broad daylight had not so much as managed to form into companies. It is certain that a midnight descent upon the tavern by an unorganized host of gallant officers and unsteady men, each one more or less manoeuvring on his own, would have spread consternation and confusion far surpassing that of the affair in Mrs. Sharpe's garden. But whether this effect would now be to the government's advantage was doubtful in the extreme.

The meeting decided that MacNab's plan might damage the prestige of their cause and so invite further uprisings in the province. Hagerman said that if their first attack upon the rebels did not end in decisive victory, the government's position was hopeless. Fitzgibbon quit the Archdeacon's council of war, in a very black temper, before it was over. Early Thursday morning, however, he was told that MacNab had released Sir Francis from his promise of the command. There was to be an attack today, and Fitzgibbon was to lead it. He set to work immediately.

"It was now broad daylight and I had to commence an organization of the most difficult nature I had ever known. I had to ride to the Town Hall and to the Garrison and back again, repeatedly. I found few of the officers present who were wanted for the attack. Vast numbers of volunteers were constantly coming in from the country without arms or appointments of any kind, who were crowding in all directions in my way till at length the organization appeared impossible." For a moment the strain of his week's struggle against inertia and his three nights' lack of sleep, together with the most recent indignity offered him, were too much to bear. "My mind was burning with indignation at the idea of Colonel MacNab or any other officer being thought of by his Excellency for the command. I became overwhelmed with the intensity and contrariety of my feelings. I walked to and fro without object, until I found the eyes of many fixed upon me, when I fled to my room and locked my door, exclaiming audibly that the Province was lost, and that I was ruined, fallen." The poor man fell on his knees to pray.

When he emerged again from his room he found that some miracle of Providence had moved one company to form of its own volition. His heart lightened, and he marched the company immediately down to the space in front of the Archdeacon's palace. With this unit as a nucleus, he managed to arrange all his twelve hundred men into companies, arm them, assign them officers, and draw them up beside the first.

Sir Francis Head trotted out before the array on his big stallion. At the officer's request, on the stroke of noon, he gave the order for a general advance. The first column wheeled north, and Yonge Street was soon one long parade. To the thump and tune of two bands, and the accompaniment of much cheering from windows and flag-waving from rooftops, the brave boys were tramping out to uphold the Empire and the honour of their new young Queen, Victoria. Such a stirring righteous sight it made that several of the Mackenzie radicals in the crowd joined the shouting with more than perfunctory enthusiasm.

At the head rode Colonels Fitzgibbon and MacNab; in the midst, Sir Francis, stiff and tiny, a hero again for the day, and black-cloaked John Strachan with a young priest attendant. Two cannon rolled north under the watchful eye of Major Carfrae, an artillery officer utterly content in his call from retirement. As the militia disappeared through the distant Bloor toll-gate, the sun glinted on bayonet and musket, and made sudden yellow flares of the brass, whose music carried away out of the city's sound and across the fields on a fresh rising breeze. The last glimpse from St. James' spire was of a straggle of spectators as they followed the silent army up Gallows Hill, eager for a view of battle.

The evil genius who had chiefly inspired the military pomp and wrathful, resolute patriotism now closing upon Montgomery's tavern, spent his morning in an agony of frustration and fitful hope. His renewed proposal for an attack had been squashed again, and all he could do was wait and watch for the reinforcements which in the end never came.

Mackenzie's chosen commander, however, old Colonel Van Egmond, was as good as his word. He arrived from Lake Huron at eight o'clock and with warm welcome was sat down to breakfast in the tavern beside the rebel leaders. It was not long before a commotion broke out in the breakfast room, clearly audible to those outside. The old veteran had expected to command something more like an army than the few hundred badly equipped volunteers he was given. But with a good will, he began to outline a plan for defending their position until help should arrive from the back country. Mackenzie told him it was an attack, not a last stand, that he had been invited to undertake. Van Egmond's temper stirred a little. To attack was stark madness, he told Mackenzie. Blunt and bitter words were exchanged, in the course of which Mackenzie threatened to have the old gentleman taken out and shot. Lount managed to make explanations to Van Egmond, and quiet Mackenzie. They then agreed to send sixty of their best riflemen down to the Don Bridge to cut off the eastern end of the town and to divert the government from its plan of action, whatever that might prove to be. The meeting over, Van Egmond tried to review his troops, but without much esthetic effect or noticeable change in morale. He then explained to them what should be done in case of an early enemy attack.

A scout arrived who said he had seen the militia leaving the city. The report was discounted; several false alarms had been received earlier in the morning. For an hour or more the men mostly idled in and about the stableyard of the tavern. The noon sun was hot in spite of the season and had melted the powdering of snow on the frozen ground. Several of the men dozed. Their party of riflemen was still absent, and only two hundred of those left behind were armed at all.

A little way down Yonge Street one of the sentinels thought he heard music. It seemed as if it had come from below Gallows Hill. In a moment musketeers appeared on the distant brow. He relayed word back to the tavern and followed swiftly after.

The news burst upon the stableyard. "Seize your arms, men! The enemy's coming, and no mistake!" Mackenzie and Van Egmond galloped down to a point of vantage from where they could see company after company rising over the brow of the hill.

One hundred and fifty rebel troops were hustled half a

mile south where they took up positions in a small wood on rising land to the west of Yonge Street. Several dozen more were sent just off the road to the east, to place themselves behind stump fences and brush heaps. The rest of the rebels were without arms, and stayed behind to take cover in the tavern with the prisoners.

As the rebels opened fire upon them, the first militia columns spread out on both sides of the road, and then continued their steady advance. Major Carfrae stopped and methodically turned his guns around. The heavy shot began crashing into the rebels' wood, followed by a scattering of musket fire. The whistling of the shot overhead and the crack of falling timber unnerved the rebels and shook their aim. But they suffered no casualties for several minutes and managed to hold their ground.

It was then that Colonel Fitzgibbon's foresight quickly settled the issue. He had sent two detachments out of the city on either flank of the main body, several hundred yards from Yonge Street. The western flank, itself as large as the whole rebel force, suddenly appeared close in to the right of the little wood. The rebels abandoned their ground and began a retreat towards the tavern. Several were dropped by the militia's muskets. A cannon ball chased along the field after them, bumping and rolling into their midst, with no damage done but terrifying effect. Rifles were abandoned and the retreat looked as if it would fail to stop at the tavern. The cannon were moved north and a ball flew straight through Montgomery's dining room window and out the other wall. The two hundred unarmed rebels swarmed out of doors and windows and scattered into the fields to the north. The prisoners had already been freed a minute earlier. Mackenzie and the other leaders galloped off northwards in full flight to escape capture. The battle was lost in less than half an hour. The rebellion was immedicably broken.

Sir Francis Head rode up to the tavern and ordered that it should be burned to mark the death of "that perfidious enemy, responsible government". But several of the enemy's henchmen were still at large. Affairs would not be easily settled until William Lyon Mackenzie was captured. Fitzgibbon and several other officers chased him up Yonge Street and across the fields for several miles, but in the end they lost him. A proclamation was composed while the flames still shot high from the tavern roof, and a four-day hunt began across the province.

Mackenzie and a group of companions struck out for the western part of the province, crossed the Humber River not far from Toronto on a small unguarded footbridge, and with posses of loyalists scouring the countryside for them, tramped from one friendly farmhouse to the next, taking shelter, supper, change of clothes and finally the night's rest, which were warmly offered them.

The next day they decided to separate and head two by two for the American frontier. Mackenzie and his partner, a husky lad of nineteen, walked west in broad daylight along a concession parallel to the main road for Dundas and Niagara. A number of people were spoken with, all of them friendly, whether they had heard of the rebellion or not. An American-born farmer and his wife stopped the two fugitives to give them dinner and sent them on their way with a horse, a farm wagon, and an Irish servant to drive. With more regard for luck and the natural goodness of man than for common sense, Mackenzie directed their course right on to the main Dundas highway, still saluting passersby, many of whom knew perfectly well who he was.

He saw bills being posted offering a thousand pound reward for his capture, learned that he was wanted, inevitably, for high treason, and was told that Colonel Chisholm and three hundred of the hottest Orangemen were divided into parties searching the district for him. The warning and the bills did nothing to dissuade him from travel by highway and the light of day. "York was the county which I had been chosen seven times to represent by its freeholders." If anyone was outlaw here, in Mackenzie's mind, it was Colonel Chisholm and his Orangemen. He surveyed the landscape as it jolted slowly past his creaky rustic substitute for a coach and four, glaring proudly about him as if he owned every farm.

The pride of rightful possession did not abstract Mackenzie entirely from the business at hand, which was to avoid the enemy. Of a sudden his sharp eye picked out a mounted patrol coming up the road to their rear. It was still a tolerable distance back, but closing on them rapidly. Mackenzie snatched the reins from their Irish driver, and the cart went careening towards the bridge at the Sixteen Mile Creek. A glance over the shoulder and he could see that the horsemen were armed and gaining on them. Almost to the bridge, they saw another company of horsemen making ready to receive them on the opposite side. But before this bridge guard could warn or shoot, Mackenzie and the younger rebel dived from the hurtling cart and scrambled into the forest.

At the first clearing they asked a labourer for the road to a north-easterly village to throw their pursuers off the track, and a minute later dropped down into the deep ravine of the creek in the thickest part of the forest to the west. The heavy November rains and a snowfall or two had turned the stream into a brimming torrential river. There was no alternative but to try fording it.

"We stripped ourselves naked, and with the surface ice beating against us, and holding our garments over our heads, in a bitterly cold December night, we buffeted the current, and were soon up to our necks. I hit my foot against a stone, let fall some of my clothes (which my companion caught) and cried aloud with pain. The cold in that stream caused me the most cruel and intense sensation of pain I ever endured. We got through, though with a better chance of drowning. The frozen sand on the bank seemed to warm our feet when we once more trod upon it."

Mackenzie knew the country well enough to discover in the dark another friendly farm, where they received food and warm flannels and a short rest while the farmer's sons and daughters took posts around the approaches to the house, watching through the long bitter evening, and ready to pass on the alarm to the house should a search party draw near.

Just before 11 p.m., the fugitives set out again, negotiated the Twelve Mile Creek on a fallen tree about midnight, and after dodging off the road into the woods to watch a party of armed horsemen gallop by, reached Burlington near the head of the lake by daybreak. Mackenzie's young companion, by now suffering from shock and exhaustion, was left at the house of a friend. Mackenzie went on alone. It began to snow and his tracks showed plainly. He was refused admittance at one place which had been searched twice already by Allan MacNab's men. Another farmer led Mackenzie to his barn, but instead Mackenzie chose to hide on a tiny thatched peaserick which stood on a little knoll and which the pigs had undermined all round. In no time the district sheriff, Colonel McDonell, was searching the premises with his posse, and Mackenzie looked on while they poked into every building and stack on the property except the one he was crouching on.

"When the coast seemed clear, my terrified host, a wealthy Canadian, came up the hill as if to feed his pigs, brought me two bottles of hot water for my feet, a bottle of tea, and several slices of bread and butter; told me that the neighbourhood was literally harassed with bodies of armed men in search of me, and advised that I should leave that place at dark, but where to go he could not tell me. After I had left his premises he was arrested, but he had powerful friends, gave bail, and the matter ended there." Before setting out again Mackenzie found his feet so swollen that he had to leave his boots behind and make his way in a pair of large borrowed slippers.

The dangers of the flight and the concentration of his will upon a simple, possible purpose evoked a calm and complete sanity in Mackenzie for the first time in several weeks, as well as a virtuoso's skill in eluding the enemy and drawing closer to his goal.

It was a late silent Saturday night when he passed through

Dundas, where he had once profitably purveyed books and medicines from his well-kept small store. A stranger hailed him on the road and passed quickly on. There was a guard stationed at the hotel but Mackenzie went by unchallenged. Crossing the square, he glanced towards the large, prosperous-looking house he had built and brought his young wife to fifteen years before. He forded the creek which ran right beside the house, and made for the high land of the Niagara escarpment above him.

A man near Ancaster lent him a horse, but it did him little good at that point for he spent the night wandering in a thick wood, leading the animal about by the halter, and for the only time on his journey, hopelessly lost. A Negro cottager put him on the right way in the first grey of the morning. Riding into a village he did not know, he was startled to find himself greeted by name in a manner that caused him to give his horse the spur, though he later discovered that all was well intended.

He took breakfast with a burly Orangeman from Belfast and his large family, who gave no sign of recognition or suspicion. The horse was watered and fed and the Orangeman began to conduct him, at Mackenzie's request, down to the main road to the frontier. Suddenly Mackenzie protested that he was surely being led the wrong way. " 'Not to the road,' said I. 'No, but to Mr. McIntyre, the magistrate,' said he. Here we came to a full stop."

But it was not for a rebel that he was taken. The big Irishman's "leading idea was that I was in the habit of borrowing other men's horses; since I had come to his house on a Sunday morning, with my clothes torn, my face badly scratched, my horse all in a foam, paid a dollar for a very humble breakfast, and was making for the frontier by the most unfrequented paths on one of the finest horses in Canada."

Mackenzie now had a loaded revolver with him, but he chose not to use it. Rather than risk the man's life by a violent attempt to escape, he decided to sound out his captor's political opinions. "I talked to him about the civil broils, Mackenzie, party spirit and Dr. Strachan; and found to my great surprise that, though averse to the object of revolt, he spoke of myself in terms of goodwill." Delighted, Mackenzie showed the initials on his watch and his linen to the astonished Ulsterman, and was sent on his way with a hearty blessing.

Mackenzie travelled over half the length of the Niagara peninsula that Sunday morning, slowing down and pretending as best he could to be on his way to church when in sight of a patrol. Along one stretch of road he asked his way of Methodists who were bound for their meeting. Some of these put an armed party of horsemen on his trail, not, Mackenzie believed, for the sake of the Governor's reward, but out of deference to conscience and to Egerton Ryerson's opinion of Radicals. The pursuers were slipped again by Mackenzie's swift turn on to the road for St. Catharines and then a sudden doubling back into a friend's stable from where he watched them charge past and on out of sight.

He took dinner at the farm house and here met one Samuel Chandler, a wagon-maker, who insisted on conducting Mackenzie personally to the border, although he risked the noose or a trip to Australia, and disaster for his family of twelve, by doing it. They reached the Niagara River on foot by Monday morning after dodging more guards, only to find all the bankdwellers' boats seized and removed by the authorities, and an order out to halt or fire on Canadian craft discovered in the river.

Chandler found a certain Captain McAfee, however, who had locked one of his boats in the shed, and who offered to row the traitor and his accomplice across, the more readily because his Yankee forebears had done some sniping at the British in 1776. The Captain's wife placed a huge breakfast in front of the three men to prepare them for the hazards and exertions of the river. Before eating, Mackenzie stepped outside to scan the river road. To his dismay he spotted, but a few hundred yards away, what he concluded to be Colonel Kerby, the Customs Officer, jogging down the road with his troop of green-coated dragoons, their carbines obviously ready for use. Captain McAfee rushed to his shed, the boat was hauled to the water. The three men were scarcely afloat when the Colonel trotted up to the front yard and dismounted to make a routine inquiry. Mrs. McAfee and her daughters were out to greet him. They talked with desperate invention while over the Colonel's gold brocaded shoulder they saw their lord and master pulling furiously out into the swift Niagara current. For a dreadful five minutes the boat lay in easy range of the dragoons, and doubtless would have been fired upon had Colonel Kerby, unlike a few of his men who turned judiciously away from what they glimpsed in the river, been able to divert his attention from Madam and the Misses McAfee.

The boat steered for Grand Island and after a few more desperate minutes it was out of range, then out of sight. Within the hour Mackenzie was safe on the American shore.

When a politician reaches his early forties it is not unusual for his friends to begin describing him as "young". His political apprenticeship is over; the rewards of his labour and the achievements of his ambitions lie just ahead. At forty-two, Mackenzie's political career was finished.

He could look forward to spending the years of maturity, sometimes in jail and always in debt, in a country which he found the more foreign the longer he lived there. He would pass his time first in plotting an invasion of Canada, then in composing pathetic letters of penitence and pleas for the right to come home. And always, when he could put his hands on a few dollars and a printing press, compulsively, almost in the manner of an addict, he would publish, expose, hang out his neighbours' dirty linen for them with all possible publicity.

The exile left behind him a countryside in which, as his last journey testifies, he was more widely known than any other politician of his own day and perhaps of any other. He left, too, something of that veneration which an unsophisticated people pays to the saints, even to the cantankerous ones. His impetuosity, his courage, his unselfishness, and his capacity for indignation and suspicion were all so bold in outline, so much larger than life, that they were plain and appealing to the simplest of country folk, and to these indeed more than any. The omnipresent image of Mackenzie had become pasted and affixed on the community mind like the layers of political posters which remain after a hard-fought campaign.

Mackenzie left behind him, too, a bookselling business, prosperous enough to have given most men pause to think about the wisdom of an agitator's career in the first place, and, with these, his newspaper, a fine new press, and several thousand dollars' worth of credit notes and property.

It cost him no little anguish to put upon his large and dependent family the anxiety they felt for him through early December of 1837. For all his persistent life-long refusal to put their well-being ahead of his own concern for public justice, Mackenzie was far more deeply attached to wife and mother and children than are most men. He had no intimate friends and there were few whose acquaintance was not primarily of a political nature. Beneath his fiery outward manner—his way of shying at a world which had no place to fit him—he reserved all his tenderness and affection for his little flock at home. One must admit that such a lot as this is almost a commonplace in the biographies of public men, but it is no less poignant for that. For the Mackenzies, their exile would mean that the worry and small hardships of life in Upper Canada would give way to years of penury and heartbreak in a foreign country. Such bearable ills as cold and hunger and disease would visit them, and the death of a little girl. Perhaps saddest of all were the long and increasingly frequent spells of silent fixed unapproachability in the man whose quick spirits and ebullient hopefulness in the old times could take the chill from the bitterest days and the bleakest of prospects. In the coming years in the Mackenzie household, a whole month might pass without the sound of children's laughter, though there were many children and they had once laughed, like their father when he was among them, a great deal.

Mackenzie's ruin was more than a personal one. If the rebellion itself exhibited certain features of the comedy of errors and the comedy of manners, it appeared in its dénouement to approach the level of high tragedy, for it involved the undoing of noble men and a whole society to suffer the event.

The good Colonel Van Egmond, for whom the sequel to Waterloo was the battle of Montgomery's tavern, far from being allowed to fade away in a gentle glory, after the fashion of old soldiers, most emphatically died, several days after his capture, from an illness caught in the cold and filthy Toronto jail cell. Besides a wife and eight young children, Captain Anthony Anderson left a reputation for courage and kindness which was a legend in his neighbourhood long before 1837. But he was a traitor and doubtless would have been executed had he survived. Samuel Lount was tried, convicted and sent to the public scaffold. Pleas for mercy from his wife and friends were rejected by the new Governor, a professional administrator called Arthur, for he was concerned to furnish a public example of the response of British justice to high treason. There were other executions in the course of 1838, much to the satisfaction of the more vindictive Tories. Ninety-two men were sentenced to be transported as convicts to Van Dieman's Land at the other end of the world. To the hundreds of labourers whom the activities of Sir Francis Head and the hard times of 1836-37 had set moving to the United States must be added the many who escaped like Mackenzie or who voluntarily decamped, and never set foot in Canada again.

The loss of some of their boldest and most outspoken spirits in dozens of little communities through the province had scarcely the most salutary effect upon the communities themselves. And there was a time of suspicion and meanness, of guilt proven by simple accusation, and of accusation commonest against those most generous in their past criticism of the Family Compact's Canada. In spite of the coming tides of immigration one wonders if these things did not leave some small mark on the temper of the country, if they did not help put a premium upon caution and upon that unimaginative and narrowly conceived self-interest which is not peculiarly, but yet still quite typically Canadian.

One further loss must be recorded. Marshall Spring Bidwell, though he was in no way involved in the uprising, was summoned by Governor Head and given the choice of immediate exile with the promise never to return to Upper Canada, or of standing trial and facing implication in the rebels' plan, a case in which Attorney-General Hagerman would have been only too anxious to invent and prosecute. He chose to return to his native country and never so much as asked to come back. So Canada lost the man who most clearly of all the characters in this portion of her history ought to have been Prime Minister, and of all her Prime Ministers might well have been one of the best.

Upper Canada was a very different place in the 1840's. Through its thick woods and icy rivers there fled with Mackenzie that December a whole era of Canadian politics. A political temper had disappeared: violent, crude, tawdrily melodramatic, over-quick to take offence, but not lacking in the barbarian's vivid sense of honour and justice. Bishop Strachan and Chief Justice Robinson retired from politics to perform full time beneath the mitre and the high curled wig. MacNab, though he erupted once more, was a spent volcano and his antediluvian Toryism was replaced by the conservative moderation of Robert Baldwin. The Orangemen and their proliferating lodges continued to thrive but they now upheld the Empire with the twin pillars of moral law and the suspicion of Rome, and no longer by the big stick and the bloody cockscomb. And within a month of Mackenzie's last hurried passage through his home stamping-ground Sir Francis Head resigned for the last time, as usual as a threat to his shallying, temporizing superiors, and his resignation was finally accepted.

The aristocracy and the common people disappeared as the two political polarities and soon merged their identity and their ideals in an amorphous middle class. The parties which once stood for principles, and thrived on such fundamental issues as that of democracy versus paternalism, were on their way to being replaced by the parties which are brokers in public opinion and like two big department stores cater tolerably well to all tastes and needs in the same market. The era of Tories and Radicals was to give way before that predominance of liberal-conservatives and conservative liberals which the Clear Grits and their heirs have never really broken.

The short hills and comfortable farms of southern Ontario, so Edenic in their greenness and so serenely unnoticing of the taut angularity of their Puritan inhabitants, were restored again to their paradisal untroublement. The brothers and sisters of peace took forever the pledge against the cheap gin of rebellion and political wildness. At a slow summer pace the land began a century's growth of elms and fat barns and Holsteins, of caution and sobriety and decency, and the begetting of generations of those who, for all their asperity of aspect and straitened conception of the permissible, were mild, solid, kindly men and women.

CHAPTER FIFTEEN

THE SPIRIT of rebellion crossed the Niagara with Mackenzie. It had quit the country, perhaps forever. But if rebellion was over and done with in Canada, it had only just begun for the Americans along the border. Mackenzie, once he was among them and had slept his first unharried sleep in a fortnight, was quite ready to join them in their enthusiasm for his cause. He arrived in Buffalo to find its citizens in a state of high excitement, ardently hoping for the success of this new American revolution. One of his own letters, sent on to a Buffalo newspaper just before the final battle, arrived several hours ahead of him, to confirm their opinion of the rebels' purpose.

> Reformers of this part of Upper Canada, [wrote Mackenzie from Montgomery's tavern] in defence of the principle of independence of European domination, have taken up arms—in plain words, they wish this Province to be a free, sovereign and independent state. They request all the assistance which the free citizens of your Republic may choose to afford.

On the night of his arrival, several of Mackenzie's American friends summoned a huge public meeting. The crowd was plied with rhetorical questions. Would they help a man whose cause was the same as that which bought their freedom and made them a nation? Or would they send him back to face British tyranny alone? A Canadian Patrick Henry had put his life in their hands: would they give him liberty—or death? Like Patrick Henry himself, Mackenzie was eventually given neither choice; but the crowd roared out the right answers. This done, they were promised that Mackenzie in person would appear before them the following night. A guard of young men volunteered to defend the house where he slept from seekers after the British reward, and the meeting broke up in a fervour of indignant satisfaction.

Mackenzie spoke to the largest crowd that had ever assembled in Buffalo. He was not the man to resist telling a sympathetic audience what it was disposed to hear. When he was finished, one Thomas Jefferson Sutherland rose to say that he was crossing the border to join the Canadians in their fight for independence. He invited volunteers to come with him. A friend of Sutherland's announced that he was arranging for contributions of arms and ammunition: would they be left, please, at the Eagle Tavern.

The following day, less than a week after he had fled the battlefield, Mackenzie was again on Canadian soil, this time as the chief of state of a new Canadian republic. The first volunteers crossed with him to Navy Island, near the Canadian mainland and three miles from the brink of Niagara Falls, on December 13th, 1837. Here Mackenzie raised the Patriot tricolour, with its twin stars for the two Canadas, and, as "Chairman, *pro tem.*" of the provisional government, promised rewards of Canadian land and silver for every new recruit.

It was like Mackenzie—he had done the same thing on becoming Mayor of Toronto—to occupy himself immediately with the designing of a Great Seal. This emblem, featuring the device of a new moon breaking through the darkness, was placed on a long proclamation which called on Canadians to rise against their oppressors, and offered a reward of £500 for the bringing of Sir Francis Head to justice for his crimes against the people. Copies were to be printed and broadcast through Upper Canada. It was also like Mackenzie to decide that one of the first requirements of a new nation was a printing press, and some stirring handbills for its intended citizens.

He had not been long on Navy Island before he had news that Duncombe's rising was long since put down and all Patriot activity in the province abandoned. As for the strength of the Loyalist government, he could fairly well see for himself the growing numbers of Colonel MacNab's militia as it patrolled the Canadian shore in wait for him.

Although British residents of the United States were at first in the majority among the Navy Island volunteers, the fate of the adventure lay increasingly in the hands of the American public. From this source there proceeded a generous anarchy of enthusiasm. "There is excitement here," wrote a visitor to Rochester, "forty soldiers marching the streets today under drum and fife; two pieces of cannon went off this morning, and three-fourths of the people here, I learn, are encouraging and supporting the cause of the patriots." The scene in Rochester was typical of what happened in a hundred towns in upstate New York during that December of 1837.

Mackenzie on Navy Island received a deluge of letters every day, beginning "Dear General" or "The Honourable W. L. Mackenzie" and announcing the dispatch of such items as a brass cannon, 117 loaves of bread, $311.00, fourteen kegs of powder, two loads of beef and pork, or a caravan of supplies—"the country folk are doing wonders." An anxious mother wrote to say she was sending "five blankets in a box, one for John Sheldon of Lockport and the remainder for any destitute volunteer." Long and learned counsel on the defence of Navy Island or the secret of success in surprise attacks, or the principles of war, was freely given by an American militia officer, by a West Point graduate, by a former colonel in the Prussian army. One who had "followed the greatest cavalry officer in the world, Murat, from the deserts of Africa to the plains of Russia", promised, though old and poor, if they would give his boy a commission in the cavalry, to "send you my son, the last descendant of a noble line of warlike commanders of France."

Surgeons offered to come and attend the wounded; secretaries of little societies plied Mackenzie with invitations to speak at recruiting drives. Two young men, freshmen, one suspects, at Harvard or Princeton University, offered themselves earnestly "for liberty, and against a cruel tyranny that has slaughtered hundreds", not failing to add that they could obtain any necessary references from Garret D. Wall, United States Senator, or Peter P. Vroom, ex-Governor of New Jersey. "We are both about twenty years of age and it may not be improper for us to state that our families are amongst the most respectable in the state of New Jersey" and that "our fathers hold high stations in its government". The young gentlemen had the Honour to be, With great respect, Mr. Mackenzie's Most Obedient Humble Servants, Clinton Westcott and Beakes Rossell.

The great volume of promises, when translated into things and men that actually reached the river and were ferried to Navy Island by the paddlesteamer *Caroline*, meant that towards the end of December the new republic had acquired a tolerably equipped and almost comfortably supplied, if shivering, army of two hundred volunteers. The provisional government had also acquired a military commander who had taken entire charge of the situation, and effectively blocked Mackenzie's urgent requests for an immediate invasion of Canada. This was a somewhat dissolute person by the name of Rensselaer Van Rensselaer, the scion of an illustrious old family with an estate on the Hudson River, and son of the General Van Rensselaer who had fought Brock in the War of 1812. He hoped to gain for Canada the same independence Sam Houston had just won for the new sovereign republic of Texas. By virtue of his father's military reputation, and some stories which were invented about his own, he managed to acquire full command of the forces on Navy Island. Dr. John Rolph, who was appealed to in Lewiston, would take no direct part in the venture, but he did give Van Rensselaer his blessing, along with the advice that he should arrest any member of the executive who tried to interfere with military operations—meaning, of course, Mackenzie. He considered

Mackenzie's rashness during the fall of 1837, not his own prudent hesitation, to have been the chief cause for the failure of the rebellion.

When word reached the Mackenzie household that its lord and master was safe in Buffalo, it was the first time since mid-November that his family could be tolerably certain he was out of harm's way and Tory clutches. The news was followed swiftly by the intelligence that he had crossed back to Canadian soil and was established on Navy Island. Isabel decided that she at least would be one citizen of the new state of Upper Canada to stand at her husband's side. She left the children and old Mrs. Mackenzie with her sister, and set out alone for the frontier. There was a story told among her grandchildren that she overheard two men talking of the rebellion as the coach neared Buffalo, and that they were speculating on a new rumour that Mackenzie was dead. Her heart stopped a moment. But when they decided he must be either drowned or hanged by now, she was hugely relieved, certain again that he was safe. She knew he would never meet death by rope or water: he had been born with a caul, his head hooded in the unbroken membrane at birth. His wife's and mother's deep-rooted conviction that he led a charmed life may indeed have been one reason why it was second nature for Mackenzie himself to face every peril with such reckless impunity.

"Isabel Mackenzie," wrote her son-in-law, "was the only female who spent any length of time on Navy Island. She remained nearly a fortnight with her husband (until ill-health obliged her to leave), making flannel cartridge-bags, and inspiring with her courage, by her entire freedom from fear, all with whom she conversed."

The trip of the S.S. *Caroline* on which Isabel Mackenzie was ferried, along with a load of cannon, to Navy Island, was to be the steamer's last. That night, the next but two to the end of the year, Colonel MacNab ordered his naval subordinates to cross to the American shore, seize the steamer, cut her loose, and destroy her. The job was not done without a skirmish, in which one American was killed and several men on both sides were wounded. Mackenzie, still up and about on Navy Island, around 1:00 a.m. observed a fire rise from the American shore, then move out towards him into the main current of the river, where he saw it to be a flaming ship. It then floated swiftly away down river towards the Falls. Several minutes later the distant fireship was suddenly engulfed by darkness.

If American opinion was excited before the *Caroline* affair, it was dangerously angry for weeks afterwards. British troops had invaded United States territory and destroyed life and property. The frontier towns cried out for war with England. The Governor of New York and President Van Buren, who had just begun making some attempts to restrain the Patriots and prevent them involving the country in war, were now compelled to ride a little way with the tide of public indignation in the frontier towns. Prosecutions for breach of American neutrality laws would have to be postponed until quieter times. In Canada, public expressions of hatred for all things American, and enthusiastic celebrations over the burning of the *Caroline* did nothing to reduce American indignation. And to set an official seal on the episode, Colonel MacNab was knighted for his exertions in defence of the frontier.

Months later Mackenzie was still doing his best to fan the coals of American indignation, by the publication of a paper called *The Caroline Almanac*. A nightmarish picture of the *Caroline* all aflame, with her bow about to dip into Niagara's giant horseshoe, garnished the front page. Mackenzie pointed out to his American readers the horror-stricken passengers at the ship's rail, being borne to their double doom of fire and water. Yet he must have been told by then that there was no one aboard the *Caroline* once she was cut loose, even if he had never troubled to find out that in fact she sank in the river long before reaching the Falls. Pen in hand, however, Mackenzie could not easily resist a dramatic effect, above all when it corresponded to the scale of the grand dramatic purpose he intended it to serve. It is useless to complain that Mackenzie was by now growing increasingly dishonest. He now habitually indulged in the disarming practice of convincing himself in advance that whatever he chose the facts to be, just that they were.

In January of 1838, pressure from the American authorities was quietly put upon the committee of Buffalo citizens who were engaged in forwarding supplies and volunteers to Navy Island, to discontinue their activities. When they went to an auction to buy another steamer, the United States commandant in that region outbid them for it, and purchased the ship himself.

Two weeks after the burning of the *Caroline* the Patriots were forced to abandon Navy Island and return to the United States. They lacked adequate equipment and their morale was dismally lowered by MacNab's steady bombardment and much bickering between Mackenzie and his military commander. The troops' arms, some of which had been stolen from American arsenals, were seized by the United States army. Rensselaer Van Rensselaer was arrested as he stepped ashore, for breach of the neutrality laws. The Canadian Republic evaporated. It was no longer alive by so much as a single handbill, or the enthusiasm of one designer of Great Seals.

Van Rensselaer received a letter of rebuke from the first celebrated victim of the Family Compact, Robert Gourlay, who was banished to the United States nearly twenty years earlier.

> Never was hallucination more blinding than yours, [wrote Gourlay]. At a moment of profound peace, putting on armour and led by the little editor of a blackguard newspaper, entering the lists of civil broil, and erecting your standard on Navy Island, to defy the armies of Britain! David before Goliath seemed little; but God was with him. What are you, in the limbo of vanity, with no stay but the devil?

In spite of this advice, Van Rensselaer headed for the St. Lawrence River border with a party of volunteers as soon as he was free to do so. He even asked "the devil" to go along but the invitation was curtly refused. The fever of American indignation mounted higher. It spread into Ohio and Michigan and northeastern New York, and for two years the frontier from Prescott to Detroit was alive with incident.

On leaving Navy Island Mackenzie refused to have further dealings with Van Rensselaer, although he was invited on the next expedition. He pledged his gold watch to raise the price of a one-way trip to Rochester for himself and Isabel, and they took up residence there. He was soon publishing a newspaper again, on borrowed money. During the rest of 1838 and on into 1839, he still agitated for the cause of Canadian independence by means of his inflammatory journalism and by speaking to a series of mass meetings in New York, Philadelphia and other cities in the northeastern states. Sometimes at first, the old hope flared up again that Canadian independence could be gained by a series of raids along the miles of unguarded frontier. "To defend it," he wrote in the spring of 1838, "would be ruinous to the government of Great Britain, still more to that of Canada. The end will be a break-up, and I mean to stick to them like wax, as do the others of our party." Certain of the Patriot leaders, however, decided that Mackenzie was a dangerous nuisance, and did their best to exclude him from their plans. He was unable to keep a secret, and he apparently planned on one occasion a scheme for blowing up Brock's monument and some locks on the Welland Canal, for which purpose he is said to have carried a keg of explosives on his back some distance, before the project was abandoned.

Mackenzie eventually became disillusioned about the benefits to be gained by frontier raiding. He grew as distrustful of the raiders' motives as they were of his tactics. "I'm glad I'm free of it all," he wrote, "it will end in picking some folks' pockets." Some of the raiders, in fact, were men whose chief aim in life was to make their fortune and were not overscrupulous about cutting a throat to gain their desire. Others liked the prospect of future power or present rank and position, as in the case of the invaders in the

Detroit area whose platoons possessed enough generals and colonels to have commanded a goodly portion of the United States Army. Unfortunately for the Patriots, the officer of that organization who arrived in Michigan to prevent the generals and colonels from supplying themselves out of the federal arsenal had a full quota of infantry along with him.

As long as the border incidents continued, captured rebels in Canada were open to vindictive punishment in court, and known Reformers liable to be victimized in a hundred petty ways by influential Tories and every sort of government official. At its worst, whether it meant turning down a man's request for licences and permits, or refusing him a piece of business, or having his premises ransacked and himself jailed on the hint of suspicion, the persecution was conducted in a mood of grisly but jubilant jingoism. Sentiments such as those of the Cobourg *Star*'s editorial in verse were commonly expressed:

> Now that the rebellion's o'er
> Let each true Briton sing
> Long live the Queen in health and peace
> And may each rebel swing.
>
> But still for Mac there's one more step
> To end his life of evil
> Soon may he take the last long step
> From gibbet to the devil.

The jails were full of accused traitors, and all through the spring and summer of 1838, the trials for treason continued. Chief Justice Robinson presided and the fierce legal battle for each rebel's life was usually fought out between prosecutor Hagerman, the "hungry tiger" as one Reformer called him, and Robert Baldwin, chief counsel for the defence. One of Lount's young riflemen, who was scheduled at first for a one-way passage to the penal colony of Van Dieman's Land,⸴ described the fortune of the group of prisoners he was with, which included Montgomery the tavern-keeper:

William Lyon Mackenzie

We were never brought to trial at all. They did better for John Anderson and old John Montgomery. They gave them what they called a trial and sentenced them both to the gallows. John Anderson took his sentence quietly, but they say that old John Montgomery [who thought his jury was packed against him] turned on the chief justice and the lawyers and said:—"You think you can send me to the gallows, but I tell you that when you're all frizzling with the devil, I'll be keeping tavern on Yonge Street." We were all kept in jail on Toronto Street until June the 8th, when they packed us off to Kingston on the steamboat. John Montgomery and John Anderson were pardoned, [that is, their sentence was commuted to transportation to the penal colony] and they were in the crowd that marched down to the Yonge Street wharf. We thought it was Van Dieman's land sure. The mothers and wives of the rebels crowded around to see the last of us as they thought. I tell you it was hard parting with the old folks, who stood there on the wharf looking after the steamer until we were out of sight.

The prisoners tunnelled through a wall to freedom while they were being kept at Fort Henry in Kingston, and after wandering half starved for a week they found a boat and crossed the river to the United States. In spite of fracturing his leg in a cannon pit just outside the prison, Montgomery escaped with the rest, and he lived long enough to be pardoned and keep tavern again at the old spot on Yonge Street, just as he had promised. What came of his prophecy for Hagerman's future is a question somewhat beyond our present scope.

There were others not so fortunate as Montgomery. Samuel Lount, the Holland Landing blacksmith, in company with another leader, Captain Peter Matthews, was captured and sentenced to be hanged for high treason. Their trial and the pleas for pardon from all over the province which subsequently deluged the Governor made up an issue that shared the keenest public attention for a time with the question of Mackenzie and the border raiders.

Poor Mrs. Lount took a petition with five thousand signatures on it to Governor Arthur, and went down on her knees in his office to plead for her husband's life. The Colonial Secretary, Glenelg, had already given the new Governor some hesitant general counsel on the need for moderation and mercy in settling the province. But Arthur's own inclination, strongly fortified by the leading members of the Compact, was to let the law take its course and so afford a public example of traitors receiving the only kind of justice they deserved. For four months Lount and Matthews were ironed and kept in the darkest cells in jail, and given blankets that were sometimes wet and frozen as their only defence against the cold. In spite of this, they refused to complain or be downhearted. Lount kept up the spirits of those in the cells around him by telling them cheerfully that they had contended in a good cause and that "Canada would yet be free". The Governor promised him his life if he would furnish evidence that would bring other men to trial, but he refused to give it, or to make any statement except that he would join the rebellion again if he had the chance. When his day came he mounted the scaffold firmly, and before kneeling to take the hood and the cord over his head, and say his prayers, he bowed across the square to the prison windows where his companions in the rebellion were watching him. Peter Matthews died beside him, and they were buried together in the Strangers' Burying Ground, often called "Potter's Field", near Yonge Street beyond the limits of the town. Matthews left a widow and fifteen children, and Lount left a family of eight. Lount's treason, like his whole life as blacksmith and member of parliament, was strongly moved by courage and a sense of justice, and more than either, by a simple generosity towards his neighbours. "An axe was a big thing in the bush in those days," wrote one of his soldiers, "and if a man had not money Lount used to make him an axe and trust him for the pay. He made axes for the Indians up there, and some of them came down to Toronto to see if they could not save him, but of course it was no use, poor fellows."

Mackenzie, it has been said, must be held responsible for the death of several of his followers, and for the sufferings of hundreds of other men and their families. In a sense this is completely true. Mackenzie was from first to last the moving spirit of the rebellion. Beforehand he was its chief and sometimes only planner. His method of planning and of inspiring others with his own enthusiasm are not above reproach or suspicion. In the fall of 1837 there is no doubt that he greatly exaggerated to Rolph and his Toronto friends the state of the country radicals' readiness for rebellion. To Lount and the York farmers in turn he misrepresented the degree to which Rolph was committed to his own plans.

Then, once the rebel army was assembled, Mackenzie contributed to its confusion and ultimate downfall by his frenzied and erratic behaviour. As for the Navy Island affair and the border raids, they would scarcely have cost the lives they did, would perhaps not have materialized at all, but for Mackenzie's presence in the United States and his enthusiasm for a Canadian revolution. Nor would the reign of vindictive punishment and suspicion in Canada have lasted so long. But of all the bad bits of a sorry business, the misfiring of strategy at the beginning of December which brought some of the rebels out four days early, to find neither arms nor provisions ready, must have appeared worst of all in the eyes of his followers. They knew it had damaged the rebellion's strong chance of success but not that Mackenzie was, at least in this respect, blameless.

Yet in spite of everything there was little recrimination at the trials, when recrimination would have paid off handsomely or would have been justified. The rebels remained deeply loyal to Mackenzie throughout the rebellion's dreadful aftermath. His memory was cherished in the home counties and the western districts for many years afterwards. They remembered the madman who stamped about Montgomery's tavern in a fit, or the little bandit stuffed in greatcoats who raved at them from his white pony. But they also remembered the editor who once spoke their minds when times were hardest, and denounced some local justice or land office man they dared not speak against themselves. They remembered the first member of parliament who ever walked the woods to attend their town meetings or take their petitions to the King. They remembered the agitator who spurned the warning of justices—and assassins; the firebrand whose tongue had kindled their hearts' desire for a better and a just Canada. As long as they lived, they would remember the strange little man who had come among them.

In 1838 the *Christian Guardian* published the statement that Samuel Lount, before his execution, had denounced Mackenzie for deceiving him. Mrs. Lount wrote to tell Mackenzie that the truth was quite otherwise. She saw her husband on each of the last three days before he died. Instead of berating them, she said, he spoke well of his friends, and prayed for their success, as he did for his country's freedom. Always "he taught his family to respect Mr. Mackenzie as one of the most honest and honourable men he ever met with." It was such a lesson as this that other families in the farms beyond the ridges must often have been taught about Mackenzie. In the days after the rebellion, groups of captured rebels were roped two and two together and marched into Toronto past Mackenzie's house in York Street. Every pair of them in succession, as they reached that spot, slowed their pace, and gravely raised their hats.

In the summer of 1839 when the American public's enthusiasm for revolution in Canada had cooled, Mackenzie was put on trial in Rochester for his part the year before in inciting American citizens to an attack upon foreign territory. He made a rousing defence speech; he claimed that the liberation of Canada had always been the goal of American foreign policy, and he played to the gallery by presenting himself as the victim of "British influence and British gold" and by describing Her Majesty Queen Victoria as "that girl". As we might well expect, the performance excited a violent flurry of interest and sympathy. A Rochester newspaper reported that he so gripped the courtroom audience that they would have declared him innocent if they could. But the jury was composed of cooler heads and they found, quite correctly, that Mackenzie had violated the law of the land. He was sentenced to eighteen months in Rochester jail and served a year of his sentence before the deluge of petitions for his pardon stirred President Van Buren into ordering his release.

In spite of a crotchety jailer and "the howling and yelling from the female dungeon" whose door was five feet from his, in spite of the dark and rank condition of his own quarters to which he was confined for the first few months without a single period outdoors, Mackenzie managed to continue writing pleas for Canadian independence, and to have them published from time to time in an edition of his newspaper.

His two oldest girls came to visit him almost daily and to bring him some of his meals, but he was not permitted a single visit home, even when his mother took to her deathbed. John Montgomery, who was keeping an inn in Rochester, managed to have Mackenzie summoned out of jail for an afternoon as witness in a trial and by this expedient he was enabled to see Elizabeth Mackenzie and receive her blessing before she died. She had summoned all the strength of her tiny ninety-year-old frame to stay alive until her son should come to her. She talked with him vigorously while he was there, and assured him she was happy in the prospect of eternity. After he had gone she never spoke again. He had to watch her funeral procession from the window of his cell. The loss of the one who had been his only parent, and such a thorough one, was very bitter for Mackenzie. Nor was he the sort of person to take any comfort in the ordinary consolations about a long and full life.

Mackenzie never came to easy terms with circumstance. This was all the truer of him after his release from jail and throughout the rest of his long exile in the United States. He persistently refused to trim his sails before the winds of adversity. His own stubbornly pursued and often eccentric notions of what constituted honourable conduct, or what occupations were suited to his particular talents and temperament, meant that he several times rejected the chance to make an adequate living for his family. He refused two or three offers of newspaper jobs because he would never take a position subordinate to anyone in the editorial room. He was offered the owner-managership of a substantial printing business, on excellent terms, but, against the advice of friends and family, he turned it down because it would require him to take a partner. A Democratic party manager asked for his assistance in the work of a presidential election campaign and offered to pay well for it, but he was sent away because Mackenzie feared for his own freedom of speech and action if he attached himself to one particular political party.

Mackenzie thought it only fitting that his family should have a large house; and so the family usually had a large house, even if they were forced to live in one room in wintertime for lack of fuel to heat the others. Lyon and Isabel struggled to keep the children particularly well dressed, and to send them to schools which satisfied their father's educational standards, even at times when the family was living without adequate food or fuel or necessary household furnishings.

They kept a young Irish servant girl at one period, and she stuck loyally by them although the Mackenzies usually found it impossible to pay her. Mackenzie melted down the huge gold medal given him by the electors of York, but, because he had to pay off a debt, there was only a few dollars left over to spend on the needs of the family. Yet he had no compunctions about continuing to borrow heavily from any acquaintance who would lend him something. Often as not the money would be poured down the drain of some new publishing venture, while the family was still living off the sale of press and type from the last one, or surviving on whatever small debts Mackenzie could collect from his old subscribers.

To add to the hazards of Mackenzie's existence in Rochester, there was at least one attempt by a gunman to assassinate him. He was a tempting prize, furthermore, for anyone in need of the Canadian Governor's £1000 reward.

The only requirements were a small posse, quick enough to catch him and strong enough to hang on to him, and a boat that could dock in town and cross Lake Ontario. Several times Mackenzie's friends heard of plans to kidnap him and managed to send him a warning. James Mackenzie, too, wrote a letter from his printing office in Lockport begging his father to take precautions. "The thing I fear most," he said, "is your own utter fearlessness." But for one reason or another, though not because of any elaborate care on Mackenzie's part, the plots all failed. Fear that her husband would be snatched back to Canada and hanged for treason was one painful emotion that Isabel Mackenzie was spared. She, like his mother, knew by the sign at his birth that he led a charmed life.

For Mackenzie and his wife and their seven daughters there was, during the 1840's, little else to mitigate their daily struggle for survival than the very substantial cheer of each other's company. Many times they were literally without bread for a whole day at a time. Once when this happened on Janet Mackenzie's thirteenth birthday, they celebrated, young and old, on a birthday supper of hot raw tea, the only provision in the house, and twitted Papa for not having had this much on his last birthday; which prompted Papa to retell the story of the time he groped over to the cupboard without a candle one night the previous winter, his mouth all set for a morsel of something, and how he improved on Mother Hubbard only to the extent of finding a dusty old book, which proved by firelight to be titled *The Dark Ages*. This line of the story, complete with Papa's chopfallen grimace to illustrate, produced peals of laughter from the whole company and dispelled for the moment the sensation of an empty stomach or the pangs of nostalgia for birthdays as they once were in the beautiful stone house in York. As was their custom in wintertime, the children were kept up late that night, around the last embers of the stove, before being all piled together under the covers and canopies of two big double beds, where they usually stayed until the morning sun was high enough to take the frost off their room.

In spite of the obvious physical and emotional hazards of this sort of family existence, and in spite of a father who was subject to moods of the blackest depression and to fits and starts of what mere common sense would call lunacy, the Mackenzie family was, in some deep uncanny sense, a happy one, and it was their strange ebullient little chieftain who was the centre and fountainhead of their content.

One of Mackenzie's last attempts at a career in Rochester was to set himself up as a lawyer. Neither his voluminous knowledge of constitutional and international law, however, nor his forensic manner of pleading a case, encouraged clients to trust him with the sort of small legal transactions which bring in fees. In fact, he had no clients at all. After four years in Rochester, Mackenzie confessed that they were "starved out". He borrowed enough money to get his family out of town, and on to an Erie Canal barge for the passage south to New York City. It was there that the Mackenzies passed almost all the remaining time of their exile, from 1842 to 1850.

Mackenzie's first position in New York was that of actuary for the Mechanic's Institute, a job just vacated by a Columbia College professor. He gave it up within a year, after receiving a vote of thanks for his services, to look for a more attractive position. His name and cause were sufficiently well known that he received many callers and several offers of a job. His mail was often addressed simply "W. L. Mackenzie, New York"—a commentary on the size both of the city and of Mackenzie's reputation.

The son of John Tyler, the new President of the United States, came to visit the Mackenzie home, and there was much scurry and bustle to entertain him in as genteel a fashion as the one properly furnished and heated room in the house would allow. Young Tyler promised Mackenzie that his father would appoint him collector of customs for the port of New York.

With this good prospect in view, Mackenzie immediately moved his family into a large house in a fashionable district in the city; whence they were all forced to pack out again almost as suddenly upon learning that the position could not be given to a British outlaw. President Tyler, however, did secure him a clerkship in the custom house archives by way of consolation.

After being engaged but a short period in his new duties at the archives, Mackenzie's busy zeal led to a new adventure. He read through a large bundle of papers which were left there by a former customs chief. This man, Jesse Hoyt, was a well known politician who had his finger in a number of public pies, from which he had managed to extract nearly a quarter of a million dollars. His papers formed a sort of case book of all the contemporary varieties of shady practice in state and federal politics. Now a certain degree of political corruption passed, among professionals, as a privately accepted, rather effective technique of doing public business, and Hoyt thought nothing of leaving his letters behind him at the customs house. But the level of morality which they presumed contrasted sharply with the high principles of American political mythology; and it was not just another case-hardened government jobholder that was delegated to read and file them away. The discovery of these letters confirmed Mackenzie in his growing mistrust of American politics. They inspired in him both horror and a kind of holy glee. In the name of truth these private letters must be published. If anyone should condemn him for doing so, Mackenzie was ready with his reply. "The sun is not to be blamed," he wrote, "as the author of that stench which arises when he shines upon some putrid substance." Mackenzie quit his job, and, with the permission of officials who did not know what he would do with it, he took along his juicy harvest from the Hoyt papers. He went back to penury again and to living off small loans, in order to prepare a book for publication.

A few days after it had reached the bookstands, it became a best-seller. "What a rush there is for that publication!" wrote a friend of one of the Canadian exiles. "In steamboats and railroads you see it with travellers. At Philadelphia it is placarded and talked about as much as in New York. Here in Harrisburg even, the demand for it, and for the New York papers respecting it, exhausts quickly the supplies at the periodical and news depot. I never recollect such a rush for a book."

By a court order, publication was suspended after 50,000 copies had been put on the market. The price of used copies immediately doubled. Mackenzie refused to touch a penny of the huge profits, however, even to repay his creditors. With one dramatic stroke of the pen, he made over all rights in the book to his publishers, lest anyone think his motives in the business were a whit less unselfish than a desire to proclaim the truth.

Miraculously, he escaped all further judicial attempts to indict him for writing his book, and he was soon borrowing funds to prepare the exposure of another sinner. The new victim was no less a person than the former President of the United States, Martin Van Buren, the heir of Mackenzie's great Democratic hero, Andrew Jackson. Mackenzie discovered that Van Buren too—though a certain delicacy kept him closer to the leeward side of the law than Hoyt and his friends usually bothered to sail—Van Buren too was a consummately skilful politician. For this Mackenzie could never forgive him. Like the Fathers of the American Constitution, Mackenzie was dedicated to the belief that political parties, and their appeal to self interest as a means to gain power, were nothing but unnecessary evils. He could hardly have heard the remark his own hero, Jackson, made on gaining the Presidency: "To the victors belong the spoils." Nor would he have been happy, had he been aware of it, about the discovery of nineteenth and twentieth century experience that political parties, with all their venial sins, are the only known basis for the successful operation of a democracy.

The longer Mackenzie lived in the United States, the more disappointed did he become with its politics. He discovered that he had been judging Upper Canada as he knew

it, not by the standard of American democracy as it really
was but by some such ideal of American democracy as may
have existed in the mind of God—or of Thomas Jefferson. But
if the reality of the eighteen-forties was not what he had
expected, he resolutely refused to abandon the ideal. He
even quoted a text from Jeffersonian gospel to fortify himself in his own perseverance. "The times will alter," Jefferson prophesied during the dawn of freedom in the War of
Independence, "our rulers will become corrupt, our people
careless . . . they will be forgotten therefore and their rights
disregarded." To this Mackenzie added his own question,
"Is it not now?"

The task was clearly to recall Americans to their lost
heritage, and the way, though it might lead through the mire,
was to show them their sins. He justified his scandalous
attack on Van Buren by telling his readers a Scottish folk-
tale.

> It is a traditional belief among the Highlanders that at
> certain times all the adders of the moors assemble to
> form from their slime an incrustation called an adder's
> stone, which receives its crowning beauty from the king
> of the adders passing through it and leaving on it the
> trace of all his shining glories. Happy is the shepherd
> that, beholding the operation, waits till all is finished and
> then steps in and secures the prize. He is henceforth held
> in the highest respect, as possessing an infallible antidote
> against deadly poison. But he does not gain the prize
> without risk, being pursued by all the venomous brood
> and obliged to seek his safety in flight. If he does not
> throw some one of his garments to the adders to occupy
> their attention and divert their rage, they cease not their
> pursuit until they recover their lost treasure or obtain
> the body of the plundered.

Mackenzie himself was the shepherd who snatched the
precious stone of truth out of the corruption of the political
adders, even though they might pursue him at law for doing
so, even though it might be his fate to be "given up to the
chilling slimy folds of the reptile tribe, to share the fate

of Laocoön, who was strangled before the altar by serpents while warning the Trojans against the wiles of the Greeks". It was a time such as Isaiah had prophesied, wrote Mackenzie: "None calleth for justice, nor any pleadeth for truth." He would see to it that there was at least one voice crying in the wilderness for repentance.

If the book did not begin the purge of American politics Mackenzie intended, it did contribute in some measure towards ending Van Buren's career, and preventing his return to the Presidency in 1848. The morality of his own behaviour, in publishing whatever private correspondence he could lay his hands on, was never a problem for him. Mackenzie had a violent quarrel with a friend in New York when the friend denied him the chance to publish a personal letter he had received from Henry Clay, the man who would rather be right than President. Clay would be neither, Mackenzie determined, if he could have his way. In the matter of keeping his own and other people's hands clean, Mackenzie at times seems almost in Lady Macbeth's condition. He was obsessed with every speck of corruption that he saw, and only by publishing could he relieve his feelings.

Mackenzie's highly spiced style and his obvious ability to find good newspaper copy brought him a job in 1846 with one of the great American newspapers of that day, the New York *Tribune*. Its editor, Horace Greeley, once ran on the Democratic ticket for President, and is remembered for telling young men to go west and fill out the country. He befriended Mackenzie and made him his special correspondent in Albany, the state capital. Here, true to form, Mackenzie was not content merely to write about politics, he had to participate in them himself. A convention was in the process of rewriting the state constitution, and Mackenzie advised the delegates to increase the number of offices open to direct popular election. By telling them of his bitter experience of the Family Compact's monopoly of office in Upper Canada, Mackenzie was partially responsible for the introduction of the practice whereby New York State judgeships, to this day, are regularly competed for by the two political parties. This plea for popular control of the judges shows him holding more strongly than ever to Jefferson's belief in the good judgment of the common man, even after the experience of American politics might have given a greater realist than Mackenzie cause to abandon that faith.

If he never lost his faith in the American ideal of direct democracy, his disillusionment with America as he found it increased steadily. "After what I have seen in Albany," he wrote to his son, James, "I frankly confess to you that had I passed nine years in the United States before, instead of after, the outbreak of the Upper Canadian rebellion, I would have been the last man in America to engage in it." Greeley asked him to go to Washington as the *Tribune*'s congressional correspondent. Mackenzie, however, though he remained on Greeley's staff as long as he was in the United States, was now more interested in doing what he could to obtain his pardon and return home to Canada.

In the latter part of the 1840's, he wrote continually to the British and Canadian authorities to express penitence for his part in organizing the rebellion and the subsequent border raids. But until 1849 his pleas were cruelly ignored. The first letters he sent to the Colonial Office were shoved aside, unread, by one of the clerks. All the other rebels but Mackenzie had been pardoned in 1843. But because of the British authorities' correct surmise that Mackenzie had done more than anyone to plot and organize the rebellion, he was not included in the general amnesty. To continue to bar Mackenzie from Canada over ten years after the rebellion, and after all his letters of contrition, was surely harsh treatment, even if not intentionally so. Here in part is one of the letters he wrote to the Colonial Secretary:

> A course of careful observation, during the last eleven years, has fully satisfied me, that, had the violent movements in which I and many others were engaged on both sides of the Niagara proved successful, that success would have deeply injured the people of Canada, whom I then believed I was serving at great risks; that it would have deprived millions, perhaps, of our own countrymen

in Europe, of a home upon this continent, except upon conditions which, though many hundreds of thousands of immigrants have been constrained to accept them, are of an exceedingly onerous and degrading character. [This is a reference to widespread American dislike of "foreign" immigrants and the activity of various Native American pressure groups.] No punishment that power could inflict or nature sustain, would have equalled the regrets I have felt on account of much that I did, said, wrote, and published; but the past cannot be recalled. . . . There is not a living man on this Continent who more sincerely desires that British Government in Canada may long continue, and give a home and a welcome to the old country-men than myself. Did I say so or ask an amnesty, seven or eight years ago, till under the convictions of more recent experience? No; I studied earnestly the workings of the institutions before me, and the manners of the people, and looked at what had been done, until few men, even natives, had been better schooled. The result is—not a desire to attain power and influence here—but to help, if I can, and all I can, the country of my birth.

Mackenzie also wrote to the new Canadian Governor-General, Lord Elgin, recalling his services to his country in the Assemblies of Upper Canada in the eighteen-thirties.

Never in the legislature, crude as my ideas often were, did I allow any measure to slip that I believed would promote good government. I worked like a slave. I was in my place late and early. Often did the servants complain to the Speaker that I kept them from their rest. And never, either in England or Canada did I ask for the smallest personal favour or office.

It was in 1849, during Lord Elgin's term of office, that the Reform ministry of Robert Baldwin, the first responsible government in Canada, passed a bill granting the rebel's pardon. Mackenzie was free to come home at last. For his pains in the matter, Baldwin was burnt in effigy at a Tory street meeting. The first night Mackenzie was back in Canada on a brief experimental visit, he was kept up by a small but howling mob of fanatics which camped outside his brother-in-law's house, and at one stage attempted to break in and lynch him. The violence of feeling was only a temporary surging up of the past, however, and times were peaceful again on the day in early May of 1850 when Mackenzie and his family moved home to Toronto to stay, after thirteen years of exile.

It was a different Canada to which they returned. Lord Durham had paid his visit, and his great Report on the condition of the colony had sealed the doom of the Family Compact and vindicated the ideas of the political moderates. The most obvious change had taken place in 1840, when Upper and Lower Canada were united under one government and one Parliament. In 1848, after a false start or two, the era of responsible government came in at last, with a Reform majority in Parliament and the accession to power of the Reform ministry of Baldwin and his French Canadian colleague, Lafontaine. A wise Governor-General, Lord Elgin, summoned all his tact and wisdom to bring in the new order by removing his own office from the rough-and-tumble of practical politics. The followers of Sir Allan MacNab and his Tory diehards revived their spirits sufficiently to pelt the Governor-General with rocks and rotten eggs for his trouble. A Tory mob attacked the Parliament Buildings in Montreal one night while the Assembly was in session, drove the members out, and set fire to the place because Elgin signed the Rebellion Losses Bill which his ministers had introduced and passed there. But this sporadic outburst of the old bitterness was soon finished. The flames merely lit a funeral pyre; the honourable day of the old strongly-principled Toryism expired in this last burst of disgraceful splendour. In its place rose the spirit of a new liberal conservatism, identified most closely with a young lawyer-politician from Kingston named John A. Macdonald.

It is true that there was by 1850 in Canada West a vital new group of radicals, the Clear Grits, who gained their earliest and most powerful support from the farmers who had once followed Mackenzie. But they increasingly derived their leadership from Toronto's fast-rising and aggressive business community. One feels that the Grits were happier about their connection with Mackenzie and his tradition after the man himself was safely dead, and could be fixed firmly in a place where he would stay put, among the party's patron saints.

Mackenzie's first public act after his return to Canada was to administer a political drubbing to the man who would soon be the powerful editor of the Toronto *Globe* and the Grits' greatest leader, George Brown. Mackenzie was no sooner settled in Toronto than he craved to begin again, at the age of fifty-six, another political career. He launched his own newspaper and impatiently sought out the first parliamentary seat open to contest, rather than wait for the general election that would allow him to stand once again before the voters of County York. The first opportunity that presented itself was a by-election in the spring of 1851 for the county of Haldimand, an area with which he had never had a very close personal connection. Nothing daunted, he put his name up and entered the campaign. When the votes were all in, Mackenzie was found at the head of the poll, with George Brown and a Tory candidate trailing him. His name and his presence still could work their magic with the Western Ontario farmers.

Only a few weeks after he had taken his seat in the House, a motion made by Mackenzie led straight to the break-up of the great Reform ministry. The Reformers from Canada West (as Upper Canada was now called) had been growing restive under the careful, temperate leadership of Baldwin. When Mackenzie demanded an investigation into the Court of Chancery, a majority of members from Canada West, though not a majority of the House, supported him. Since Baldwin regarded his reorganization of Chancery two years before as one of his great achievements, the support given to Mackenzie's motion was a particularly severe blow to him. He resigned from the ministry immediately and soon retired for the last time from public life.

Once during the eighteen-fifties, Baldwin's successor at the head of the Reform ministry, Francis Hincks, expressed the fear that Canadian politics would again become the battleground of the ultra-Tories and "men of Mackenzie's stripe". But it was an unlikely prospect. Mackenzie's part in the defeat of Baldwin was no real indication of his position in Parliament. Sometimes a group of the Clear Grits supported him in one of his incessant attacks upon some special interest group that he thought was making use of the government, or in one of his demands to look into some suspected area of inefficiency or corruption. The back country Clear Grits followed him in his attack on those privileges of the Trust and Loan Company, for example, which were necessary for its successful contribution to a more complex and highly developed Canadian economy. His chief constructive work was his participation in the critical review of government operations conducted by the House's Public Accounts Committee, which he chaired in 1854. But on the whole Mackenzie went his own way in Parliament. He would have been a happier and more formidable figure in the American Congress than he was under the newer system of cabinet government. "I confess I do not view Mackenzie's return with much apprehension," wrote Lord Elgin after his Haldimand by-election victory. "He will I have little doubt be about equally troublesome to every party." Elgin's shrewd guess proved substantially correct.

Mackenzie was often as not in a minority of one in the opinions he expressed in the Assembly. He could still rock the House with laughter on occasion with his quick chattering manner, his captious retorts, or his joking references to the events of 1837. But it was hard to tell sometimes whether members were laughing with him or at him. More often his constant criticism outlasted their patience and grated on their nerves. The Honourable Amelia Murray, one of Queen Victoria's maids of honour, when she visited the Canadian House of Assembly in Quebec, described Mackenzie as "a singularly wild-looking little man with red hair, waspish and fractious in manner, one of that kind of people who would not sit down content under the government of an angel. He has evidently talent and energy; but he seems intent only in picking holes in other men's coats." Many members would have vouched for the accuracy of the description. They regarded Mackenzie, in short, as a public nuisance.

Mackenzie did not help his own present causes much by dwelling frequently, both in his published works and his speeches, on events of the past, in an effort to raise and settle to his own satisfaction the old issues of 1837. He had a violent quarrel, of his own picking, with Dr. John Rolph, also a member of Parliament, over the matter of who had let the rebel side down. As we might expect, Mackenzie's attack on Rolph's participation in the flag of truce mission in 1837 quickly broadened into a questioning of Rolph's present political motives. He noted regularly in his newspaper whenever Rolph voted with the Reform ministry, which Mackenzie heartily disliked, and imputed to him a desire for mere personal gain when he took a government position. "If cringing servility and abandonment of principle deserve reward under a bad system then Rolph should be provided for." If Rolph did not commit himself on an issue or was absent from the House, Mackenzie would call him "the artful dodger" or place a notice at the bottom of his column on Assembly business:

☞ ROLPH was just then ☞ INVISIBLE.

As the eighteen-fifties progressed, Mackenzie grew less penitent than he had been near the end of his American exile, and more clearly concerned to justify everything he had done. He became more radical as he grew older. This, even more than his personal idiosyncrasies, was the basic reason he did not figure as a major political power in the eighteen-fifties. He rejected responsible government, the premise of the whole new system, as a mockery of true justice and the people's interest. Nor could he bring himself to tolerate the easy morals of the politics of this new brand of democracy or to abide those small political vices which helped to smooth the path of a government reaching out to develop the country.

> A wharf or a lighthouse is to be built—a canal or railway to be made—public printing to be given out—Indians out west to be tranquillized—a commission is to be filled up—a hundred things I needn't mention are to be proffered. . . . Who shall be Queen's counsel, and who shall have the fattest picking of such jobs as the above? Who but the members of the Assembly and their near relations! See how a sop of this kind has tamed editors and how the shutting off the huge trough hath set them roaring again.
>
> Our Lower Canadian brethren seem to have no sense of shame in such matters. From a province of patriots, when out of place, they are transformed into a province of placemen. If anyone complains, all who have axes to grind howl at him in chorus. Is *this* reform? Is *this* responsible government? "Of course it is [they reply]; have we not the majority of the House at our back?"

Mackenzie denounced the government's ambitious programme for building the Grand Trunk railway, as the largest item in a whole programme of political jobbery. "This is a dishonest scheme to take control of $12 million, borrowed in Britain on the security of every house and farm in Canada, away from the country and give it to a few crafty land jobbers, bankers, sharpers etc. It bought up Speaker of the House MacDonald whose family got sixty miles of it to construct."

When Mackenzie saw a list of the things purchased by the Assembly from the merchants of Quebec, he fixed upon the item "rat-traps" and commented: "Rats we certainly had among us but if the people do not catch them at the polls, the traps will never do it. We had bugs also in the Legislature, and Mussen the apothecary demands a dollar for exterminator. The election purge would be more apt to work a cure. Chloride of lime would never neutralize the odours from Hincks and Co."

Mackenzie's concern roved from the homeliest and most particular of questions to the most lofty and remote, provided always that they excited his own passion for justice. He moved in the House, against the wishes of the ministry, for example, for a petition to the Queen to release Irish political prisoners condemned to the penal colony to which many Canadians had once been sentenced. One might regard this motion as meddling in other people's business and taking an unbalanced view of what was after all a legal necessity —or on the other hand one might call it a humane concern for an ideal which transcended the boundaries of mere legalism and the commonsense demands of the ordinary conscience. Both ways of putting it apply to Mackenzie.

The older he grew, the more he pressed his impossible demands, like a tiny, fretting, old Samson attempting to rock down the temple of the new Philistia. In spite of all his efforts, he scarcely succeeded in dislodging more than a few loose stones. "Behold, I cry out of wrong, but I am not heard," was a text he circled in his Bible. "I cry aloud but there is no judgment."

In 1858, Mackenzie's own constituents decided that they needed a branch line railway more than they could afford a representative who denounced the kind of political pressure that might procure them such a favour, and they told him so. They would doubtless have re-elected him anyway, had he stood at the general election, but Mackenzie was too broken in spirit to try again. He retired from the Assembly, stating that he could no longer endure the struggle there, and though he continued to publish *Mackenzie's Weekly Message* as often as his dwindling funds and waning strength would allow, he never returned to public life.

In his last three years, after his retirement, Mackenzie's personal fortunes reached a new low. He sank deeper into debt, and though he continued to borrow incessantly, there was little his friends could do persuade him to arrange his affairs properly or spend the small sums he procured wisely. They managed to take up a collection to buy the Mackenzies a house on Bond Street, and this is where Mackenzie spent his last years. He had a quarrel with the committee which was managing the fund; he wanted some of the money to travel to Scotland and it was refused him. The upshot of this was that he inserted a public notice in the newspaper asking that contributions to the fund be stopped. The committee of friends doled out what little money was left over from the house purchase to the family, when they saw fit.

Near the end of his American exile, Mackenzie had suffered a personal blow from which his spirits never fully recovered. His twelve-year old daughter Margaret died in 1848, after a painful illness, in spite of all the loving care and watchful nursing that her mother and father could give her. He wore Margaret's watch around his neck after that and he always kept the memory of the dead little girl, according to his son-in-law, with an almost superstitious veneration. In spite of his bereavement, he could write in 1850 to comfort his son James who had sorrows of his own:

> Cheer up—do not despond—there are moments of pain and anguish which time only can alleviate, and of these you are seemingly to have your share; but there are also green spots in the desert of life, and you and I may fall upon one or two of them yet: after the darkness comes light. The Bible tells us that they who have loved on earth shall meet in a land where pain and sorrow are no more. So let us play our part here like men, fearless and faithful, trusting that "in due time we shall reap if we faint not."

Many times during his last years did Mackenzie seek recourse to his own advice, and urge himself along the heartbreaking, lonely path of what he conceived to be public service. But by the beginning of 1861, there were things that even his courage and recurrent hopefulness could not accomplish. He began to keep to his house, like a recluse, lest by going out people should notice how much he had failed. He took to his bed, his hope and his physical and mental powers draining away together, as if he were suffering the effects of slowly paralyzing stroke. By the summer of 1861, he was incapable of holding a pen to write with. He still had enough of his stubborn independence left to disobey doctor's orders and refuse all medicines and stimulants.

Soon all that was left of the old busy activity that had so continually agitated his small frame were the disconnected daydreams that flew in incoherent snatches through his once vigorous mind. What images were there can only be guessed at. But perhaps, with all the dim fighting out of ancient battles and quarrels, and all the sighing over old sorrows and despairs, things that returned to trouble and then pass from his consciousness for the last time, perhaps there came too the remembrance of earlier, sweeter moments: the roar of the voters at the Red Lion Inn, and the boys printing his New Year's message over the coal fire in the sleigh just ahead, and the gold chain and medal at his proud breast, and how the cheers of defiance went up before Colborne's place, and then, by torchlight, how they carried him home on their shoulders; and on market day the clumps of weatherbeaten faces gazing up at him on his wagon while the words and the good warm rage poured from his throat; and the cholera cart he wheeled around Toronto and the look on one man's face when he went back to tell him that his wife was out of danger; and the day Isabel gave birth to their baby boy in London; and the night in the Lords the Great Reform Bill passed; and the formal splendour of the White House and the rough warm handclasp of Old Hickory Jackson in the midst of it; and the day he first shook Sam Lount's hand at Holland Landing; and the curious root and flower in the Lake Simcoe country whose name no one could tell; and the garden of the house on York Street, and the cool deep well ("of the purest water in the town," he always said), and the trees on a summer morning; and Isabel standing in the early mist on the pier at Quebec; and his stern tiny mother waving good-bye from the door in Dundee; and from the cottages the smell of cooking oatmeal mingling with the smell of the harbour and the sea; and the roughness of heather on small bare legs, and the castle where the fairies were, and the hearth fire, and the huge black Bible, and his mother leaning over his bed one bright morning to tell him there was snow, and his mother in her widow's black and his mother's arms and the midsummer twilight and the tolling of the bell-buoy in the harbour as she rocked him to sleep.

In the last week of August, 1861, William Lyon Mackenzie entered a deep coma. He died on the twenty-eighth of the month, towards evening.

EPILOGUE

THE LEGENDS of William Lyon Mackenzie have survived him and proliferated. Much of the folklore of Southwestern Ontario—sparse as it is—has gathered around his name. There is a wide swath of land from County York west to the London district still liberally sprinkled with cellars and attics, barns and dining rooms, where Mackenzie hid, re-clothed himself, changed horses, took gruel through a tube, or dined with three kinds of wine and the blinds down. Few owners of a really old log barn or cabin within twenty miles of his escape route to the American border will not tell a stranger the story of how William Lyon Mackenzie slept there. Six generations of Dundas school children have visited the caves which sheltered him from his hunters.

There is about Mackenzie the shadowy suggestion of an Upper Canadian Robin Hood, fighting the battles of the poor. There is a touch of the elf, Robin Goodfellow, wreaking capricious mischief on the countryside. But he is chiefly remembered in the manner of Bonnie Prince Charlie: always away or in the hiding, the incarnation of impossible loyalties, the secret hope hidden at the heart's core.

Such myths as these present the imagination with essential truths about the man, however much they may do violence to the details of historical fact. It is the shallower and more official myths which are objectionable. Mackenzie will never quite do if we expect him to play the role of a sort of grandfather of Confederation, or to function as a schoolbook cause of all our modern political conveniences.

229

William Lyon Mackenzie

He is not the cornerstone but the chief gargoyle on the sober edifice of our public history.

It is true that the indirect results of his rebellion were basic to the future of the Canadian nation. Responsible government, Confederation, the Commonwealth idea, universal suffrage, and an efficient professional civil service—these were all made possible by the rebels of 1837. It can even be shown that Mackenzie advocated each one of these things at some period in his career. But the point is that for him none of these came first. When responsible government became a reality he denounced the idea and the men who made it work as fiercely as he had ever denounced the Family Compact. Responsible government, like the other things, was only a device to achieve limited political objectives. For Mackenzie devices and limited objectives were not enough. Politics was not the art of the possible but the means of bringing in the kingdom of heaven on earth. His solution for political problems was not a mechanical but a moral one. Politics was continuously and entirely a branch of morals, morals verging on the Apocalypse, and political actions were to be judged accordingly.

Sir John A. Macdonald jovially prided himself on being a skilful political craftsman, a "cabinetmaker" as he signed himself at Charlottetown. The very idea would have horrified Mackenzie. Mackenzie did not want to solve the Canadian puzzle by intelligent limited devices nearly as much as he wanted to change human nature.

The result, of course, was abject and sometimes ludicrous failure. His high purposes and actual achievements were so far apart that in the crises he was driven to distraction. If we are to cherish Mackenzie as one of the heroes of Canadian history, it cannot really be for those later historical achievements which he helped to bring about. It must rather be for the vast eccentric proportions of what he wanted and tried and failed to achieve. His stature is that of the grand national mistake.

There is a phrase of Oscar Wilde's which can be applied to the solid and comfortable success story of Canadian history and to Mackenzie's place in it. "We die daily of a kind of creeping common sense and only discover when it is too late that the only things one never regrets are one's mistakes." Mackenzie could never be said to have suffered from creeping common sense. He died heartbroken because his countrymen were not moved to abide by his own very uncommon sense. By the ordinary sensible political standards he was one of our mistakes. But it is by such mistakes that a nation's history is illuminated and given meaning.

BIBLIOGRAPHICAL NOTE

IN SPITE of the loss in the rebellion of most of Mackenzie's own papers previous to 1837, the primary sources are fairly good, though by no means extensive. Dent's *Story of the Rebellion* and Lindsey's *Life and Times of William Lyon Mackenzie* are so largely based upon the oral and written testimony of the chief witnesses and actors of the events described, and were written such a short time afterwards, that they may well be considered primary sources. They contain a great deal of information obtainable nowhere else. Lindsey was, of course, himself a witness to the events of the 1850's in Canada.

Dent is more scholarly and his conclusions are based on a painstakingly careful investigation of almost all the available evidence. His great personal antipathy to Mackenzie, while it spurred him to establish, once for all, some unpleasant home truths, and to clear away a good deal of mythology, often of Mackenzie's own making, led to a final judgment upon the man which is one-sided and rather unfair.

The Lindsey biography, on the other hand, is entirely sympathetic. His work is based chiefly on his own recollection of Mackenzie, on Mackenzie's own writings, and on the reminiscences of members of the Mackenzie family. In spite of its uncritical character, it remains the most useful single source for the life of Mackenzie.

The *Lindsey Papers* in the Ontario Archives, the largest extant collection of Mackenzie's papers, include a number of interesting letters to Mackenzie from his son, James, which are invaluable for a study of Mackenzie's character. Though there is material here dating back to 1822, including letters from both Bidwells, Ketchum and others, to Mackenzie, the bulk of the papers cover the period after 1837. The *Neilson Papers*, in the Dominion Archives, contain an interesting series of Mackenzie's letters, and are one of the best sources for a study of his political ideas. There are photostats of Mackenzie's letters to Neilson in the *Lindsey Papers*.

Of the other primary source material listed in the bibliography, the *Grievances Report*, Mackenzie's *Sketches*, and the files of three of his newspapers, the *Colonial Advocate*, *The Constitution*, and *Mackenzie's Weekly Message*, are the most useful. The Canadian Library Association has also recently made Mackenzie's American newspapers available on microfilm. Robertson's *Landmarks*, (and the anthology of this long work by Kyte) and Scadding's *Toronto of Old* have also been relied upon heavily for the purposes of this book. Margaret Fairley's *The Selected Writings of William Lyon Mackenzie* is a wide-ranging anthology of his work in one volume.

Among the secondary works, William Smith's highly intelligent, vivid sketches of Mackenzie, Strachan, Robinson, Head and Ryerson (in his *Political Leaders of Upper Canada*), and Wallace's interesting and authoritative book on the *Family Compact* have been very useful, and are strongly recommended to anyone interested in Upper Canadian history. Of the general surveys of Canadian history, Lower's *Colony to Nation* is particularly helpful on this period. Sisson's *Life and Letters of Egerton Ryerson* and Landon's *Western Ontario and the American Frontier* provide an invaluable picture of certain aspects of Upper Canada in the eighteen-thirties and are essential reading for any student of Mackenzie's career. LeSueur's unpublished biography of Mackenzie presents a detailed, scholarly, and intelligent account of his political career. It is much fairer to Mackenzie than Dent's book, but is, on the balance, somewhat lacking in sympathy for its subject. The best recent study of Mackenzie is Lillian F. Gates' article in *The Canadian*

Historical Review, XL (1959), pp. 185-208. The only definitive and thorough work on the whole period is Gerald Craig's *Upper Canada: 1784-1841* which also contains a useful bibliography.

The general view of Canadian political history expressed in the Introduction to *The Firebrand* and at certain other points in the book owes a great deal to the periodical articles of Professor F. H. Underhill. His "Reflections on the Liberal Tradition in Canada" may be said to have inspired—and provoked—much that has been written here.

BIBLIOGRAPHY

MANUSCRIPT SOURCES

Lindsey Papers, Ontario Archives.
Neilson Papers, Dominion Archives. Photostats of relevant por-
tions in the Ontario Archives.
LeSueur, W. D., Unpublished biography of William Lyon Mackenzie in the University of Toronto Library.
Lesslie Papers, Dundas Historical Society Museum, Dundas, Ontario.

NEWSPAPERS

Colonial Advocate, 1824 - 1834.
The Constitution, 1836 - 1837.
Mackenzie's Gazette, Rochester and New York, 1838 - 1840.
Mackenzie's Weekly Message, 1853 - 1860.
New York Examiner, 1843.
Volunteer, Rochester, 1841 - 1842.
The Welland Canal, December, 1835.

PRIMARY SOURCES

Durand, C., *Reminiscences of the Rebellion of 1837.* Toronto,
1898.
Durham Report, (Methuen). London, 1922.
Early Travellers in the Canadas. G. M. Craig, ed. Toronto, 1955.
The Elgin-Grey Papers, 1846-52, Sir A. Doughty, ed. Ottawa, 1937.
Fairley, Margaret, *Selected Writings of William Lyon Mackenzie,
1824 - 1837.* Toronto, 1960.
Gourlay, Robert F., *Statistical Account of Upper Canada,* 2 vols.
London, 1822.
Head, Sir Francis Bond, *A Narrative.* Second edition. London, 1839.
Head, Sir Francis Bond, *The Emigrant.* London, 1847.
Howison, John, *Sketches of Upper Canada,* 3rd ed. Edinburgh,
1825.
Jameson, Mrs. Anna, *Winter Studies and Summer Rambles in
Canada.* J. J. Talman and E. M. Murray, eds. Toronto, 1943.
Journals of the House of Assembly of Upper Canada 1829 - 1837.

Bibliography

Kyte, E. C., *Old Toronto: a selection of excerpts from* LANDMARKS OF TORONTO *by John Ross Robertson.* Toronto, 1954.

Langton, John, *Early Days in Upper Canada, Letters of John Langton from the Backwoods of Upper Canada.* W. A. Langton, ed. Toronto, 1926.

Lindsey, Charles, *The Life and Times of William Lyon Mackenzie, with an account of the Canadian Rebellion of 1837, and the subsequent frontier disturbances, chiefly from Unpublished Documents,* 2 vols. Toronto, 1862.

Lindsey, Charles, *William Lyon Mackenzie,* (*The Makers of Canada,* vol. XI.) This is the 1862 Life as abridged and added to by G. G. S. Lindsey. Toronto, 1909.

Mackenzie, W. L., *The Catechism of Education.* York, 1830.

Mackenzie, W. L., *Head's Flag of Truce,* published as *Mackenzie's Weekly Message Extra.* Toronto [the 1850's].

Mackenzie, W. L., *The History of the Destruction of the* Colonial Advocate *Press,* York, 1826, W. S. Wallace, ed. Toronto, 1937.

Mackenzie, W. L., *A New Almanack for the Canadian True Blues with which is incorporated the Constitutional Reformer's Text Book; For the millenial and prophetical year of the Grand General Election for Upper Canada and the total and Everlasting Downfall of Toryism in the British Empire, 1834, by Patrick Swift, Esq., M.P.P. Professor of Astrology, York.* Toronto, 1834.

Mackenzie, W. L., *The Life and Times of Martin Van Buren.* Boston, 1846.

Mackenzie, W. L., *The Lives and Opinions of Benjamin Franklin Butler, United States District Attorney, and Jesse Hoyt, Counsellor at Law, formerly Collector of Customs for the Port of New York.* Boston, 1845.

Mackenzie, W. L., *The Seventh Report from the Select Committee of the House of Assembly of Upper Canada on Grievances.* Toronto, 1835.

Mackenzie, W. L., *Sketches of Canada and the United States.* London, 1833.

Scadding, Henry, *Toronto of Old, Collections and Recollections.* Toronto, 1873.

Scherk, Michael George, *Pen Pictures of Early Pioneer Life in Upper Canada.* Toronto, 1905.

Strachan, John, *The John Strachan Letter Book: 1812 - 1834.* G. W. Spragge, ed. Toronto, 1946.

Theller, E. A., *Canada in 1837 - 1838,* 2 vols. Philadelphia, 1841.

Traill, Catharine Parr, *The Backwoods of Upper Canada.* London, 1846.

SECONDARY SOURCES

Bethune, A. N., *Memoirs of the Rt. Hon. and Rev. John Strachan.* Toronto, 1870.

Clark, S. D., *Movements of Social Protest in Canada*. Toronto, 1959.

Corey, A. B., *The Crisis of 1830 to 1842 in Canadian-American Relations*. New Haven, 1941.

Cowan, H. I., *British Emigration to North America, 1783 - 1837*. Toronto, 1928.

Craig, G. M., *Upper Canada: The Formative Years: 1784 - 1841*. Toronto, 1963.

Creighton, D. G., *The Commercial Empire of the St. Lawrence*. Toronto, 1937.

Creighton, D. G., *John A. Macdonald, The Young Politician*. Toronto, 1952.

Coupland, Sir Reginald, *The Durham Report*. Oxford, 1945

De Celles, A., *Papineau*. Montreal, 1905.

Dent, J. C., *The Story of the Upper Canadian Rebellion*, 2 vols. Toronto, 1885.

Glazebrook, G. P. deT., *A History of Transportation in Canada*. Toronto, 1938.

Guillet, E. C., *Lives and Times of the Patriots*. Toronto, 1938.

Guillet, E. C., *Toronto Illustrated*. Toronto, 1939.

Hamilton, M. W., *The Country Printer, New York State 1785 - 1830*. New York, 1936.

Hodgetts, J. E., *Pioneer Public Service*. Toronto, 1954.

Jackman, Sydney, *Galloping Head*. London, 1958.

Kerr, D. G. G., *Sir Edmund Head*. Toronto, 1954.

King, John, *The Other Side of the Story*. Toronto, 1886.

Landon, Fred, *Western Ontario and the American Frontier*. Toronto, 1941.

Lizars, Robina, *Humours of '37*. Toronto, 1899.

Longley, R. S., *Sir Francis Hincks*. Toronto, 1943.

Lower, A. R. M., *Colony to Nation*. Toronto, 1946.

New, C. W., *Lord Durham*. Oxford, 1927.

Ouellet, Fernand, *Louis-Joseph Papineau, un être divisé* (C.H.A. Brochure No. 11). Ottawa, 1960.

Robinson, Maj.-General C. W., *Life of John Beverley Robinson*. London, 1904.

Robertson, T. B., *The Fighting Bishop*. Ottawa, 1926.

Robertson, John Ross, *Landmarks of Toronto*, 6 vols. Toronto, 1894 et seq.

Sissons, C. B., *Egerton Ryerson: His Life and Letters*, Vol. I. Toronto, 1937.

Smith, G. C. M., *The Life of John Colborne, Field-Marshal Lord Seaton*. London, 1905.

Smith, William, *Political Leaders of Upper Canada*. Toronto, 1931.

Somervell, D. C., *English Thought in the Nineteenth Century*, 5th ed. London, 1947.

Bibliography

Wallace, W. S., *The Family Compact (Chronicles of Canada Series*, Vol. 24). Toronto, 1915.

Wallace, W. S., *John Strachan*. Toronto, [1930].

Wallas, Graham, *The Life of Francis Place*. New York, 1919.

ARTICLES

Brown, G. W., "The Durham Report and the Upper Canadian Scene". *Canadian Historical Review*, Vol. XX, no. 2.

Creighton, D. G., "Economic Background to the Rebellions of 1837". *Canadian Journal of Economics and Political Science*, Vol. III, no. 3.

Gates, Lillian F., "The Decided Policy of William Lyon Mackenzie". *Canadian Historical Review*, Vol. XL, no. 3, pp. 185 - 208.

Gibson, James, "The 'Persistent Fallacy' of the Governors Head". *Canadian Historical Review*, Vol. XIX, no. 3.

Kilbourn, William, "Notes on Three of Mackenzie's Later Newspapers". *Canadian Library Association Microfilm Project Bulletin*, Series I, Vol. 1, no. 6.

Kilbourn, William, "Review of *Selected Writings of William Lyon Mackenzie* ed. by Margaret Fairley". Toronto *Globe and Mail*, Mar. 25, 1961.

Mackay, R. A., "Political Ideas of William Lyon Mackenzie". *Canadian Journal of Economics and Political Science*, Vol. III, no. 1.

New, C. W., "Lord Durham and the British Background to his Report". *Canadian Historical Review*, Vol. XX, no. 2.

Reed, T. A., "The Story of Toronto". *Ontario Historical Association Proceedings*, 1934.

Talman, J. J., "The Printing Presses of William Lyon Mackenzie Prior to 1837". *Canadian Historical Review*, Vol. XVIII, no. 4.

Underhill, F. H., "Reflections on the Liberal Tradition in Canada". *Canadian Historical Association Report*, 1946.

NOTES ON THE TEXT

CHAPTER 1

The view of York presented in the first part of the chapter is a composite one for the eighteen-twenties. A few of the things named, however, such as Gooderham's windmill, Upper Canada College, and the Orange "walks", were not in existence until the early eighteen-thirties.

Bateaux were long, narrow, wall-sided flat-bottomed barges, sharp-pointed and slightly higher at both ends. They generally had a crew of five, and carried three to four and a half tons of merchandise. They were propelled by square sails, oars and poles. The Durham boat was similar but much larger, not quite flat-bottomed, with a keel and rounded bow. The York boat was commoner in Hudson's Bay country, a light, forty-foot, shallow, keel-boat. See Glazebrook, *A History of Transportation in Canada*, 66-7 and 219.

The Family Compact. Mackenzie used this phrase in his *Grievances Report*, xlii, 1835, and it has become common since. The term was not used in the 1820's but it is, of course, an apt one when applied to that period.

"not apologies for cravats. . . ." Scadding, *Old Toronto*, 132.

Church parade to St. James'. The regular place of worship for the soldiers was St. John's Garrison Church near Fort York.

"John Strachan." The arrangement for dividing Upper Canada into two archdeaconries within the huge diocese of Quebec, had been made in 1824. Strachan was promised the archdeaconry of York. The Letters Patent were not actually issued, however, until 1827. Upper Canada did not become a separate diocese until 1839, when Strachan was consecrated Bishop of Toronto, but in many practical matters his position, and the way he used it, were episcopal in character long before 1839 or even before 1827.

Mackenzie in church. In later years, as a Member of the Assembly, Mackenzie used to appear occasionally in St. James' on a Sunday morning. "Up to his seat in the Parliamentary pew," wrote Dr. Scadding, in his *Old Toronto,* "we have seen Mr. William Lyon Mackenzie himself hurriedly make his way with an air of great animation, and take his place to the visible discontent of several honourable members and others." Mackenzie's curiosity, especially on his travels, led him to sample every variety of religious service from Roman Catholic to Quaker, and from that of Orthodox Judaism to those of the stranger sects. He had usually a good thing to say for every one he attended, although the limits of his own liberal Protestant viewpoint seem to have prevented him from understanding the worship and beliefs of many of them and from realizing how little he really knew about them.

The description of Mackenzie's bookstore, and its window decorations is derived from R. Lizars, *Humours of '37,* 57. Although he must have quickly mastered the rudiments of the trade, Mackenzie was not, so far as is known, a printer himself, and normally left this operation to his employees. However, at least one contemporary editor, Francis Collins, used to compose articles straight from his head into the type case, and it is the sort of thing one might well expect Mackenzie to do in an emergency. The author wishes to make it clear that this particular detail is purely the result of a guess.

"keen, restless, piercing blue eye." Lindsey, *Mackenzie,* I, 35. The phrase "when they met your gaze at all" is interpolated on the basis of other evidence and is not in the Lindsey text.

CHAPTER 2

"some of the first families in Scotland." Lindsey, *Life and Times,* I, 20.

"a bright boy with yellow hair. . . ." Ibid., I, 22. Almost all the surviving information on Mackenzie's first ten years is in his son-in-law's biography: Lindsey's, *Life and Times,* I, 1-28.

Somersaulted down the staircase. This is a story which Mrs. H. M. Lay, Mackenzie's granddaughter, remembers her mother telling her.

For the full list of books read by Mackenzie between the ages of eleven and twenty-four, before his emigration to Canada, see Lindsey, *Life and Times,* Appendix A. To emphasize the quantity and scope of Mackenzie's reading it should be noted that many of the 957 titles listed were composite ones. The complete works, for example, of Shakespeare, Molière, Pope, Sterne, Benjamin Franklin ("read very often since"), were given only one number apiece. He also counted as a single title each collection of the back works of the periodicals he read such as *The Spectator* of Addison and Steele, the *Edinburgh Review,* and the *Quarterly Review.* For the influence of the British liberal periodicals on

Mackenzie see below, Chapter 9, and R. A. Mackay, "The Political Ideas of William Lyon Mackenzie", in the *Canadian Journal of Economics and Political Science*, Vol. III, no. 1. The phrase, "Mackenzie the filing-system" is R. A. Mackay's.

"lest the laddie read himsel' out o' his judgment." Elizabeth Mackenzie, quoted in Lindsey, *Life and Times*, I, 26.

"Mackenzie and Lesslie." The evidence in the *Lesslie Papers*, Dundas Museum, would indicate that Mackenzie was at most promised a partnership in this firm, but never given it because of a veto by the head of the Lesslie family. Certainly, however, he was the manager of the Dundas store until he broke with the firm and went into business for himself.

"efficient weapons in the hands of free men." Mackenzie, *Sketches*, 284. Mackenzie says, in the same place, that he distributed up to 40,000 of his own Almanacks annually.

"I cannot boast a talent for mechanics." Mackenzie, *Sketches*, 217.

"System is everything." Mackenzie, *Sketches*, 186.

Mackenzie's switch from druggist to publisher did not involve such a total change in vocation as might first appear. Eventually, when he moved his press to York, he returned to selling books and drugs as a means of supporting some of his publishing ventures. It may be worth noting that the apothecary-book-dealer was a common calling for the lay intellectual in medieval and early modern Europe. Like the village witch doctor or tribal medicine man, he was a sort of practical physician to both body and mind.

Chapter 3

The hotels were "badly conducted. . . ." Patrick Shirreff, *A Tour through North America 1825*, quoted in Lower, *Colony to Nation*, 190.

Strachan on Maitland ". . . he now sees things more clearly." Bethune, *Strachan*, 72-3.

The War of 1812 was fought to "liberate" Upper Canada. There were, of course, other causes as well.

Chapter 4

"I had long seen . . . a desert." Mackenzie during his American exile writing to a friend, quoted in Lindsey, *Life and Times*, I, 40.

"mothers came to America and were purchased. . . ." Colonial *Advocate*, May 18, 1826.

"No. 7, Peter. . . ." Mackenzie, *Sketches*, 406 reprinted from the *Colonial Advocate*.

"His Majesty's butcher and baker." Colonial *Advocate*, June 10, 1824.

"Generally in the evening . . . then come the remarks. . . ." G. W. Brown, *Building the Canadian Nation*, 237.

"3¼ lb. tooth. . . ." Colonial Advocate, July 18, 1833.

Mackenzie's advertisement of drugs for sale. The Constitution, September 14, 1836, and in twenty issues following.

The stray cow. The Colonial Advocate, July 18, 1833.

Two letters from James Laidlaw, January 8, 1827 and March 17, 1827. The originals are in the *Lindsey Papers*, Ontario Archives. The first of the two was printed in the *Colonial Advocate*, January 18, 1827, and reprinted in Mackenzie's *Sketches*, 468-71.

"When we entered the church . . . Mr. Ryerson never forgets his index." Colonial Advocate, January 12, 1826, quoted in Sissons, *Ryerson*, I, 19-20.

"A short time since a happy pair . . . have not lived together since." Mackenzie, *Sketches*, 33-4.

"an old curmudgeon. . . ." Ibid., 282-3.

Reverend Lorenzo "Crazy" Dow. Ibid., 34.

"Sam Patch . . . inhales when he leaps." Ibid., 99.

"Be diligent . . . touch not, taste not, handle not." Ibid., 350-1.

"America is a good country but . . . full of Rougs. . . ." James Laidlaw to Mackenzie, January 8, 1827, *Lindsey Papers*, Ontario Archives.

"Four-fifths of the journals are in raptures. . . ." Mackenzie's speech in his own defence on a libel charge before the House of Assembly, December 11, 1831. Text in Lindsey, *Life and Times*, Appendix B.

"Our wood-paying subscribers. . . ." The Cornwall Observer, December 18, 1835, quoted in G. W. Brown, *Building the Canadian Nation*, 237.

Marshall Spring Bidwell as Advocate agent. Correspondence during the late 1820's, *Lindsey Papers*, Ontario Archives. There is a much more warm and personal series of letters from Bidwell's father, Barnabas, to Mackenzie during the same period, praising and encouraging Mackenzie for his editorials, and later, for his work in the Legislature.

"On your part you should not call . . . Mr. McAlly Barber." Jesse Ketchum, in York, to Mackenzie, June 12, 1826, *Lindsey Papers*, Ontario Archives.

"I have no fear . . . you will scold W.L.M. no more." Mackenzie, in Queenston, to Matthew Crooks, June 12, 1826, *Lindsey Papers*, Ontario Archives.

"It may be said I am proof of freedom. . . ." Mackenzie to John Neilson, December 28, 1835, *Neilson Papers*.

CHAPTER 5

I have deliberately, if reluctantly, transplanted the scene of the opening of Parilament in 1829 from the temporary quarters on King Street, where it actually met in that year, to the new Parliament Buildings whose construction was, by January, 1829, not yet completed. It seemed best to describe members in the general setting in which most of the later incidents in the Assembly did, in fact, take place, that is, in the new building. And yet it did not seem at all wise, for the purpose of telling the story effectively, to hold back the description of Parliament until later on in the narrative. The quotation used is from Anna Jameson's description of a prorogation of Parliament, March, 1837. Jameson, *Winter Studies and Summer Rambles*, 34.

"the most pleasing voice. . . ." Anna Jameson, *Winter Studies and Summer Rambles*, 34.

"never mind the law. . . ." W. S. Wallace, booklet, *John Strachan*.

"men who were notoriously disloyal. . . ." Dispatch from Lieutenant-Governor Maitland to Sir George Murray, August 12, 1828, quoted in Dunham, *Political Unrest*, 117-18.

"I can truly say . . . I felt like a bird escaped from a cage." Letter from Mackenzie to John Neilson, York, March 23, 1829. In the *Neilson Papers*.

Verse from Gore Mercury. Quoted in Mackenzie's speech before the House of Assembly, December 11, 1831, in Lindsey, *Life and Times*, Appendix B.

"I have paid our legislators a visit. . . ." Letter from John Langton, Fenelon, to his father, February, 1834, Langton, *Letters*, 78.

"Many of these legislators are qualified to sign their name. . . ." Letter from Mackenzie to Earl Dalhousie, 1827, quoted in Le-Sueur, *Mackenzie*, 141.

"little mannikin from York." Dent, *Story*, I, 236.

Mackenzie's trip to Quebec. See Mackenzie, *Sketches*, 172-92.

Mackenzie's trip through County York, and quotations concerning this. Mackenzie, *Sketches*, 237-47.

"a sycophantic office. . . ." *Colonial Advocate*, November 24, 1831.

Mackenzie's speech in his own defence. Lindsey, *Life and Times*, Appendix B.

Chapter 6

Description of the by-election of January 2, 1832, Mackenzie Sketches, 298-304. Details concerning Mackenzie's arrival home, Lizars, *Humours of '37*.

"choice fruit trees . . . stabling for the horses." From a "to let" notice, inserted by Mackenzie in *The Constitution*, regularly during the winter of 1836-37.

There is a pathetic letter. . . . Letter from his solicitor to Mackenzie, December, 1824, *Lindsey Papers.*

"A lady sat on a castle wall. . . ." The author is indebted to Mrs. H. M. Lay, Mackenzie's granddaughter, for this reminiscence.

The hanging of Charles French. There are slightly conflicting versions of this story in Lindsey, *Life and Times,* I, 117-20; and in two places in Robertson, *Landmarks,* I and III. See extract from the latter, with comment, in Kyte, *Old Toronto,* 170-2. One further eyewitness' detail in Scadding, *Old Toronto,* 104-5.

Contract signed by James Mackenzie and his father, April 6, 1836. In the *Lindsey Papers,* Ontario Archives.

"My dear father, why embroil yourself. . . ." Letter from James Mackenzie, Lockport, N.Y., to W. L. Mackenzie, Aug. 6, 1838. In the *Lindsey Papers,* Ontario Archives.

"Every market day . . . how the people listened." Robina Lizars, *Humours of '37.*

The assassination attempt. Mackenzie, *Sketches,* 390-404.

York Courier's account of Mackenzie tumbled from his wagon. The event described took place on March 23, 1832.

"If these persons in England. . . ." Mackenzie, *Sketches,* 243.

"Now our Willie's awa'. . . ." Lindsey, *Life and Times,* I, 254-5.

CHAPTER 7

Mackenzie aboard the Ontario. Mackenzie, *Sketches,* 213-20.

"the hero of Waterloo, pelted with mud. . . ." For his descriptions of London during the Reform Bill crisis, see Mackenzie's Letters in all numbers of the *Colonial Advocate* for July and August, 1832.

"My library was a sort of gossiping-shop. . . ." Wallas, *Life of Francis Place,* 177.

"Give me place for my fulcrum. . . ." Ibid., 177.

"There upon that three-footed stool. . . ." Ibid., 188-9.

"Mr. Mackenzie has now laboured for more than seven years to create discontent. . . ." Dispatch from Lieutenant-Governor Colborne, York, to Lord Goderich, June 18, 1832, quoted in Le-Sueur, *Mackenzie,* 286.

"five foot nothing and very like a baboon. . . ." Letter from John Langton, Fenelon, to his father, April, 1835, Langton, *Letters,* 101.

"he was perfectly satisfied that Mackenzie was as vain. . . ." Goderich, quoted in Lizars, *Humours of '37,* 78.

"When my mind and body are active . . . how little sleep we require. . . ." Mackenzie, *A Catechism of Education,* 1830.

"The longer I remain here the more clearly I see that the Whigs and Tories. . . ." Letter from Mackenzie, London, December 17, 1832, quoted in LeSueur, *Mackenzie,* 263.

"It is needless to look beyond Mr. Mackenzie's journal. . . ."
Dispatch from Lord Goderich, Downing Street, to Lieutenant-Governor Colborne, November 8, 1832, in *Grievances Report*, 225.

"An elegant piece of fiddle-faddle. . . ." Upper Canada *Courier*, quoted in Lindsey, *Mackenzie*, 231.

"They begin to cast about for some new state. . . ." Ibid., 234.

"Mr. Mother Country. . . . There are rooms in the Colonial Office. . . ." Somervell, *English Thought*, 177.

Lords contained three to one more bald pates. Colonial Advocate, August 16, 1832.

"I would rather spend a winter in Upper Canada. . . ." Mackenzie, *Sketches*, 345.

"that scared the Romans so." The phrase is D. H. Lawrence's. Lawrence, "Benjamin Franklin", in his *Selected Essays*, Penguin Edition.

CHAPTER 8

"Rational freedom must now prevail. . . ." The Quebec *Gazette*, some time in 1830, as quoted by Mackenzie, *Sketches*, 193.

President Jackson and the "agile little Irish lad. . . ." For Mackenzie's account of his meeting with the President, see Mackenzie, *Sketches*, 46-8.

" 'I saw a sturdy-looking farmer. . . .' Who would not exchange Colborne for a governor of this sort?" Mackenzie, *Almanack for 1834*.

"I am less loyal than I was." Letter from Mackenzie to John Neilson, Toronto, December 28, 1835, in *Neilson Papers*.

Mackenzie's severest modern- critic: LeSueur. The comment referred to here is in LeSueur, *Mackenzie*, 265.

Our Lord, "a person of moderation". Archdeacon Paley, *Evidences of Christianity*, quoted in Somervell, *English Thought*, 192.

Methodists voted Reform. It was the common opinion that they did, but there is no very carefully established evidence to this effect.

Ryerson, "a man of profound hypocrisy. . . ." Gore *Mercury*, June 9th and September 15, 1831, quoted by Mackenzie in the House of Assembly, December 8, 1831, in Lindsey, *Mackenzie*, 192.

"Methodism is opposed to democracy. . . ." Reverend Jabez Bunting, British Wesleyan Methodist Conference, 1829.

Ryerson's distinction could be planted . . . if there were a public quarrel. Professor G. S. French has kindly provided me with extracts from several of Ryerson's letters, in the Records of the Wesleyan Methodist Missionary Society (Reel 24, microfilm, in the Archives of the United Church of Canada), as evidence for the statements made in this paragraph of my text. On November 13, 1833, Ryerson wrote from York that since Mackenzie's mission to England "the object and tendency of [his] writings and proceedings were to unite with the French party in Lower Canada and make an effort to separate this Colony from the Parent Government. I felt it my duty to do what I could indirectly to neutralize this influence . . . by showing the dangerous character and tendency of radicalism in England." He went on to say that "it has produced considerable excitement or rather pain in some of our societies" [since the rank and file were strongly inclined to Mackenzie and Reform] but it "will not be of long duration. It may blow off some of the chaff in *some* places."

"ANOTHER DESERTER!" . . . . *Colonial Advocate,* second edition, Wednesday night, October 30, 1833.

"You have got Mr. Mackenzie very low down. . . ." Jesse Ketchum, speaking to the House of Assembly, November 25, 1833, as quoted in LeSueur, *Mackenzie,* 300.

Mackenzie's jingle. Quoted in Lizars, *Humours of '37,* 59.

CHAPTER 9

"He who first fixed on this spot. . . ." E. A. Talbot, a visitor to York, in 1820, quoted in the Hamilton *Spectator,* March 3, 1956.

"a gentleman walking on King Street espied a hat. . . ." C. C. Taylor, *Toronto Called Back,* 59-60, quoted in Guillet, *Lives and times of the Patriots.*

"streets well-paved and lit with gas. . . ." Charles Dickens, *American Notes,* quoted by T. A. Reed, "The Story of Toronto", *Ontario Historical Association Proceedings,* 1933-34, 207.

". . . baneful domination of the Mother Country. . . ." Letter from Joseph Hume, London, to Mackenzie, March 29, 1834, quoted in the *Colonial Advocate,* May 22, 1834.

"The most extraordinary collection of sturdy beggars. . . ." Mackenzie, *Almanack for 1834,* 3.

Methodists' acceptance of government money. It should be noted that Ryerson was opposed to the idea, and that the payments were made to the British Wesleyans in London, for their Upper Canadian missionary work. None of it was paid to normal Methodist congregations in Upper Canada, which were self-supporting.

"Ye believe these doctrines. . . ." Mackenzie, *Almanack for 1834,* 23.

"a strong desire in Canada to become rich. . . ." *Appendix to the Colonial Advocate,* April, 1825.

"The question whether a people should be educated. . . ." Mackenzie, *A Catechism of Education,* 1830.

Stanza from Burns. Quoted in *Almanack for 1834,* top margin.

Our farmers are indebted to our country merchants. . . ." *Colonial Advocate,* May 18, 1824 (1st issue), quoted in Mackay,

"Political Ideas of W. L. Mackenzie", *Canadian Journal of Economics and Political Science*, Vol. III, no. 1.

"*the sweepings of some second-hand London bookshop . . . the age requires.*" Mackenzie, *Sketches*, 183.

"*The loss of the North American provinces. . . .*" *Blackwoods Magazine*, quoted in Mackenzie, *Sketches*, 383.

"*The road to honour . . . is public opinion.*" Mackenzie, *Sketches*, 171.

"*The smoke of their steam-engines darkens the heavens. . . .*" Mackenzie writing from Dundee, April 15, 1833, quoted in Lindsey, *Life and Times*, I, 286.

"*. . . farmers make the laws . . . war may be the game of statesmen. . . .*" Mackenzie, *Sketches*, 467.

"*There are several degrees of liberty. . . .*" Mackenzie, *Sketches*, 19-20.

"*Ask a Canadian. . . .*" Mackenzie, *Sketches*, 155.

"*If there had been no display of force. . . .*" Speech by Joseph Hume at Manchester, reported in the London *Times*, November 3, 1833, quoted in Mackenzie, *Almanack for 1834*, 1.

Chapter 10

"*there is a greater amount of Mackenzie spirit. . . .*" Letter from Egerton Ryerson, London, England, to Sir George Grey, June 3, 1836, quoted in Sissons, *Ryerson*, I, 336.

The interviews:

    with Lieutenant-Colonel Rowan, *Grievances Report*, 1-8.

    with the Honourable G. Markland, *ibid.*, 76-9.

    with Strachan, *ibid.*, 81-8.

    with Van Egmond, *ibid.*, 26-7.

Mackenzie and responsible government. Question. "Would not the British Constitutional system by which the head of the government" must "choose his Counsellors from men possessing the confidence of the popular branch of the Legislature, be more suitable . . . than the present irresponsible mode of government?" *Ibid.*, 8, and in most other interviews. For Mackenzie's use of the term, "responsible government" see further his correspondence with John Neilson and his introduction to the *Grievances Report*, xxvi-xlviii. He often used the term in a wider sense than Baldwin but he understood Baldwin's principle well enough to advocate it when advocacy was expedient, and to criticize it effectively when he wished to press for a far more radical reform of politics than the introduction of Baldwin's simple mechanical device would allow.

Chapter 11

The appointment of Sir Francis Head. I am grateful to Mr.

Notes on the Text

Sydney Jackman of Bates College, for recent information on this point. His doctoral dissertation for Harvard University and his forthcoming book on Head suggest that Sir Francis Head was definitely the man intended by the Colonial Office for the Lieutenant-Governorship of Upper Canada. His brother, Sir George, had published only the one book, and, unlike Sir Francis, was not widely known as an author. More important, Sir Francis was apparently well-known in Whig circles (Brougham recommended him for the post of Poor Law Commissioner) and to King William himself.

Professors D. G. G. Kerr and James Gibson, in their biography of Sir Edmund Head have made out a strong case against the likelihood of Sir Edmund having been offered the governorship. The story that Sir Edmund was the intended appointee rests chiefly on certain remarks of Sir Francis Hincks. See Kerr, *Sir Edmund Head,* and Gibson, "The 'Persistent Fallacy' of the Governors Head", *Canadian Historical Review,* Vol. XIX, no. 3.

"The government were so intoxicated with the insane theory of conciliating democracy. . . ." Head, *Narrative,* 31.

"with Mr. Mackenzie's heavy book of lamentations. . . ." Ibid., 32.

"I was no more connected with human politics than the horses. . . ." Ibid., 32.

"Mr. Mackenzie's mind seemed to nauseate. . . ." Ibid., 34.

"Although too small to fill the chair. . . ." An eye-witness, quoted in Lizars, *Humours of '37,* 200-1.

"in plainer language." Head, to a deputation of Toronto Reformers, March, 1836, quoted in Lindsey, *Mackenzie,* 298.

"The moment we establish responsible government. . . ." A. McLean, in the House of Assembly, March, 1836, quoted in Lindsey, *Mackenzie,* 298.

"The people detest democracy. . . ." Head, *Narrative,* 110-11.

Stirred to action by Mackenzie's exhortations. There is no evidence for this in the usual places, but on December 31, 1850, Mackenzie wrote Baldwin to say that it was he who had persuaded the Reformers to cut off supply, chiefly as a vote of confidence in Baldwin. Letter in *Baldwin Papers,* quoted by LeSueur, *Mackenzie.*

"Gentlemen: No one can be more sensible than I am. . . ." Head, in reply to an address of the electors of Toronto, March, 1836, quoted in Lindsey, *Mackenzie,* 313-14.

"Do you know why a little weasel. . . ." Dispatch from Lieutenant-Governor Head, York, to Sir George Stephen, April, 1836, quoted in Smith, *Political Leaders,* 140.

"In South America, truth and justice carried me through. . . ." Head, *Narrative,* 100.

"The Governor is such a masterly hand. . . ." Letter from S. S. Junkin, Toronto, to Egerton Ryerson, May 1, 1836, quoted in Sissons, *Ryerson*, I, 327.

"To put the multitude at the top. . . ." Head, *Narrative*, 465.

"The people appeared as anxious I should ride good horses as I was myself. . . ." Head, *The Emigrant*, 49-50.

"Can you do as much for yourselves as I can. . . ." Sir Francis Head in reply to an address from the electors of Toronto, March, 1836, quoted in Lindsey, *Mackenzie*, 314-15.

"All along we expected to straighten things out at the polls. . . ." Thomas Anderson, quoted in Kyte, *Old Toronto*, 114.

"If you had been in London. . . ." Robert Davis, *The Canadian Farmer's Travels in the U.S.A.*, 14, quoted in Landon, *Western Ontario*, 160.

"The ripstavers. . . ." St. Thomas *Liberal*, January 10, 1833, quoted in Landon, *Western Ontario*, 157-8.

Bishop Macdonell's vigorous campaigning. See evidence for this in the *Grievances Report*, 28-44.

CHAPTER 12

"I am hot and fiery. . . ." Letter from Mackenzie, *en route* from Quebec to Montreal, to John Neilson, November 18, 1835, *Neilson Papers*.

"Try to moderate . . . I cannot. . . ." Letter from Mackenzie *en route* from Quebec to Montreal, to John Neilson's son, Samuel, November 18, 1835, *Neilson Papers*.

"I turn to the dark." Letter from Mackenzie to John Neilson, February 1, 1836. The full context will make the meaning more precise: "You look at the fair side of things done by the British government in and for Canada. I turn to the dark. . . ."

"this bold, dangerous, but delightful course. . . ." *The Constitution*, June 28, 1837.

"Tories! . . . Profligates!" *The Constitution*, August 1, 1836.

"God send down fire. . . ." *The Constitution*, March 22, 1837.

"Small cause have Highlanders. . . ." Mackenzie, quoted in Lindsey, *Mackenzie*, 318.

"The low grovelling principles of democracy." Head, *Narrative*, 273.

"the days of brass money and wooden shoes. . . ." *The Constitution*, 1837, as quoted in Creighton, "Economic Background to the 1837 Rebellions", *Canadian Journal of Economics and Political Science*, Vol. III, no. 3 ,1937.

"EXCHANGE YOUR BANK NOTES. . . ." *The Constitution*, May 17, 1837.

"Labour is the true source of wealth." *The Constitution*, May 24, 1837.

Notes on the Text

Declaration of the Toronto Radicals, July 31, 1837. Full text in Lindsey, *Life and Times,* Appendix D. First published in *The Constitution,* August 2, 1837.

"When a government is engaged in oppressing. . . ." Resolution at a meeting in the township of Caledon, August 9, 1837, quoted in Lindsey, *Life and Times,* II, 27.

"We all separated . . . meek as lambs." Letter to *The Constitution,* August, 1837, quoted in Guillet, *Lives and Times of the Patriots,* 10.

"There is rage in men's minds. . . ." Mackenzie, quoted *ibid.,* 10.

"The author has been in Canada . . . disappointed." Robert Davis, *The Canadian Farmer's Travels in the U.S.A.,* 3-4, quoted in Landon, *Western Ontario,* 159.

"Mike and I then lived at the mill. . . ." Thomas Sheppard, quoted in Kyte, *Old Toronto,* 116.

"Three or four hundred men and boys. . . ." Lizars, *Humours of '37,* 93.

"The captain of lancers was proprietor of the village store. . . ." Ibid., 94.

"One invention of '37 was the fuddle-o-meter. . . ." Ibid., 94.

"without a display of force. . . ." See Note, Chapter 9.

Chapter 13

"A brave stroke for liberty. . . ." Message from Papineau taken to Mackenzie by Jesse Lloyd, October 9, 1837, quoted in Dent, *Story,* I, 378.

"Those who persuaded Head. . . ." Mackenzie's speech to the radicals at Doel's, October 9, 1837, quoted in Lindsey, *Mackenzie,* 348-9.

"I said the troops had left. . . ." Ibid., 348-9.

"I do not apprehend rebellion. . . ." Head to Fitzgibbon, in Fitzgibbon, *Appeal to the People of Upper Canada,* 10, quoted in Dent, *Story,* II, 25.

The draft Constitution. Full text in Lindsey, *Life and Times,* Appendix E, and in *The Constitution,* November 15, 1837.

"I am sorry to see you alarming the people. . . ." Robinson to Fitzgibbon, in Fitzgibbon, *Appeal,* 12, quoted in Dent, *Story,* II, 28.

Mackenzie's handbill INDEPENDENCE! For full text see Lindsey, *Mackenzie,* Appendix F.

"Not fifty people. . . ." Hagerman to official meeting, Toronto, December 2, 1837, quoted in Dent, *Story,* II, 30.

"You do not mean to say. . . ." Judge Jones, at the same meeting, *ibid.,* II, 31.

Attorney-General Hagerman. He advanced to this office from the Solicitor-Generalship in 1837.

"The Orangemen . . . little Mac's for it now. . . ." These expressions are of the author's manufacture. It is hoped that they increase, rather than detract from, the historical verisimilitude of the narrative.

"The Monday night before the fight. . . ." Thomas Sheppard, quoted in Kyte, *Old Toronto,* 116.

"as men of honour. . . ." Mackenzie to Alderman Powell, Monday night, December 4, 1837, quoted in Dent, *Story,* II, 56.

"the rebels have shot Moodie. . . ." Moodie's companion to Powell, the same night, quoted in Dent, *Story,* II, 57.

"I walked along King Street. . . ." Head, *The Emigrant,* 169.

"Once or twice I thought he was going to have a fit. . . ." A rebel survivor, quoted in Dent, *Story,* II, 94.

"There are rich men . . . feel their strength." From Mackenzie's handbill *INDEPENDENCE!* See Lindsey, *Mackenzie,* Appendix F.

"He had his family out in the Bay. . . ." Mackenzie, *Flag of Truce,* quoted in Dent, *Story,* II, 62.

The pikes. These weapons often were made up to 30 feet in length, but in the rebels' army the pikes used were only from 10 to 20 feet long.

On a little white mare. Dent says that Mackenzie had now switched to a bay stallion. This may be incorrect since Mackenzie did not capture the mails and a certain bay coach horse until Wednesday, December 6th. For this reason, and because it suits my description, I am keeping Mackenzie on the white pony he rode for a time earlier in the day.

CHAPTER 14

One poor woman "he robbed of her all". Notes to Toronto reprint, 1838, of Mackenzie's Navy Island *Narrative,* quoted in Dent, *Story,* II, 107.

"bold . . . course." See Note above, Chapter 12.

"It was now broad daylight. . . ." Fitzgibbon, *Appeal to the People of Upper Canada,* quoted in Dent, *Story,* II, 116-17.

"Seize your arms. . . ." Silas Fletcher's words, as recalled by survivors of the rebellion, quoted in Dent, *Story,* II, 123.

The death of "that perfidious enemy, responsible government." Head, *The Emigrant,* 185.

Mackenzie's account of his escape. Full text in Lindsey, *Mackenzie,* 381-401.

CHAPTER 15

"Reformers of this part . . . afford." Letter from Mackenzie to

the Buffalo *Whig and Journal,* Yonge Street, December 6, 1837, quoted by Dent, *Story,* II, 177.

"There is excitement here. . . ." Letter from Marshal Garron to N. P. Beaton, quoted by Lindsey, *Life and Times,* II, 126.

Letters to Mackenzie and Van Rensselaer on Navy Island. The *Lindsey Papers.*

Mackenzie's caul. Most traditional lore has it that the caul protects from drowning, but the Mackenzies, at least, added hanging to the tradition.

"Isabel Mackenzie . . . the only female on Navy Island." Lindsey, *Life and Times,* II, 163.

The Caroline *incident.* For Mackenzie's treatment of this in the *Caroline Almanack,* see Dent, *Story,* II, chapter 31.

"Never was hallucination more blinding. . . ." Letter from Robert Gourlay to Van Rensselaer, Cleveland, Ohio, January 17, 1838, quoted by Dent, *Story,* II, 227.

"To defend it would be ruinous. . . ." Mackenzie, quoted in Lindsey, *Life and Times,* II.

Mackenzie's scheme for blowing up the Welland Canal. The evidence for this and for the Patriot leaders' distrust of Mackenzie is printed in Dent, *Story,* II, 271-2.

"Now that the rebellion's o'er. . . ." Cobourg *Star,* February 7, 1838, quoted in Lizars, *Humours of '37,* 10.

"We were never brought to trial. . . ." Thomas Sheppard's account of the rebellion from Robertson, *Landmarks,* quoted in Kyte, *Old Toronto,* 119.

"An axe was a big thing in the bush. . . ." Thomas Anderson's account of the rebellion from Robertson, *Landmarks,* quoted in Kyte, *Old Toronto,* 115.

"he taught his family to respect Mr. Mackenzie." Letter of Mrs. Lount, Utica, N.Y., to Mackenzie, December 8, 1838. In the *Lindsey Papers,* in the Ontario Archives.

". . . your own utter fearlessness." Letter from James Mackenzie, Lockport, N.Y., to his father, February, 1839, in the *Lindsey Papers,* Ontario Archives.

Mackenzie, his mouth set for a morsel. The original of the story is rather more grim. He went to the bare cupboard to get food for the children who had not eaten that day. Mackenzie could change or embroider a story for the sake of good cheer as well as to make a political point.

"The sun is not to be blamed. . . ." Mackenzie, *Martin Van Buren,* 4-5.

"What a rush for that publication. . . ." Letter from a friend to Dr. O'Callaghan, quoted in Smith, *Political Leaders,* 121.

"Is it not now?" Mackenzie, *Martin Van Buren,* 6.

"It is a traditional belief among them. . . ." Ibid., 5.

"After what I have seen. . . ." Letter from Mackenzie, Albany, N.Y., to his son James, March 5, 1846, quoted in Lindsey, *Life and Times,* II, 290.

"A course of careful observation. . . ." Letter from Mackenzie, New York, to Earl Grey, February 3, 1849, quoted in Lindsey, *Life and Times,* II, 291.

"Never in the legislature. . . ." Letter from Mackenzie, New York, to Major Campbell, Lord Elgin's secretary, February 14, 1848, quoted in LeSueur, *Mackenzie,* 484.

"men of Mackenzie's stripe." Letter from Francis Hincks to Egerton Ryerson, 1854, quoted by Sissons, *Ryerson,* II, 277.

". . . he will be equally troublesome to every party." *Elgin-Grey Papers,* 821.

"a singularly wild-looking little man. . . ." Honourable Amelia Murray's comment on the House of Assembly at Quebec, 1853, quoted by LeSueur, *Mackenzie,* 544.

"If cringing servility . . . the artful dodger . . . ROLPH WAS INVISIBLE." *Mackenzie's Weekly Message,* 1853, in University of Toronto Library.

"A wharf is to be built. . . . Is this responsible government?" Letter from Mackenzie to his constituents, Quebec, January 13, 1853; *Mackenzie's Weekly Message,* January, 1853; quoted in LeSueur, *Mackenzie,* 541.

"This is a dishonest scheme. . . ." *Mackenzie's Weekly Message,* 1853, in the University of Toronto Library.

"Rats we certainly had. . . ." *Mackenzie's Weekly Message,* July, 1854, quoted in LeSueur, *Mackenzie,* 543.

Public Accounts Committee. See J. E. Hodgetts, *Pioneer Public Service.*

"Cheer up, do not despond. . . ." Letter from Mackenzie to his son James, October 3, 1850, quoted in Lindsey, *Mackenzie,* II, 296.

The second last paragraph. The device of surveying recessively certain moments in the subject's life is derived from the closing paragraph of Lytton Strachey, *Queen Victoria.*

General Note on Direct Quotations, All Chapters. It was decided not to pock-mark the text with dots to indicate gaps in passages quoted directly from Mackenzie. This inevitably gives the reader a slightly distorted impression of his style. A greater distortion would result, however, if the gaps were all marked, or if the author had abstained from dropping any of Mackenzie's phrases.

Epilogue. Part of the last sentence is derived from a lecture by Alan Bulloch on Gladstone. Oxford, 1950.

INDEX

254

Index

Index